In Search of Limits

Also by Mark Bles

Non-fiction

The Kidnap Business
Child at War

Fiction

The Joshua Inheritance
Hearts and Minds

IN SEARCH OF LIMITS

Climbing the Alpine 4000-metre peaks

MARK BLES

Hodder & Stoughton
LONDON SYDNEY AUCKLAND

First published in Great Britain in 1994
by Hodder and Stoughton Ltd,
a division of Hodder Headline PLC

British Library Cataloguing in Publication Data

Bles, Mark
In Search of Limits: Climbing the Alpine
4000-metre peaks
I. Title
796.522094

ISBN 0-340-59614-7

Typeset by Hewer Text Composition Services, Edinburgh
Printed and bound in Great Britain by Mackays of Chatham plc

Hodder and Stoughton Ltd,
A division of Hodder Headline PLC
338 Euston Road
London NW1 3BH

Just for
Claudia and Madeleine

The life that I have
is all that I have
and the life that I have
is yours

The love that I have
for the life that I have
is yours and yours and yours

A sleep I shall have
a rest I shall have
yet death will be but a pause

For the peace of my years
in the long green grass
will be yours and yours
and yours.

Leo Marks

CONTENTS

Foreword by
H.R.H. The Duke of Kent
Patron

York House
St. James's Palace
London S.W.1

In our sedentary modern age, when so much entertainment is passive or man-made, it is reassuring to find that there are still people whose idea of amusement is to seek adventure in wild places.

The Scots Guards expedition ALP 4000, which set out to climb all the four-thousand metre Alpine peaks, something never previously achieved in a single season, was both ambitious and at the same time entirely in keeping with the military tradition of adventurous projects. That it also helped to raise money for research into cot deaths, gave it both justification and added impetus.

Mark Bles, who led the expedition, gives a thoroughly entertaining and lively account of the team's Alpine exploits. In spite of some distinctly interesting, not to say alarming moments, it is clear that the climbers made highly impressive progress, at one stage climbing as many as six peaks in one day. But this remarkable vertical agility was too good to last and with some forty-eight summits under their belts, all climbed in the space of a few weeks, the mountaineers were forced by the early onset of bad autumn weather to abandon their project.

These bare facts actually conceal a remarkable saga of courage and determination. The climbing team had to face a daunting sequence of challenges: obstructive officialdom, departmental red tape, the vagaries of Alpine weather, ferocious hut wardens and terrifying glaciers. All had to be surmounted, or circumvented, though not without pain and anguish and, on several occasions, serious danger. The writer makes light of most of these difficulties but even his restrained description often makes one feel quite glad (if a shade guilty) to be reading about it in the comfort of one's armchair.

Although the ALP 4000 team did not in the end succeed in their goal of conquering all the four-thousand-ers in a season, they accomplished a great deal: an entirely amateur team, some of whom had only limited climbing experience, dispatched a total of forty-eight of the highest Alpine peaks in a little over eight weeks, without guides. They admit that they learned a great deal, about the mountains, about snow conditions, about their own limits. Above all, in the best British Army tradition, it is clear that they all enjoyed the experience hugely. Without that element of fun, it would surely not have been worth doing.

I feel proud to have been associated with ALP 4000. I congratulate the whole team, and only wish that when I visited them on the Weissmies I had been able to climb just one peak. That would assuredly have been an adventure.

H.R.H. The Duke of Kent, KG Patron

ACKNOWLEDGEMENTS

Many people were involved and support came from all directions, actual and moral, much of which was crucial.

Principally, I am indebted to His Royal Highness the Duke of Kent for agreeing to be the patron of our climbing, and I hope that when he has read this account, he will not be too appalled to find out what went on.

Without Tim Spicer and Jean-Daniel Mudry we could not have done what we did. The Scots Guards were a pleasure to work with and the generosity of the Swiss Army was truly humbling. I am indebted to them both for the opportunity to climb all summer in the Alps.

I want to thank all the climbers and the base support group for making this an unforgettably enjoyable five months. We made lasting friendships: Stewart Barron, Tim Boyle, Peter Copeland, Mark 'Death' Cowell, Douglas Glen, Christopher 'Gonzo' Martin, Charlie Messervy-Whiting, Dave Moore, Michael Nutter, Gary Parker, Justin Ramsay, Darren 'George' Roper, Nigel Taylor, Simon Whittaker and Nikki Hatrick.

Others deserve a special mention for their help which covered a wide spectrum of involvement: Russell Brice, Alistair Bruce, Tom Coke, Anne Diamond, Ingrid Gottschalk, Bev Hickey, Michael Hollingsworth, Hans Immer, Henry Jones-Davies, Roger and Ursula Mathieu, Graham Messervy-Whiting, Caroline Spicer, Al Stenner, Harry Taylor, Bill and Rachel Thatcher, Aldwyn Wight, John Williams, Sarah Wollaston.

I want to thank all the sponsors of equipment and the officers whose support was crucial to obtaining cash from various Army funds, without which we might not have been able to continue climbing. By the same token thanks go to everyone who generously dipped into their pockets to give something to the Foundation for the

Study of Infant Death Syndrome for cot-death research. We would have liked to raise more, but every bit helps.

I hope others whom I have not mentioned here (but may be in the text) will forgive me, especially all the Danes. Your support was invaluable – I shall wear it always. MB

1

EARLY DAYS

In the beginning, all creatures had the power of speech and were gifted with reason.

Geronimo, in his autobiography

The sea was suspiciously smooth, the path of reflections from the sunset too perfect. I gazed over the rail of the ship which was cutting through the glassy water towards Hamburg and tried not to be superstitious. After two years of struggle, planning and preparation, I was leaving England to climb all the big mountains in the Alps 4000 metres above sea level. There are sixty-one, they had never been climbed all in one year, and I was suddenly sensitive to every omen of the future.

My head was filled with mountains. Initially amused, then disbelieving and finally resigned but supportive, my wife Rebecca became used to my bedtime reading. Night after night, she watched me absorbed in the excellent series of little Alpine guide books published by Collomb, several important ones now sadly out of print, and poring over endless photographs of tantalising snowcapped mountains. I researched in the Alpine Club library in its depressing new offices in a less than savoury corner of Shoreditch. After exhaustive analysis of every peak, gorged with the images and route descriptions of the most famous and many more unheard-of Alpine summits, I estimated we would have to walk around 700 kilometres and ascend the equivalent of Mt Everest twenty times. That, at least, was the theory. I thought this would take us four months, maybe five, but everything depended on the weather.

Before we started, I knew that the 'met' forecast, the science of clairvoyance, would rule our lives all summer. These mountains are not like the Scottish Munros, which by and large can be 'done' one after the other, whatever the weather. The big Alpine peaks, all of them, deserve more respect, and of all the factors affecting a climb, the weather would be the first to consider. Already on our Channel crossing I was absurdly searching the skies for a portent of what lay in store for us.

'Plans get you into things, but you got to work your way out,' said Will Rogers. Not for the first time, I felt vulnerable, dwarfed by the immensity of what we had taken on. Watching the ruffled white spume slide past the ship's hull far below me, I was impatient to be in the mountains. Of course, like everyone else in the world, I see myself as well-balanced, an ideal combination of artistic imagination and practical common sense, but, like everyone else, I secretly know my birth sign and read the Stars in the newspapers, which are as reliable and certainly more entertaining than any weather forecast. I confess I would not go so far as to dip my hands into a stomach-ful of chicken entrails to predict the future, but I do believe in vibes. I've been on too many trips in the past which have started badly and fulfilled every awful premonition. Sailing serenely across the Channel in the golden reflections of a perfect sunset, I thought of all the risks on the big Alpine peaks, the crevasses, hanging séracs, huge drops into space and avalanches, and the placid comfort of the start of our adventure seemed too good to be true.

'*Vogel*,' declared Simon Whittaker, interrupting my suspicious interpretation of the cloud formations.

'Bird,' I answered, dredging up some very rusty German. '*Das Vogel, die Vögeln*.' We were revising and I was taught to learn the plural with the singular. The Germans insist on it.

Simon nodded looking through my vocab cards, but before he could decipher my appalling handwriting to ask another question, I fired one at him, 'What's an eagle?' We were going to the High Alps, where the maps were littered with Eagles' Nests, Needles and Cols.

'A big *Vogel*,' he said without hesitation.

Simon is rather laid-back. Good-humoured and naturally philo-sophical about things, he is not one to seek hidden meanings in the shape of clouds. More to the point, he is athletic and excellent on rock, having great natural balance, and I was depending on him to lead the way on various rock ridge climbs we planned for later in the summer, such as the traverse of the Täschhorn and Dom, which rates as one of the best expeditions to make in the whole Alps.

'My bonny lies over the ocean, my bonny lies over the sea! My bonny lies over the ocean, oh bring back my bonny to me!' chanted a brassy German blonde later that evening in the bar. Her black leather suit stretched voluptuously over generous curves as she gyrated on the circular dance floor. Glittering with *bonhomie* under the bright lights, she introduced a Bulgarian–Turkish combo who skilfully worked their way through a strange, old-fashioned mixture of 'Oh Susanna!', 'When the saints go marching in!' and 'She'll be coming round the mountain when she comes!' The words seemed to augur well and I relaxed. Beer, music, and three pretty dancers flaunting their long naked legs under peasant red-check Dirndl dresses soothed away my worries about the next months on the mountains far away to the South.

At the end of the show, the blonde hostess in black leather, all false promise with stick-on eyelashes and rouged lips glued to the mike, sang lustily in a delightful German accent, 'Peck up your troubulse in your old kit beg!' An odd choice for a modern cabaret, but that famous song from the First World War seemed to summarise our plans rather neatly. We slept like lambs that night and woke to brilliant sunshine in Hamburg docks.

The team gathered in Hohne, an hour from Hamburg and temporary home of the Scots Guards while they were based in Germany in a camp next door to the infamous Bergen-Belsen Konzentrationslager. Eighteen months before, Tim Spicer, who was the Commanding Officer of their 1st Battalion and a good friend, had heard me talking about my plans during my last liquid lunch in the London Travellers' Club before I resigned, regretfully, on the grounds of the enormous annual subscription. Very possibly influenced by several bottles of Club claret, he at once volunteered to join in. I was impressed, flattered and delighted. Once a regular officer myself, I have sat on the Army sidelines in the SAS Reserve for more than twelve years and watched the British Army so reduced in numbers that those left are terrified of making decisions which might jeopardise their careers. Where once the bold reaction was,

'Let's go for it!', now all you hear is the sound of air cautiously sucked through teeth, and a negative, 'Not sure there's an AGAI on that one, old boy.' Like a good sauce, reduced any more and the British Army will end up a congealed mess.

Tim is an unlikely Guards Colonel, probably because he spent some years as a civilian working in the City before joining up. He had his ear pierced by someone at a dinner party with two ice cubes and a red-hot needle, less in the spirit of punk rock than in the style of Mike Cumberlege, a wartime Naval officer (and friend of Patrick Leigh Fermor) who also pierced his ear for an attractive girl and, in a spirit of delightful eccentricity long gone in the services, wore her ear-ring in the hole at all times, including with his Naval uniform. Similarly, Tim's eclectic background allows him to see the British Army in the context of its increasingly small place in society, and he is energetic, which puzzles some Guards officers. He happily stamps on the complacent bridges of those who work for him to see if they hold up, he has great political acuity and intelligent charm and makes friends in high places. The Chief of the General Staff, Sir Peter Inge, was impressed to learn of our plan to climb the Alpine peaks in a summer, and described it as 'in the best traditions of the SAS and the Scots Guards', presumably bearing in mind that the late founder of the SAS, Colonel David Stirling, was himself a Scots Guards officer and also supported several Everest expeditions.

However, the SAS is terrified of publicity. Although there is nothing remotely khaki or 'classified' about climbing in the Alps, we were told we could not breathe a word about the 'SAS'. Sad, really. The SAS need some clean-shaven PR to offset the public conception of brutal black-clad anti-terrorists (sic) taking no prisoners. But Army officers, especially in the SAS in my experience, are notoriously unable to handle PR, good or bad. The expedition was therefore mounted entirely by Tim's Scots Guards. For the purposes of the expedition, the three of us from the SAS Reserve squadron in Hereford which I commanded for years, Simon Whittaker, Gary Parker and I, all became Scots Guardsmen on that most auspicious day in the calendar, All Fools' Day.

At the end of April, Simon and I drove from Hamburg docks to Hohne, and joined the three Scots Guardsmen who would make up the full six in our climbing team: Peter Copeland, Douglas Glen and Stewart Barron. We also met the small group of nine others who would support us in our base camp. We stuffed climbing gear, skis, arctic rations and of course vast bottles of NATO duty-free drink into two very well-used army Land-Rovers and an eight-ton truck, all painted a most bizarre gentian blue to 'civilianise' them for Switzerland, and then drove south in a balmy spring heat wave.

The good weather did not last. On the last leg of the journey, the eight-tonner had to turn back on the Furka Pass which was blocked by late snowfall. To avoid a long detour round the mountains via Lake Geneva, they went instead for the Kandersteg–Goppenstein drive-on-drive-off railway tunnel through the Lötschberg mountain. Tim Boyle, our vehicle mechanic and heavy goods driver, only just squeezed the eight-tonner onto the flat-bed with an inch to spare all round. A Swiss railway official at the other end watched aghast as this enormous blue 'thing' emerged from the tunnel and drove off into the Valais under lowering clouds and drizzle.

All the same, I wanted to get started. On the last day of April, the climbers left the Base Camp party to settle into our quarters in Brig and we drove to the top of the Simplon Pass for our first day out. We disappeared into thick, bone-chilling cloud at about 2000 metres. This was only half the height of the big mountains we had come to climb.

'The worst föhn since records began,' said the met office smugly when I rang Geneva to find out when we could begin climbing for real. The 'föhn', a warm front from the Mediterranean, was pushing masses of snow-laden clouds over the mountain frontier crest between Italy and Switzerland and dumping huge quantities of snow all over the Alps. There was more than a metre of fresh snowfall at altitude and climbing the 4000ers was out of the question. First, we had to wait for the snow to stop and then give the new snow time to consolidate. Already, on our first day, I felt the pressure was on. If only the weather would allow it, I felt sure we could climb all those mountains. If only.

Avalanches are not a risk on the top of the Simplon and in miserable white sleet we skinned uphill on our newly issued Swiss Army mountaineering skis in a stolid line behind our new *Bergführer*, or mountain guide, Roger Mathieu. He had come with us to assess our skiing ability, and for that matter have a good look at everything else. We were very slow. After one and a half hours zigzagging back and forth up soggy snow slopes and around outcrops

of wet, black rock, we had climbed only 250 metres. Roger stopped
by some level rocks gleaming with damp in a thick mist reminiscent
of Scotland.

'We shall practise with the avalanches,' he announced, taking
off his light civilian mountaineering skis and stuffing the ends
in the snow. Roger is slight, a fit thirty-three with a neat fair
moustache, and takes his duties as a guide seriously. He took
my Pieps avalanche transceiver which I had strapped to my chest,
checked it was transmitting and vigorously threw it away onto an
open slope of soft wet snow, where it disappeared. I wondered who
had signed for it.

He turned to us and announced gravely, 'This is not the time to
masturbate.'

Indeed. Expressionless, we glanced at each other and waited to
see what other fascinating insights into Swiss avalanche rescue
procedure might be revealed.

We were none of us sure whether he had been making a joke or
had misused a word. Equally, we could not imagine what word he
had intended to use. Maybe later, when we got to know him better,
we could ask.

Blissfully unaware of the impact he had made, Roger took his
own Pieps, which is an orange transceiver the size of a Walkman,
switched it to receive and energetically demonstrated how to find
a 'lost skier'. By a repeated sequence of decreasing the range and
sensitivity of the receiver, he crossed back and forth, up and down
the area where the 'skier' was thought to be buried. With his Pieps
beeping strongly each time he passed the area where he had thrown
mine, he worked closer and closer and finally reached down to
pull my Pieps out of the deep soft snow. A simple but impressive
demonstration. I hoped very much we would not have to do this
for real.

'You must work fast,' he told us. 'Recent research shows that a
person is likely to freeze to death within fifteen minutes.' No way to
die. I looked at the wet soggy snow and shivered in the cold mist. We
all took our avalanche rescue practice more seriously after that.

At the end, we stood about and warmed up with hot coffee from
flasks. Roger declared no one could find their way about on the
hills in such poor visibility. He was emphatic. I hesitated, unwilling
to provoke an argument, but the gloom, damp and awful snow

reminded me so much of innumerable days spent on the Scottish and Welsh hills, I could not let that one pass, and said, 'Any British soldier who can't map-read his way in conditions like these should be shot!'

Roger, shocked by this insight into British military discipline, persisted all the same. There followed a competitive and ludicrous comparison of Swiss and British mist. I merely wanted to put down a marker that although we were not UIAGM qualified guides, we had some years of useful mountain experience between us, climbing in Britain, the Himalayas, Norway, North Africa, Alaska and the Alps. All in good humour, we circled each other verbally, like dogs meeting for the first time, but as soon as Roger conceded a point on map-reading, I backed off. There is, after all, no real comparison between Scotland and the great Alpine mountains we wanted to climb.

He got his own back when we skied down. Heavy wet snow, off-piste, is not anyone's choice for their first day back on skis. Emphatically not if it is your first time on skis ever. The mist saved public embarrassment, as the few hardy souls hidden from view on the main road at the top of the Simplon Pass could not see us tumbling about in the snow, but we took as long to ski down as we had taken to skin up and Roger realised that Peter and Stewart were complete beginners.

Peter and I were last down, hidden from the rest of the group by the mist but clearly audible. A disembodied stream of rich language floated downhill through the mist as I tried to coax Peter off his back, sides and head, and down his first ever ski run. Below, in shock again, Roger shook his head at my instructional techniques, doubtless appalled by this further evidence of British military lunacy.

He and I talked about it later, in Brig in the Rhône valley in our office in the building the Swiss Army had given us to use as our base camp, and I was obliged to face facts. Peter was Tim Spicer's Communications Officer and had been too busy running the battalion's radio net in Northern Ireland and on training exercises for Bosnia to squeeze in even a single weekend's skiing during the winter, and Stewart had been brought onto the team at short notice, owing to other personnel changes, leaving no time for his own ski training. Roger's conclusions after our first day out were no surprise.

'They must not go on the high mountains,' he said. There was no criticism in his tone. Just the straightforward statement that Peter and Stewart, with the utmost determination, would not be able to ski on the mountains we wanted to reach on skis while the snow lasted. Fitness and enthusiasm, which they had in plenty, were not enough. Even skinning uphill, which on the face of it sounds merely a question of endurance, they would constantly fall over and slow us down till they had learned the balance required to execute kick-turns on steep slopes, or edge the skis on icy off-piste conditions. More telling, they would take hours to 'ski' downhill, which might well turn a pleasant day's mountaineering into an epic struggle for survival. Taking them down a crevassed glacier when they could not properly turn or stop did not bear thinking about. Time is of the essence on mountains and closely linked to safety. Inescapably, they could not come with us on skis. It remained for me to tell them.

This was not a good start. From a team of six, we were suddenly down to four after only our first day out and our credibility with the Swiss, through Roger, was in doubt. He was going to report on us and I needed him to understand why our climbing group was such a mix of experience.

'The mountains should not be the reserve of elitists,' I said without preamble, stating the fundamental principle that had guided Tim Spicer and me when we decided to take three people from his battalion, volunteers all, with very little climbing between them.

Roger said nothing but watched me over his cup as he sipped his coffee. I plunged on, 'The mountains belong to everyone. Not just to the rock stars and big-route super-athletes.'

'Or the people who want to control access to the hills with paper qualifications,' interjected Gary, an accountant in the SAS Reserve who had the most climbing experience of us all.

'Everyone should be allowed on the mountains,' I agreed. 'They are as much part of our environment as the lowlands, the lakes and woods where we all go without a second's thought. In fact, everyone should be encouraged to go into the mountains and learn from them. The mountains belong to us all.'

This was a crucial moment. Roger was to be our mountain guide and the link on all climbing matters with the Swiss who were being so generous to us. In the silence after I finished, I recalled French guides I had seen literally dragging clients up the Goûter arête by the rope that linked them, and the story of the Saas guides quietly condoning an outrageous plan by their local councillors to raise a platform on the summit of the Fletschhorn which would turn it into another lucrative 4000er. Alpine mountain guides are skilled, qualified and experienced but the modern commercialism of guiding, ironically the direct corollary of increasing popular interest in the mountains, has had a terrible impact on their behaviour and reputation. What sort of guide was Roger?

'Not everyone can be a Reinhold Messner,' he said smiling, and put down his coffee cup. 'The mountains are not so complicated as people think.'

This, from a guide, was exceptional. So many maintain the mystique of danger and inaccessibility merely to protect their jobs.

He told a story of a Swiss Army major who had trained his entire company of a hundred men, by no means all skiers, and taken them all up Piz Bernina, the easternmost 4000er we had to climb in Switzerland, over 100 kilometres from the nearest other big mountain. To my immense relief, Roger's philosophy matched ours. I looked forward to climbing with him.

Later still that evening, all six of us on the climbing team sat down and hacked over the same discussion while I explained why Peter and Stewart could not join us on skis. After thrashing about in the snow on the Simplon, they half-suspected it, they understood it, but they were intensely disappointed. Peter, small and fit with a sleek mass of dark hair, is the epitome of Guards' reserve and was quietly determined not to let the situation get him down. Stewart, a crew-cut, stocky and enthusiastic Glaswegian, was more direct.

'What d'we do now?' he wanted to know, staring at me unblinking through his steel-rimmed glasses.

'Go back up to the Simplon, or to Saas Fee, and learn to ski,' I said feebly, perfectly well aware that the chances were slim of becoming good enough in time to join us before the skiing season was over. 'And acclimatise,' I added practically. Whatever happened on skis, the rest of us would be well acclimatised to the altitude by the time Peter and Stewart joined us, though none of us could have foreseen the implications of that remark for Stewart.

I can only imagine how intensely frustrated they both must have felt watching us pack our gear in the big room we all shared for our first mountain, the Allalinhorn. The name is said to come from the Latin *Aquilina*, which means Little Eagle.

The weather had cleared over our first weekend; Roger telephoned the head of the Saas Fee guides who confirmed that skiers had already been on the mountain on Sunday, and we were all set to go. Early on Monday morning we set out, excited with the prospect of our first peak, even though the Allalinhorn is usually written off by ski-mountaineering illuminati as being one of the easiest and most accessible. All you have to do, they say, is take the Metro-Allalin railway to 3454 metres and then skin up a few hundred metres to the summit at 4027 metres. Doubtless Roger had assessed this would be an ideal start for the poor British skiers. I admit, this matched my own plan to start with an easy one. We were prepared, but not mountain fit by a long way yet, and certainly not acclimatised.

It did not work out easy at all. What the Sunday skiers had appreciated better than us was that the Metro-Allalin railway closed that Sunday afternoon for seven weeks until 19 June, for maintenance works between the winter skiing and the summer seasons. So, on Monday morning, instead of climbing only 573 metres, we were faced with 1177 metres from the next highest T-bar ski-lift, half-way up Felskinn. Worse, even though we took the first lift of the day, it was already past nine o'clock by the time we started uphill, the sun was well up and hot, the snow was softening and there was no wind. We plodded up, each absorbed in his own painful little world, finding our balance on the Swiss Army mountain skis, getting used to the skins, hoping our plastic mountaineering boots would not give us blisters, adjusting our clothes at frequent drink stops to wear the right amount so we wouldn't loose too much liquid sweating under the relentless sun nor freeze if we fell in the snow. It was a long, hot, airless and very tiring ascent to the Feejoch, the little col between the summit pyramid and the Feechopf on our right.

The antics of a sleek black chough cunningly strutting about to encourage skiers to throw it bits of picnic sandwiches and our own elation at being so close to our first peak restored our energies. I cannot pretend I enjoyed the last 200 metres of snow slope, particularly as cloud began to thicken round us, blotting the view. I worried about route-finding down through the huge crevasses we had passed on our way up the Feegletscher. I wanted to hurry, before visibility closed right in, and took the lead, but my breath was short, I was hot, sweaty and tired. I could drag my heavy Swiss Army mountaineering skis up the hill no faster.

You have to leave your skis beneath the last rocky scramble to the summit, and we put on crampons. To my surprise, I felt suddenly light, fit, unaffected by the altitude and intensely exhilarated as I stepped out onto the topmost snowy ridge and strode easily to the big old-fashioned cross on the summit. We all felt the same.

Even though the Allalinhorn was first climbed as long ago as 1856, by the Saas Grund priest Johann Josef Imseng, his manservant Franz Andenmatten and an English barrister called Edward Levi Ames, even though it has been climbed since by literally thousands of people, and even though it is rated 'Facile', or Easy, in the guide books, we felt grand. Simply, this was our first. And we had done it on our own. Our intrepid guide Roger had been ordered to Andermatt that morning to report on his day out with us on the Simplon.

On cue, the sun abruptly came out, the clouds parted, and we had a superb view of the series of rock spires rising to the summit of the Rimpfischhorn, the smooth snow summit of the Strahlhorn and towering further away on the border with Italy we saw the massive Monte Rosa group. All summits we must visit. I was struck by our insignificance even on the Allalinhorn, small by comparison with those others, and by the enormity of what we had set out to do.

2

A LEARNING CURVE

The sight looks up with pain on craggy rocks and barren
mountains wanting in shades of green to entertain it.
                                                    John Dryden

The Breithorn followed next day. There was no further snowfall, so
Gary, Simon, Douglas and I grabbed our skis and drove to Zermatt
early in the morning in our battered gentian-blue hard-topped
Land-Rover. This had German number plates so, dressed in an
eye-damaging mixture of salmon and violet Gore-Tex gear, Douglas
with a bandana round his head, wearing mirror sunglasses, we
looked like members of the Baader–Meinhof gang, fifth generation,
on holiday. Belching smoke, the ancient Rover strained up the
hairpin bends by Randa as if it had been thrashed round Germany
on every British Army exercise since the Second World War. The
steering went haywire over bumps, reducing our speed to 30 mph
and I wondered how it would last the summer.

   You are forbidden to drive into Zermatt as the village is too
small. Everyone has to leave their cars at Täsch and take the train.
Socially and ecologically, the rule is jolly sensible, like so much in
Switzerland, as visitors' cars would jam and asphyxiate Zermatt,
but the return train ride costs 11.00 SFrs which is money for old
rope. Thousands of tourists use the railway daily in the winter and
summer seasons. Fine for those holidaying in the village for a week
or two (if you can afford it), but it is a nuisance just for a day.

   At least plastic ski-mountaineering boots are easy to walk in. We

lumbered our ski gear and day sacks onto the train and marched
through Zermatt which is rather like a huge outdoor, up-market
Woolworths for the very rich. We had a game to see who could
find the most expensive watch on sale and Gary took first prize
with a diamond-encrusted gold Rolex for a snip over £70,000. We
took the lift at the other end of the village, changed into two
more lifts, stamped through the big restaurant complex for skiers
at Trockenersteg (2939m) and finally reached the Klein Matterhorn
(3883m) at eleven o'clock.

This is one of the highest ski stations in the Alps, but the famous
view of the Matterhorn just to the west was completely obscured.
Thick clouds hung around the mountain in windless air. On the
other side, the broad slope up the Breithorn was clear and covered
with parties of skiers toiling up the well-cut track zigzagging to the
summit plateau, like black insects on the steep white snow field.

We were late, as we had waited for the shops to open in Zermatt
village to buy some equipment (kit shops are terrible places for
spending money). However, we reached the summit in an hour and
a half and I was encouraged to find I was neither tired nor suffered
any altitude sickness. Feeling rather pleased with myself, I jostled
for a place on the broad summit snow cap among the numerous
other skiers and ate a bar of chocolate next to a grizzled Zermatt
guide and his client, a scrawny middle-aged American woman who
had been having difficulty on the steep icy patches near the summit.
Thinking she was a beginner, I asked, 'Is this your first time up the
Breithorn?'

'Jesus, no!' she drawled. 'My fifth!'

Chastened, as I was very much a beginner myself if I had to admit
it, I observed foolishly, 'You must like this mountain a lot?'

'No,' she corrected me. 'I use the Breithorn as a training run-out
when I come to Switzerland every year for other climbs.'

I thought this was a pity. The Breithorn is probably the most
frequented 4000er in the Alps. I suppose tens of thousands have
traipsed up it since it was first climbed eons ago in 1813, two
years before the Battle of Waterloo, especially since the Klein
Matterhorn lift was built; nowadays even grossly unfit skiers can
make the summit in little more than two hours. All the same, this
cheap reputation belies the dangers inherent on any big mountain.
Apart from the fact that the Breithorn's northern flank has some

difficult snow and ice routes, there is always avalanche risk on the hot southern side. In 1977 five German climbers, fully equipped with maps, compasses and altimeters, became utterly lost in a whiteout and froze to death on the flat Breithorn plateau. Even death, it seemed, has failed to leave its usual impact on the Breithorn's reputation.

The Matterhorn summit appeared briefly through the clouds and I turned to the American woman's guide and said, 'I 'spec you've been up there a few times?'

'Five hundred or more,' he replied, munching a garlic sausage. His expression of deep resignation suggested he would not be upset if he never climbed the Matterhorn again. Such is commerce, the downside of more and more people coming into the mountains, the same for client and guide alike.

The weather held and improved. We returned next day earlier still, took the same tiresome trek by train from Täsch, through Zermatt village, up the three lifts, and started from the Klein Matterhorn at shortly after nine o'clock. The sun shone and the eight-kilometre ski traverse to Pollux was superb, across the southern flanks of the frontier mountains, with magnificient views into Italy over range upon range of jagged snowy peaks separated by dark mysterious valleys lost in black shadows far below. The heat softened the glittering snow so we chose the rocky West-South-West Ridge on Pollux rather than struggle up steep heavy snow on the West Face.

The air was clear, the views fantastic and rather to Douglas's horror, we disdained protection as we swung about like monkeys on the fixed rope on the steep rocks near the top of the rock ridge. Douglas had done little climbing before this expedition so even this easy section appeared worrying at first sight. But he is tall, dark and powerfully built, like a stretched Rambo (but without Stallone's agreeable bank balance) and he followed easily, cursing us fiercely until he suddenly topped a short cliff to find the statue of a sad-faced Virgin Mary.

These were early days, when we all had so much to learn about our judgement of the risks which are inescapably part of mountains. Everyone perceives these risks differently. Some hate the very idea of mountains. Some, usually with the advantage of experience or a towering lack of imagination, make nothing of what terrifies everyone else. Each time we went out was a new experience, and I had already noticed that there was always something a little harder than before. The Allalinhorn had been 'Facile', the Breithorn 'Peu difficile minus' and Pollux was 'Peu difficile' with Grade II rock climbing. More than just improving our climbing techniques, each of us had to come to terms with how we would cope with the risks. Fear is a very personal thing and I wondered what would happen on the more difficult routes ahead.

But we were confident and our choice of route on Pollux was vindicated on the way down. On the steep part of the rock ridge, we met a Scottish couple, a young guy and his girlfriend, who were coming up. They had tried the snow slope on the West Face and turned back, put off by the heavy warm snow, and then followed us up the ridge. Now they were stuck by the fixed ropes. I was interested to see their perception of the exposure on the rock ridge had scared them so much that they had almost given up. They had tied themselves onto the fixed ropes with a cat's-cradle of karabiners and slings so they could hardly move at all, they had no protection left to move upwards and they were puffing like trains. Funny how people pant when they are frightened.

We helped them up, though their hands seemed glued to rope and rock, and they plainly hated it. We advised them to take the ridge in descent too. It was nearly one o'clock by then, a lovely hot day and even the snow on the summit was soft. Of course they did not take our advice. They went down by the snow slope on the West Face. During our long ski traverse back to the Breithorn Pass, Simon and I kept stopping for a breather and looking back to watch their two tiny black figures inching their way down the soft snow face. I should not have liked to make that descent in such gungy snow, and we talked about what we should do if we saw them fall. This question grew more acute the further we distanced ourselves from them. The idea of going back did not appeal. The sun was baking, we were roasting even in T-shirts, sunburned and sweating.

Besides, we had our own worries. There was still 2 kilometres of skinning under the Breithorn group to the col by the Klein Matterhorn before we could take off our skins for the downhill run to the Trockenersteg, and several small avalanches had already slid across our early ski tracks in the heat since morning.

We agreed we would have gone back, but thank God we did not

have to. Just as we skied out of sight over the Breithorn col, the black dots, hardly visible so far away across the bright snow slopes by then, reached the base of Pollux safely, doubtless very relieved.

The ski down to the Trockenersteg lift station was quite exhilarating after a long hot day. We had made a highly satisfactory start with three mountains climbed, but as I sank a large ice-cold beer in the bar sitting in the sun waiting for the others, I was conscious of all the work which remained to be done and aware not merely of the pressure to finish but in particular the pressure to decide which mountain we tackled next.

Then the weather turned, and perhaps just as well since Gary and Douglas had bad blisters. Plastic ski-mountaineering boots are excellent for keeping out the wet, for fitting speed clip-on crampons and holding your feet rigid in the downhill ski mode, but they are totally unforgiving. The inner, which comes out, is laced onto your foot and is always comfortable, but the trouble starts when you stuff your foot into the plastic shell and go walking. They are impossible to break in. You either get on with them or not. After only three mountains, Gary and Douglas had round angry red patches of bare flesh on their insteps and heels and needed a day or two out of boots to let the air harden off their feet.

Plus, we had been out every day since arriving and our personal administration, not least some stinking socks, skiddies and sweat shirts were in serious need of attention.

Back in Brig, the Base Camp party were busy in town setting up their own private Swiss bank accounts, to prove that British Army lance corporals and Guardsmen can do anything, while I spent the morning wrist-deep in soapsuds and dirty clothes in the stainless steel trough which looked like a thigh-level pissoir and passed for our 'wash handbasin'. The rooms we had were rudimentary, but immaculately clean, so freshly painted I doubt anyone had used them before, and aptly suited to our purpose. We slept in barrack rooms on the third floor and used the ground floor showers, drying room, dining-room and kitchen. The four-storey granite building stood by the railway line on the edge of town, between the extremes of a fearsomely noisy building site on one side and the Kantonal district police station on the other, where absolutely nothing seemed to happen at all. Thankfully our building did not look at all military. The car park outside, where we kept our natty blue Land-Rovers, was a short cut to the town and people wandered past all day. The Swiss Army only used the first floor offices during the weekdays, so we more or less had the run of the place and slopped about in flip-flops and shorts.

'I don't think I'll hack all this,' said Simon. I looked down to see him lying on the bottom bunk of our twin bunk-beds in the barrack room which was littered with climbing gear, ropes, harnesses, helmets, boxes of army rations, rucksacks and boots. He was reading a bulky paperback entitled *Mein Kampf* by Adolf Hitler, edited by Alan Bullock.

'Heavy stuff,' I agreed. Not my cup of tea at all, but Simon wanted to broaden his mind in between climbs. He knew all about Hitler, like everyone else, but he thought he ought to find out what the man himself had said.

Decisively, he ripped the first hundred pages off the top of the book, declaring, 'That'll be lighter.'

'I doubt it,' I replied.

He gave me a funny look, but having neatly disposed of the practical problems of genuine historical research, he added, 'Now let's go for a beer.'

We chose the Pirate, a bar nautically decked out with ships' wheels, sepia photos of the Cutty Sark and fish netting, and drank Paulaner *Weissbier*, which is made from wheat, strong and delicious, even at 5 SFrs a bottle. Quite soon, Dave Moore floated into the bar with a group of the base camp support team, dressed to kill. Dave is a Londoner, sharp and practical, with unfailing good humour, and he was our chef. I had banned all reference to rank for the duration, we were all strictly on Christian-name terms, but in real life he was a sergeant and he became the effective self-appointed leader of the Base Camp. By day he rustled round Brig looking for deals and discounts to buy our food (and anything else), using his German to good effect, and he cooked excellent meals with Nigel Taylor. At night he and all the others had a shit, shower, shave and decked themselves out to hit the town. Mike Nutter, a dedicated Scots Guardsman, and 'George' Roper, our lance-corporal medic, led another group but the single-minded aim was the same: women. Already a chart had been prepared on a white display board on the wall of our TV room to record successes.

Dave, Mike and the others very quickly established Brig contained a soldier's dream combination. The town is attractive and contained a handful of good bars all within walking distance: the Pirate, the Britannia (because the Swiss think there is something chic about a bar decorated like a London pub) which we inevitably called the Brit, Johnny's Bar, the Napoleon and the Lötschberg disco. Better still, they were all staffed by a dozen or more Danish girls. Several were really stunning, but there is nothing which makes up for beauty so much as blond hair and a liberal Scandinavian upbringing.

I am not shy of a tincture and no stranger to bars, but my own feelings were slightly different. I had left behind a wife and two little girls at home.

I wondered if the first Alpine explorers, like Edward Whymper and Geoffrey Winthrop Young, who opened up the Alps for the Swiss at the turn of the century, missed their families as I did. Later travellers, such as Eric Newby, certainly did and said so. In 1646, John Evelyn wrote that the Simplon Pass was, 'strange, horrid and fearful . . . only inhabited by bears, wolves and wild goats,' and doubtless he would have been amazed to have found so many attractive Danish barmaids when he reached Brig.

Of course, we were not explorers in the traditional sense, because all our mountains had already been climbed and the bars of Brig hardly compete with the current mountaineering fashion for derring-do in the Himalayas, but I was searching for my limits just the same, not in resisting the birds of Brig (though God knows that was tough enough), but out on the mountains all round, where there is still freedom and where bureaucracy is still happily as remote as on any mountain in the world.

Most readers will envy us, with nothing but the prospect of climbing and drinking all summer, but I was beginning to find out that when we were not on the mountains, there were unexpected constraints. We were prisoners of the weather forecast. To start with, I could not find a reliable guru. Roger gave me a Zurich number but they refused to speak English or French, even though French is an official Swiss language, and for a time we depended wholly on the met office at Geneva Airport. They forecast for pilots flying planes, not for mountaineers on the ground, so they were not ideal, but they said there was another belt of föhn going through. There had been fresh snow at altitude and we had to leave off for a couple of days to allow the snow to consolidate.

On Friday, 7 May, we tried again. We drove to Saas Fee, where Roger had suggested that we might try the Strahlhorn. The route was long, needing five hours' skiing up the Allalin Glacier so we needed to spend a night in the mountains at the Britannia Hut for an early start on Saturday morning. It was no good taking lifts first thing. They did not reach altitude till about nine, which was a waste of cold crisp early morning snow conditions which we needed for the glacier approach.

However, there was nothing cold or crisp about Saas Fee that day. Grey clouds hung round the circle of big 4000ers above the village, hiding the Allalinhorn, Alphubel, Täschhorn, Dom and Lenzspitze, snow threatened and none of the lifts was working. Fed up, we walked into the village to find a bar. The place was deserted. The skiing season was over, the bars, hotels and restaurants were closed and the streets empty. Ski resorts look very depressing closed down. The Café Central was the only place open. A pile of skis and rucksacks stacked outside testified to other frustrated ski-mountaineers whom we found cosily steamed up inside drinking schnapps and hot drinks.

I swear that all the best climbing decisions are made in the bar. Over a tasty but intrinsically foul combination of hot chocolate and beer, we discussed the Strahlhorn. The tactics were this. The weather forecast promised good mornings and poor afternoons, but if the mornings were like this the afternoons would be serious, and the idea of route-finding up a long crevasse-filled glacier in bad visibility did not appeal. Par time from the Britannia Hut to the summit in good weather was five hours up and four back. In bad, we would be into the regions of an epic in the dark.

Anyway, there was the expense. The cabin to the top of the Felskinn cost 30 SFrs each, or £14.00, (the Klein Matterhorn lift for the Breithorn cost 49 SFrs, or £23.00), and even after trying hard for eighteen months I had still not found a financial sponsor to cover these running costs. Tim Spicer and I were scraping round obscure army funds to cover what costs we could but we knew there was still a shortfall so my responsibility was to minimise our expenses, like anyone holidaying in the Alps. The Britannia Hut warden, whom I had called to check the weather and snow conditions, said we could pitch our tents by the hut, which would save hut accommodation fees, but the idea of committing ourselves to lift costs on such a slim chance of success did not appeal. We decided to bin the Strahlhorn.

We ordered another beer, convinced ourselves a pretty dark-haired girl kept making phone calls at the back of the café where we were sitting just to keep passing us at our table, and wondered what to do instead. The weather was forecast the same for at least two days, so long glacier approaches in mist were out. But we could tackle ridges. At least on a ridge you know at once if you slip off the route. We opted for the Bernese Oberland.

With typical London cheerfulness, Dave Moore volunteered to cook us breakfast at five o'clock next morning. We all regretted it. He never missed a single night out in Brig and I had made the mistake of drinking too much Hefe *Weissbier* in the Pirate. He staggered into the kitchen in flip-flops, whacked on the boogie player (I don't think he can cook unless deafened by music) and, to the sound of Whitney Houston singing, 'I'm every woman', which sounded to me more like 'Climb every mountain' (though I never said anything as the others thought I was deaf anyway), he set about producing the traditional British Army breakfast of fried egg, sausage, bacon, tomatoes and spoonfuls of the ubiquitous baked bean, an explosive carbohydrate bomb enthusiastically consumed by soldiers in every part of the world, be it desert, jungle or snow. It did not help.

Feeling ghastly, I tried to sleep as Gary drove the ancient hard-top down the valley and onto the Goppenstein–Kandersteg car-train which takes you through the sulphurous Lötschberg tunnel. From Lauterbrunnen, I lolled about half-conscious on the hard bench seats of the Wengen-Alp Bahn railway and tried to ignore dozens of Japanese tourists snapping and filming everything. This remarkable funicular rack-and-pinion railway was built from 1900 to 1912 at a cost of twenty-eight lives and after a lovely trip past Wengen and Kleine Scheidegg rises steeply along a granite tunnel through the Eiger to the Jungfraujoch at 3454 metres. All of this should have been a pleasant journey. There is no better time to see mountain scenery, lakes and glaciers than in the first clear hours after dawn, but I did not feel at all crisp.

I do not recall much of the Mönch. In nasty blowing cloud, we skinned the short distance from the Jungfraujoch across to the foot of the mountain and took the normal route, up the South Spur and

East-South-East Ridge. I felt drained, almost disorientated as the clouds closed in, reducing vis to nothing, the ridge was steep and Douglas and I moved agonisingly slowly in the steps of Gary and Simon who romped above us. At 1.30 p.m., by the time we were on the summit, the snow was unpleasantly soft and we could see nothing at all in the mist. We could have been anywhere in the world.

Our crampons balled up badly on the lower slopes on the descent to the Mönchsjoch, and I was glad to reach the Mönchsjoch Hut and feel human again with a bowl of excellent hot minestrone. I do not recommend climbing 4000ers with a hangover.

All sorts frequent the Mönchsjoch Hut. It is perched on a steel frame against the South-East Spur of the Mönch, like a large wooden shed on an oil rig. Inside, the low-ceilinged wood dining-room was warm with lean, sun-browned ski mountaineers, mostly young fit-looking French and Swiss, other less earnest groups like us who look unlikely to rise at 3 a.m. from a warm bunk-bed, parties of middle-aged couples who would look more at home in a café down in Lauterbrunnen drinking beer or watching football on telly, and two enormously fat Germans, plainly not shy of a litre or two and who do not look as though they could climb the stairs, let alone mountains.

Of course, the Mönchsjoch Hut is easy to reach: the route from the Jungfraujoch railway is an hour and a half gentle uphill along a broad track signed with stakes. The place is well run too, the staff helpful and the food good, very probably a direct result of being privately run rather than managed by staff employed by the Swiss Alpine Club.

At supper, served on long tables like at school, we sat with three US Army dentists 'on vacation' who wanted to climb the Eiger. Oddly, one had mountaineering skis like us, one had Norwegian 'Langlauf' skis and the other was on foot. Given the unsettled weather and somewhat warm snow conditions, I did not fancy their combined chances, but they were agreeable company, fresh and keen, a team of all-American dental enthusiasts. I suppose you have to be optimistic if you spend all day peering into rotten mouths.

We were given more minestrone in a large tureen, so one of the dentists played 'mother', doshing out while the other two were busy saying politely, 'No thank you. I've plenty. You have some more.'

All round the busy dining-room we could hear, '*Nein danke!*' or '*Après vous, je vous en prie!*'

Of course the pigs in our group, led by Simon who eats for two, needed no prompting to take any seconds on offer.

Curry followed, and rice. Strange how the Swiss, with absolutely no links with the East like our own tattered legacy of the Indian Empire, should think it a good idea to produce curry on a cold snowy mountain.

After this odd meal, I watched the three dentists who were sharing our bunk-bed room busy scrubbing their teeth and felt guilty. I had forgotten my toothbrush.

We left the hut at 7 a.m., which will shock the real mountaineers who like to rush into the icy dawn hours earlier, and headed for the Jungfrau. The sky was clear, the air cold and our spirits lifted. Crack the Jungfrau, we thought, then the next day we could climb the two Fiescherhörner en route to the Finsteraarhorn, and then the Gross-Grünhorn before we move on to . . .

Such plans are pie in the sky in big mountains. These splendid summits demand respect for their intrinsic beauty and for all the fascinating variables which are part of every decision you make on them, such as weather, steepness, visibility, climbing or skiing skills, fitness, time, conditions of crevasses, ice, rock and of course, snow. I surprised myself by beginning to find the constant assessment of all these factors a most fascinating part of mountaineering. Like most people, I like to think I work well under pressure and I enjoyed the ever-changing situations on mountains which present a continuous series of decisions to be made in order to achieve one's aim of climbing to the top and then finding a way safely down. I was finding that the challenge is not solely in reaching the summit: it exists in every step of the way, and in such breath-taking scenery as the vast and remote glaciers of the Bernese Oberland, on skis and free in the wind and sun, there is no greater pleasure on earth.

We passed the Jungfraujoch again which was, as usual, overflowing with camera-festooned Japanese tourists, skied hilariously downhill across to the foot of the Jungfrau and skinned up the spur towards the Rottalsattel. There we stopped. We looked over to the saddle only 200 metres away, to the bergschrund where we could leave our skis and crampon up the steep snow slope to the summit. Two hundred metres is not far, but the track crosses a slope which steepens sharply to fifty degrees and falls away into a bay of the Jungfraufirn Glacier below. The snow on that slope was nearly a metre deep, dry, loose and seriously unconsolidated.

My feeling of pleasure at the sunny day and making such good headway on our next objective vanished. Suddenly, I felt empty and my imagination took over. What did they say in the books? Expect avalanches on a slope of thirty to forty-five degrees? We were standing on a part of the spur which fitted that bracket nicely. Would the whole slope suddenly break away? I wondered what it would feel like tumbling downhill in a cascade of avalanching snow. Feeling empty, I helped Gary dig an avalanche pit, isolating a test block of snow a metre cubed. The block collapsed even as I began to slide my ski on it, sure indication of avalanche conditions.

The sun shone mockingly and we stared again at the tantalisingly short 200 metres we had to traverse to the Rottalsattel. It would be plain sailing after that, but this short distance is notorious for avalanching. People have died here. A party of British climbers were swept away some weeks later, one died and one was seriously injured. We noticed there had been another ski party at the same spot before us, probably the day before. They had dug snow profiles too, and turned back. There were no ski tracks across that tempting steep slope to the bergschrund. Gary was furious, frustrated by our failure, and prepared to risk it, but we persuaded him not to and turned back.

Our depression at this first failed attempt lifted the following day with the weather, which dawned clear and ice cold. We decided it was pointless returning to the Jungfrau, as the snow would not have consolidated enough overnight, so we opted to try the Gross- and Hinter-Fiescherhörner, 4049 metres and 4025 metres respectively. We thought we might be able to climb both in one day, but once again it was 7 a.m. before we left the Mönchsjoch hut. We skied onto an ice-hard, vast and open glacier appropriately named the Ewigschneefeld, or 'everlasting snowfield', which should have been called the Ewigkeitschneefeld, for, in the cold, translucent light of early morning, this spacious snowy amphitheatre, ringed at the top with high mountains and descending smoothly out of sight miles to the south, was the very essence of the space and freedom of eternity. Like specks on a white plain, we glided downhill, losing 400 metres of altitude over five kilometres in just half an hour. I will leave walking to others! This is the only way to travel on glaciers. Frozen but elated, we stopped at the side of the glacier under the glacier which falls from the Fiescherhorn summit ridge nearly 800 metres above us.

We fitted skins, plugged in Walkmans and set off on the long steady pull up the glacier. Doubtless the purists will have cardiac arrest to read this, but music perfectly complements the beauty of a fine mountain morning, on glittering snow with views of great peaks all round, just as a musical score enhances a film. Anyway, stuff the Luddites; we all used Walkmans and loved it.

'Don't let the sun go down on me,' crooned Elton John in my ears. His early love songs were the best.

Up ahead was a party of seven and I fixed my sights on them. Following their track back and forth around the deep crevasses, I led Douglas, Gary and Simon steadily uphill, sliding one ski forward and up after the other, watching the tips flicking into view along the grooves in the firm snow, taking pleasure in balancing my weight correctly to avoid back-slipping on the steeper sections, in keeping a long relaxed pace, and in the sheer metronomic physical repetition which set up an unexpected but powerfully seductive metaphysical rhythm inside me. I began to enjoy going uphill.

In time with our music, we relentlessly overhauled the party ahead. I wanted to time it so we overtook them just before we reached the bergschrund under the Fiechersattel. The idea of following them up the snow couloir from the bergschrund to the saddle, with snow debris cascading down on us, did not appeal.

We passed them 100 metres short of the bergschrund, and as I made the last turn, I realised the bergschrund crevasse was wider and deeper than it had appeared from below. There was something of a track, probably made the day before, but the approach was steep and the bridge across looked delicate.

I edged forward, holding myself awkwardly upright to stop my skis sliding back as I pushed with my ski sticks to ease myself up the short sharp slope to the crevasse. On the snow bridge, I tried to levitate, persuading myself I could somehow diminish my weight as I slipped across. Beneath my feet under the snow bridge, all was deep blue ice inside a dark chasm.

'Watch the ice,' I said over my shoulder to Douglas, meaning he could easily side-slip on the steep part. He slipped over, his face a picture of concentration as he peered into the depths of the crevasse below. Gary was next.

As Douglas and I moved to a suitable place on the steep slope to remove our skis and fit crampons, Gary suddenly disappeared.

I heard shouting. I looked back. Stupidly, I wondered where Gary had gone. All I could see was a big hole where the snow bridge had been and Simon moving up fast. He had flung off his rucksack and was pulling out a rope. Behind him, the guide leading the seven-man party was skinning forward with interest to see what was going on. I fancy his clients' enthusiasm for a nice day out had suddenly evaporated. The wonderful wide-open views, space, sun and freedom had abruptly closed down on reality.

Gary's stocky shape was wedged in cold ice about three metres down. His shouts were faint, muffled by the ice and snow so I could hardly hear him. He was bruised and shaken but nothing was broken, and he was using his skis to stop himself slipping any deeper, holding the edges against little ridges of rock-hard ice. Even after a few short moments he was having to shake off the bitter cold.

Simon worked very quickly and threw him one end of the rope. Below, out of sight, Gary struggled to tie himself on and then disentangle himself from his rucksack. Next, he took off his skis, which he nearly dropped into the depths below him as he manoeuvred them in the confined space and clipped them with a karabiner to the rope, all the time trying not to lose balance and fall himself.

The guide leading the party behind us arrived on the scene. Leaning over perilously close to the lip of broken snow at the edge of the hole, he peered down at Gary and enquired in English, 'You okay?'

Was this emergency aid on the mountains? Or, was the guide covering himself in case there was an inquiry? Or, was he just a man with a sense of humour? If so, he needed it. Gary was fine, but the guide's clients behind were not. Now they were closer, Douglas and I laughed to see every face etched with horror, each one wondering how on earth they were going to cross the bergschrund themselves without dying! The guide was faced with a serious loss of confidence.

Looking cheerful but relieved, Gary crawled out of his hole on Simon's rope and sat downhill of the bergschrund. Above it, Douglas had the rope he and I used and threw him an end. We yanked Simon and Gary over the crevasse by brute force. The guide watched us, but never asked if we could help him over the same way. Maybe it was pride, or maybe he felt he had to earn his pay, which was a cool 780 SFrs per client in the group behind him. He certainly had a duty to them at this price. In the Mönch hut, we had been reading a Grindelwald Bergführer guide magazine and the guide rates quite took our breath away. They charged 780 SFrs for the Jungfrau, Mönch and the Gross-Fiescherhorn (adding the Hinter-Fiescherhorn cost extra). The Finsteraarhorn cost 790 SFrs, the Aletschhorn 610 SFrs, one must suppose a similar sum for the Gross-Grünhorn while the Schreckhorn and Lauteraarhorn were rated at 920 SFrs each. So, if we took guides, the nine peaks we wanted to climb in the Bernese Oberland would cost 6,400 SFrs (nearly £3,000) each! Excluding hut and lift costs. No wonder so few people have climbed all these mountains.

We left him to it and he was still faffing about trying to entice his party to cross that crevasse by the time we were descending from the summit of the Gross-Fiescherhorn an hour and a half later.

I don't think anyone goes up the Hinter-Fiescherhorn. Even after the first ascent of the Gross-Fiescherhorn, on 23 July 1862, no one bothered to make the short traverse to visit the summit next door for twenty-three years. We saw no tracks from the saddle, nor sign of any old ones.

We left our skis in the saddle and floundered about in deep snow following the line of the bergschrund to find a way across. This took time as the crevasse was much larger than the one Gary had fallen in, but we encouraged him no end to find a suitable bridge since he was now an experienced '*bergschrund-hund*'. Finally, Simon found a dodgy-looking bridge onto an ice dome which swelled up to the ridge above. I should not like to cross this in summer when it must open up wider still as the snow melts.

The snow was dry, loose and dangerous near the summit and Simon, roped to me, led the last part on a snow-covered rock ridge convinced he would take a tumble. However, the view from the top was superb, all round the great peaks of the Bernese Oberland, especially of the much bigger Finsteraarhorn away to the south-east. The summit block stood out like a great white ship from a sea of cloud which filled the glacial valley beneath, and the final ridge, like a sail, looked steep, knife-sharp and daunting.

It's the most wonderful feeling to relax on the summit you have worked hard to reach for hours before, but always there are those decisions to be made, the innumerable elements changing every which way all the time. Clouds were encroaching fast from the south now, it was nearly one o'clock, cold and time to go.

'Let's sod off,' I said, expedition-leader-wise. You never know what can happen on the way down.

The couloir down from the Fieschersattel was soft on our descent and the snow round Gary's bergschrund equally unpleasant. Judging by the chaos of holes and tracks everywhere, the guide and his party had made a real meal of crossing the crevasse and it was not easy to see a way over. I stood in the middle pretending to fiddle with my skis, Gary and Simon cast to the right and left, while Douglas decided on the direct method. Preparatory to leaping over himself, he tied his skis together with Velcro carrying-tapes and, before I could utter a word, tossed the bundle over the crevasse, hoping the skis would stick into the soft snow below, like a spear. Murphy's law intervened, in full measure. Transfixed, speechless, we all watched the skis arc through the air, as if in slow motion. They bounced once on the snow, snapping the Velcro tapes apart, and only one ski stuck into the snow. The other seemed to hesitate, as if to underline the wickedness of its intention, then slid off downhill. In a second, it gathered speed and disappeared from view into thick cloud washing up the slope below us.

'Nice one,' I remarked after a moment's stunned silence.

We all stared after the vanished ski, where the snow merged with the cloud. We looked at Douglas, who looked at us. There was no need to say anything more.

We were still at 3700 metres, high up on a mountain and seven kilometres from the hut, it was already past two o'clock and the weather was worsening. The clouds were moving but visibility was down to less than 100 metres. Douglas would have to walk down, or at best scooter along on one ski with a crampon, which would take ages. I had visions of losing our way down the glacier in the cloud and being caught out at night. Lastly, there was no way he could get another ski to continue with us next day.

Douglas hid his feelings well. Come to that, we all did. There was no point shouting and ranting. You can't do that on mountains. There is absolutely no point. So, we all just got on with it. Gary, Simon and I put on our skis and swung wildly back and forth in big loops on the steep slopes as we followed Douglas walking slowly down, trying to keep on the tracks of another party which was ahead of us. It was not easy. The wind obscured the cuts and grooves in the snow with more blowing snow and the dense white cloud obliterated all depth of vision and contrast.

Twenty minutes later when we were feeling particularly gloomy, the clouds suddenly blew ragged, the sun shone feebly through and there, hundreds of metres below, on a seemingly smooth shoulder, I saw something sticking out of the snow. I hardly had time to shout at the others before the cloud swirled back again, but we all convinced ourselves it could only be the lost ski.

We had not been able to judge how far the object was below us, or even if we could get at it. There were some spectacular crevasses either side of our route down which the ski might have rocketed. However, speculation was academic. As long as we were struggling in a virtual whiteout, we would never find the ski again. Tantalised by this brief vision, we could do nothing but carry on down.

None of us said much. The three of us on skis were concentrating on staying upright in the softening afternoon snow and Douglas had his own dark thoughts. Abruptly, the cloud cleared again and we all shouted, 'The ski!'

The devil or Douglas's guardian angel was working overtime. The ski was sticking out of the snow on a gently sloping shoulder no more than 200 metres away on our left. I was nearest and skied over to retrieve it, a wary eye open, for we had had more than our share of 'schrunds and crevasses that day.

The ski's runaway track was plain in the snow, a straight line down the mountain, but only two metres or so from where it had stuck in the snow, it seemed to have rolled, caught the tip, somersaulted and stuck in upright. I pulled it out and, keeping clear of a large crevasse on my left, I skied back to Douglas.

Buoyed by this extraordinary piece of luck, we romped back to the hut, easily overtaking the party ahead of us on the vast open Ewigschneefeld. Douglas raced ahead, doubtless still angry with himself, and Gary said to Simon and me, 'We're SAS! Can't let the Scots Guards get away with this!'

Simon and I laughed. Then, we still felt there was a difference. Gary chased off after Douglas, but Simon and I stuck to our own good pace, and I listened to more of Elton John's early love songs on that endless open glacier called eternity, like 'Song for Guy' and 'Sorry seems to be the hardest word'.

These easy rhythms matched our mood. For the first time, we had had a good mixed day, with skiing, crevasses and rock. We felt fit and acclimatised.

Our luck with the weather did not hold. Before dawn next morning, in darkness, we peered out of the double-glazed windows of the Mönch hut to find the weather was filthy. Thick clouds were driving through the col on a fearsome wind, we could hardly see the tracks on the snow below and fresh snow was falling. We had to go down.

Douglas's devilish luck did not desert him. At Lauterbrunnen, he dropped his wallet as we got off the train and found it missing when he went to pay the car park fee. He ran back to the station office where an honest man had handed it in.

3

TIME OUT

The days come and go like muffled and veiled figures sent from a distant friendly party; but they say nothing, and if we do not use the gifts they bring, they carry them as silently away.

Emerson, *Journals* 1847

'You will have lovely conditions,' said a man looking into a cupful of tea leaves in the Geneva met office.

This welcome news came at the end of a frustrating week of appalling föhn, storms and unusually heavy snowfall, when we had climbed six mountains but before our second visit to the Bernese Oberland. I rang Roger to discuss what we might do next. Plainly he had been talking to the mountain fairies.

'I feel change in the seasons,' he declared. I visualised him casting a fey glance out of his window, across Sierre in the valley below, at the white mass of the Weisshorn and Bishorn. He was in tune with the mountains. 'I am sure the winter skiing season is over. Real spring is in the air. The snow conditions will be good. I think you can go on the Monte Rosa group and you will find it very fine.' This was a favourite expression, used on the happy assumption of its idiomatic rather than meteorological accuracy. Our relationship was still young, but I should have guessed.

Simon, Gary, Douglas and I spent another 49 SFrs each on lifts to the Klein Matterhorn. We walked onto the snow at 9 a.m. and the day augured well. The sun shone, the snow was crisp in the cold air and there was an impressive view of the mountains ranging south into Italy. Only a few white clouds lurked in the distance, hiding the Gran Paradiso.

We removed our skins on the flat Breithorn plateau and glided off on a long gentle traverse along the sparkling white southern slopes of the frontier mountains. Far away, and rising above its twin Pollux, was Castor (4228m), our objective. Almost at once, Douglas fell on hard icy ruts as we were sidling round a tricky shoulder under the Breithorn group. He slithered dramatically down the mountain before stopping himself by jabbing the end of his ski stick into the snow and coming to rest on a flatter snowfield below. Then, he had to fit skins back onto his skis to skin uphill and take them off again when he reached us. This cost time so we took an hour and a half to reach the Zwillingsjoch at the bottom of Castor. In that time, while we had been concentrating on not repeating Douglas's fall ourselves, cloud had sneaked up from the south and settled on the tops of the whole border range.

At 3845 metres, the Zwillingsjoch was clear but as soon as we fitted our skins and began traversing back and forth up the North-West Face we entered cloud and visibility dropped to ten metres. The warmth of the sun was replaced by a bitterly cold wind in our faces. Half-way up Simon and I decided we must fit harscheisen to our skis to cross the iced rubble of an avalanche which covered the slope. At this point, Douglas announced to us he had forgotten to bring his. We ignored him.

Harscheisen prevent you slipping on hard ice or snow when merely edging the skis will not hold you. They clip on the plate under the boot, so they lift as you bend your leg to slide the ski forward, but when all your weight is on the ski, with the plate and boot flat on the ski, the harscheisen crampon points extend beneath the ski and dig into the hard ice. The trick is to remember you are carrying the things, the problem attaching them on a steep slope, because everything has to come off. First the skis, stabbing them into the hard snow. Then you loop the wrist-straps of your ski sticks over one ski and, slipping your rucksack off your back you hook a shoulder strap over the other ski. Even the most famous of climbers have lost rucksacks by inadvertently knocking them as they manoeuvre about in a tight corner. Then you pull out the four little pieces of metal, the harscheisen, which must be fitted two to each ski, taking great care not to drop any. I always find the worst part is putting the skis back on, especially the second one. Bending and twisting round to fit the boot correctly into its safety binding at the heel is most unbalancing.

We all changed in silence. It was a pity not having a view, as we were at just over 4000 metres but I often think it helps not seeing where you might go if you fell. I looked down. Half visible in the mist, Douglas had put on his boot crampons, speed clip-on type, and was strapping his skis with compression straps to the sides of his rucksack. He hoisted this unwieldly package onto his back and proceeded to clamber directly uphill over the chunks of avalanche rubble. Simon, Gary and I continued to skin up, traversing back and forth across the avalanche track which had swept down exactly over our route. I was wondering if anyone had been on it at the time, when I noticed Douglas had disappeared entirely from sight in the cloud.

The three of us shouted. At first, we heard nothing. It is amazing how cloud soaks up sound. Then, we heard a faint holler. Douglas was furiously trying to tell us he had found the way. But he sounded lower than us. An argument developed. Unseen and disorientated, we bellowed at each other through the cloud. We continued this ludicrous exchange, like four actors shouting at each other off stage, until we all emerged near a steep rock section where we had to take off our skis and fit crampons anyway.

Rock climbing is awkward with skis strapped either side of a rucksack. The tips, which are tied together above your head, tend to dip forward and stick into the rock, which stops you being able to reach the next hold. Above the rock, we continued on steepening snow through a break in a large overhanging cornice onto the narrow summit ridge. Our Swiss Army mountaineering skis, which were twice as heavy as civilian ones, made balancing rather precarious.

With nil vis and fierce winds, conditions on the summit were most unpleasant. There were some fresh ski tracks in the snow, but it was evident from the easy way they disappeared downhill into the mist in a smooth straight line on the other side that the skiers who had made them were more expert than we were.

We were also conscious that time was passing. All this fiddling about, with skis off, crampons on and shouting at each other in the fog, had taken up three hours from the Zwillingsjoch. Now we had two options, both unappealing in bad visibility: first, to try and find the route down the ridge on the Italian side to the Quintino Sella Hut, or, second, ski down the Zwillings Glacier to the Monte Rosa Hut.

In the Quintino Sella, at 3585 metres, we would be well placed to continue along a part of the famous ski-mountaineers' Haute Route to the Monte Rosa summits, of which Liskamm was next, but if the weather turned really bad the descent from the hut was long, and being on the Italian side meant a long drive round the mountains back to Switzerland, possibly even having to wait a day for someone from Base Camp to drive out to pick us up. The Monte Rosa Hut is easier to retreat from but it is much lower at only 2795 metres, and to reach it we would have to ski down the Zwillings Glacier which is very crevassed – not a good look-out in thick cloud.

Hoping the tracks in front of us were not made by a party of lunatics out for a jolly day's *ski extrême*, we cautiously followed them down from the summit, turned right under some huge overhanging séracs and then turned right again, uphill a short way to the Felikjoch at 4000 metres.

After several hours peering through cloud on steep slopes, it was a pleasant change to stand safely on a flat snowfield, even though the south wind from Italy never let up. The clouds cleared around the col, seemingly wind-blown in a dome as they washed over the frontier edge of this towering crest of 4000ers between Switzerland and Italy. We stood about high on that ridge drinking hot coffee from flasks, insignificant and hidden from view inside the cloud, buffeted by the wind, and the rest of the world was quite unaware of our presence up there. This was a refreshing thought. The solution of our problems was ours alone.

Even two Frenchmen who appeared out of the mist, lost, did not spoil this feeling of detachment. They watched as we fixed up a deadman and a body belay to let Simon out on a rope over the edge where we thought he could spot the route down to the Quintino Sella Hut. This was the very edge of the frontier crest, where particles of snow blew vertically upwards, like continuous waves breaking on a sea wall. Simon leaned over, peering down, his purple jacket flapping in the wind, then casually called back that he was standing on a four-metre-deep cornice curling over a big drop. He could see no way down, nor the route below. We pulled him back.

Option One out, we had to go down the Zwillings Glacier to the Monte Rosa Hut.

'If you must go down the Zwillings, you must rope up. It's very dangerous,' Roger had said to me during our chat on the phone.

Skiing downhill roped up is hysterically funny, like something from an old black and white silent movie, the skiers jerking each other about till they wipe out, then clambering back to their feet and starting all over again. I had done it in Norway. I guess expert skiers might manage it without pulling each other over, but we were in the high mountains at 4000 metres and I doubt we would have made it down at all if we had tried it.

We fell over enough as it was, for the snow was warm in the afternoon and very heavy. In the cloud, we skied as slowly as we could and our eyes ached in the disorientating whiteness looking for the others' tracks and for crevasses. We did not use our Walkmans. Music seems to get in the way when things get serious.

We overtook the two Frenchmen, which was a great boost to our confidence. Wonderful to find there actually were worse skiers than us. Then suddenly, at about 3500 metres we skied out of the clouds.

The rest of the long descent was a question of endurance. We were tired, we fell over a lot, spent hours waiting for each other to disentangle ourselves from each pile-up, scoop snow from our necks, wipe it off our darkglasses, and fit skis, again and again.

Route-finding was no longer a problem in the sunshine, but the Zwillings Glacier was difficult. I was conscious we were descending late in the afternoon when the snow bridges over hidden crevasses are soft. Our legs muscles burned and we got to a stage when we hardly cared, just 'going for it' over obvious fault lines beneath which we could see deep, dark blue chasms.

We all fell in a crevasse of some sort. I escaped until right at the end, skiing hard for the Monte Rosa Hut which had miraculously appeared perched on rocks on the other side of a small gulley on the edge of the glacier. I shot over a rise and plunged into an ice hole which I had not seen from the other side, turning a somersault, twisting my knee, and landing in a heap in the slush. My language was truly appalling. We had all laughed till we cried when Gary had done the same earlier, but we were too tired by then.

Supper was being served in the hut as we walked in. Without a

word, wind-blown, sunburned and tired out, we sat down and began
to eat. We were ravenous.

There is a different atmosphere in the Monte Rosa Hut compared
to the Mönchsjoch Hut. The Monte Rosa is stone built, rather
gloomy and introverted and it is more difficult to reach, from
Zermatt via the Gornergrat railway. You must leave the train at
Rotboden and walk for at least two hours down the side of the
Gornergrat Ridge and then skin across the Gorner Glacier. This is
not a route for fatties, especially on the way back which is all uphill.
All the people in the hut were fit ski mountaineers with the hard faces
of men determined to assault the big mountains tomorrow. No one
seemed to mind that the food was really very poor, but perhaps that
was because we were served by a beautiful dark-haired girl who was
working in the kitchen. Later, Simon and I met a guide, a Frenchman
of course, who said she had been very nice to him indeed.

Pity she did not get up to serve breakfast, which was worse. The
black bread was solid and the water for our tea and coffee (in those
awful little sachets) had been stored from the night before in several
very old-fashioned thermos urns and was cold.

We all felt quite drained by the previous day, so we were the
last to leave the hut, at 6 a.m., and it was a long haul up the
Grenz Glacier. This glacier is one of the longest in the Alps but
it is nothing like the steep, broken Zwillings. The Grenzgletscher
is vast and open, a kilometre wide, flanked by the huge walls of
Liskamm and the Dufourspitze, and it slopes relentlessly uphill for
eight kilometres. Two big tumbling icefalls break the monotony and
are turned by zigzagging up steep, narrow snow slopes on one side
or the other. Fortunately the bulk of the Dufourspitze (4634m) on
the left kept the sun off us most of the way so we did not boil as
we had on the way up the Allalinhorn. Instead, a sharp wind iced
up my thumbs. This was a residue of skiing in Norway when they
got severely frost-bitten once, but I could do little about them as I
had to keep using my ski sticks.

We were still acclimatising and improving our fitness, so we were
pleased to overtake several other parties who were very grumpy for
some reason when we wished them, 'Gruss Gott!' as we passed. We
reached the summit of the Signalkuppe (4556m) in just under six
hours, slightly better than par time in the guide books. This was
the highest we had been and we were rewarded with fine views

of the Dufourspitze, Nordend and Liskamm, all mountains we had to climb.

Extraordinarily, a fully equipped mountain hut, called the Margherita, sits on top of the Signalkuppe. Built in the 1890s, before anyone worried about ecology or insulting the nature of mountains, the Margherita is really a terrible eyesore among Europe's highest peaks. Mont Blanc is superior but the Monte Rosa group is more massive, with five peaks over 4500 metres, and every time I saw this dark cuboid perched on the summit right in the centre of these magnificent mountains, I felt it diminished the environment.

However, we were very pleased to reach it. We staggered through the door expecting to find a welcoming warden, steaming kitchen and platefuls of hot broth, only to find a cold little wood-lined room, a couple of tables, a few chairs, two of which were broken, and mess everywhere. The rest of the hut, the biggest section which presumably contained the warden's accommodation for the summer, was behind a locked door upstairs. This was a shock, as we had very little food between us, but there was a small kitchen in one corner with several very battered and filthy pans and three large canisters of Calor gas, so we made a brew and began to feel more human.

An hour later, three tanned Italians turned up wearing the last word in ski fashion and looking very professional. They made their own inspection of the room, found a gas fire appliance attached to one of the gas canisters and lit it at once. Their attitude was quite straightforward: any fool can be cold and uncomfortable, but not an Italian. We all began to warm up.

We introduced ourselves. Luca, Stefano and Fausto skinned up mountains just in order to ski down them again. They were impressed and jealous that we could set aside the whole summer to climb and ski, and we were impressed and jealous of their expertise, hearing them talk of skiing off the summits of the Grand Combin and Mont Blanc. We still felt very much beginners.

They had a radio which they used to speak to a friend in Alagna, the village right down in the valley on the Italian side, and he said the weather was due to be stormy till Sunday. This was bad news, contradicting our Swiss forecast, but as none of us had much faith in any weather report we tried to look at our situation from first principles. We were there to climb mountains. We had some rather squashed sandwiches left over from Dave's kitchen in Brig, some brews, a large bag of tired-looking spaghetti we found in a cupboard and there were bunk-beds and blankets upstairs for more than a dozen people. We, and the Italians, decided to stay overnight. We were in a perfect place to climb seven summits all round us – Liskamm, Parrotspitze, Zumsteinspitze, Ludwigshöhe, Corno Nero (Schwarzhorn), Balmenhorn and the Vincent Piramide.

The Italians were right. A storm hit us during the night and threatened to knock the hut off the top of the mountain. There is nothing more depressing than waking up at five o'clock expecting to find even half-way reasonable climbing weather and visibility, and instead finding yourself staring through ice-rimmed panes at a whiteout of cloud. I would have dipped my hands into any quantity of chicken entrails, or anyone else's entrails come to that, to know what the weather would do next. I went back to my bunk and wrapped myself in several blankets to keep warm. The others slept on.

Fortunately, apart from a few headaches, no one was sick or suffered unduly from sleeping at high altitude. Altitude sickness is about feeling ghastly, dizzy and unbalanced, like having bad flu. In 1990, I had been stricken in Tibet at only 5000 metres on a trip to Cho Oyu and Shisha Pangma with Russell Brice, Joe Brown and Harry Taylor (the latter summited Everest in 1993), and I had been worried about acclimatising in the Alps. A very good book on mountaineering medicine edited by Dr James Wilkerson suggests that altitude sickness, called 'acute mountain sickness', or even high altitude pulmonary œdema, is possible at only 2400 metres, and climbing and sleeping above that increases the risk. Œdema is the most dangerous effect of high altitude, when the lungs fill with fluid, blocking their capacity to transfer oxygen from the air to the blood, which in turn reduces the concentration of oxygen in the blood, causing cyanosis, impaired cerebral function and finally death by suffocation. There have been cases as low as 2630 metres though most occur well above 3000 metres, and deaths seem to ensue in only a quarter of cases. Recovery is normally swift as long as the sufferer is brought down to lower altitudes as soon as possible.

At 4556 metres, we were perhaps rather high, but we were fit and had already spent some nights at altitude in the Mönchsjoch Hut at 3629 metres. I was also pleased to note that my resting pulse rate was only seventy-five to the minute, but I put that down to giving up coffee and drinking less as much as to being in good shape.

However, just acclimatising hardly makes for an interesting day and the hours passed slowly. Gary and Simon sat at the table scribbling in diaries and I sat typing up my notes on a small IBM-compatible computer called a Sharp PC3000 which was stuffed with leading-edge solid-state technology all designed by a British company called DIP Systems who had given me one to try on the mountains. The only moving parts were the keys, just large enough so I could touch-type, and the three AA batteries which jiggled about a bit in the back. It was light (weighing only 480 g), extremely hardy, lived without trouble in my rucksack, and put up with some extreme conditions of cold, hot sun and very rough handling.

Douglas spent the day restlessly walking from window to window scraping away the ice and looking out for a change in the weather. He gave us minute-by-minute updates on the gradations of whiteness he could see until, utterly frustrated, he turned his attention inside to the room. He observed an emergency radio-telephone on the wall and said, 'I wonder if that works?'

We shrugged. One of the Italians said, 'Eet ees-a only to the Carabinieri.'

Hut phones are limited to a single number which connects you directly to the emergency mountain rescue office, but Douglas is not a person to be put off by convention. Since boredom, not necessity, is the mother of curiosity, if not invention itself, he lifted the phone and experimentally dialled Roger's IDD number in Switzerland. 'We want to know about the weather, don't we?' he said at large to the room by way of an excuse.

We stopped our writing and watched. This might be the most exciting thing that happened all day. Douglas listened a moment, then he grinned, 'It's ringing!'

Distantly, we all heard a faint voice say, 'Mathieu?'

Douglas's grin broadened as he exclaimed, 'Roger!'

Our intrepid guide, sitting in the comfort of the hotel Inter-Golf which he managed in Crans-Montana, was amazed to hear where we were. We thrashed over all aspects of the weather, from facts to wild speculation, and he confirmed our analysis of the situation. The forecast was mixed, but he thought we were well placed at 4556 metres to wait and see.

The Italians had no time to wait. They had to get back to Milan to their offices, but they were delighted with Douglas's discovery about the telephone. They were certain we were not the first to use the phone and hugely entertained at the idea of the Carabinicri paying the bill. Frantic discussions in Italian ensued when they called a friend who was still in the Monte Rosa Hut far below and asked for an on-the-spot weather report. By afternoon, their friend said that as far as he could see from the hut up the Grenz Glacier, the clouds seemed less dense up to maybe 3800 metres. The Italians decided to risk a descent. They donned all their natty ski-wear, including full body harnesses as they intended to ski roped up through the cloud, clipped into their lightweight skis and slid off into the cloud. They were better skiers than us, but I did not envy them. Visibility outside the hut was down to about twenty metres at the most when looking at rocks, but when looking at the snow there was no ground-line at all. These were not the conditions for us to try finding our way back down the Grenz Glacier.

We ate spaghetti for supper, spruced up with some minestrone soup which the Italians left us. The meal was very dull, but as there was nothing else to do we deliberately made the preparation last for nearly two hours, gathering snow from outside to melt down for water, deciding when to start cooking, how long it would take, and precisely how much we should eat in relation to how long we would need to make the bag of spaghetti last, an existential analysis which broke down as soon as we had to introduce the uncertainty of the weather.

High winds battered the hut all day, but the Margherita is held in place by thick hawsers buried in the rock and stretched over the roof. You get used to the constant creaking of the wood as it grates against the outer cladding of sheet copper. This 'skin' works on the 'Faraday Cage' principle, providing a screen against extreme electrical fields, and turns the hut into a huge lightning conductor. This is just as well, for our second night was lit from dusk to dawn with brilliant flashes of lightning. In the morning, Gary got up early before dawn and peered through the window at the blackness outside to see if the vis or wind offered any chance of a sortie. From the warmth of my bunk, wrapped in grey blankets against the cold, I watched his dark figure standing at the window, hands cupped around his face against the glass. Suddenly, he was silhouetted brilliantly by a flash of lightning bursting on the hut. His hair stood up on his head as if he was being electrocuted, he staggered backwards, blinded and swearing, and fell on his bunk.

'No good out there, I take it?' asked Simon warmly from under several blankets.

'Bugger off,' Gary croaked rubbing his eyes.

Douglas slept on, snoring gently.

After a brew of hot tea which passed for breakfast, I was trying to take my mind off the inevitability of spaghetti for our next meal, since there was no sign of a change in the weather, when I decided, as is the nature of all animals, that I needed a shit. I had not been looking forward to this. Normally, I would have gone outside, dug a hole in the snow and enjoyed the spectacular view, but as our fingers froze within even a few seconds every time we went out to fetch snow to melt down, the idea of exposing any more delicate parts of my anatomy to the biting wind was out of the question. Now, the alternative was certainly warmer, but truly evil. Opposite the front door in the little passage to the kitchen was a door to a small cubicle which passed as a khazi. It was a nasty, dark little place with a mound of snow on one side where everyone pissed or shit and flung a scoop of snow on top. The result was a deeply unsavoury pyramid of rock-hard snow two feet or more high which spilled out round the cubicle and made wearing a head-torch essential if you wanted to keep your feet more or less out of the mess.

I squatted as fast as I could and nipped back into the warmer room where Gary was reading the guide book. I remarked, 'That bloody place needs a good digging out.'

He looked up and said, 'Why not?'

'You serious?'

We looked at each other for a moment and then just went out and started. There was nothing else to do and something British in us made us feel we needed to clean the place up.

Working by the light of our head-torches, Gary shovelled the awful mixture of snow and shit from the cubicle into a large plastic bag which I held gingerly by the sides, careful not to let bits drop on the floor of the passage. Then, while Gary held the double outside doors open, I carried the bag outside and threw the contents over the East Face which dropped thousands of metres sheer below one side of the hut entrance. The trick was trying to keep up-wind.

We used an ice pick and adze blade to chip away at the mound, rather like cutting out a snowhole, and took care not to let the slivers spit up into our faces. We swopped places and gradually transferred the mound outside.

One of the guide books complains, rightly, that the khazi outfall of the Margherita Hut simply drops away over the East Face. About the same time as we finally discovered the truth of this by finding and cleaning out a proper 'long-drop' hole, a panel on one side of the cubicle, which had been held in place by the iced heap of filth, fell against my leg. I bent down to pick it up.

'There's a hole in the wall,' said Gary looking past me. The fallen panel had revealed a hole low in the cubicle wall behind. We bent down and peered through. The other side was the rest of the hut accommodation, frozen into still life since the hut-warden had locked it up at the end of the season eight months before.

Gary glanced up at me, a wide grin on his face. We were through in a moment, wriggling over a plastic bag we put on the floor of the cubicle to keep clean, and found ourselves in a hallway with the kitchens beyond. Pots and pans stood on the worktops and the hob, tins sat about as if waiting to be opened and everything was covered with a white dusting of hoar frost. We wandered through into the dining area, and looked upstairs round the accommodation rooms. The place was very cold and spooky, as if the last occupants had left in a hurry before having a chance to tidy up, like the *Marie-Céleste*. We were soon chilled to the bone and crawled back through the cubicle.

On the way out, I noticed an old sepia photograph on the wall, of Queen Margherita of Italy standing on the summit during the official opening of the hut in 1893. The old bird must have been quite adventurous to have walked all the way up from Alagna, twenty-four kilometres and 3400 metres below – the photograph shows her in voluminous skirts and buttoned walking boots looking like an athletic Queen Victoria – but what struck me as the real achievement was overcoming the objections of the coterie of advisers and staff to permit her to do it all.

We were having similar difficulties with our plans for the visit of HRH The Duke of Kent. As Colonel of the Scots Guards and Patron of our climbing expedition, he had let it be known to Tim Spicer that he wanted to climb a 4000er, but given the limited time he could spend with us, we had to use a helicopter to land him high enough to walk to the summit. However, RAF Queen's Flight regulations stipulated a 'Catch-22' impasse. First, the helicopter had to have two engines, in case one failed, but the Swiss overcame this by very generously offering to fly him in a twin-engined Super Puma, as good a chopper as any. Secondly, the regulations stated that the helicopter had to be able to pull out of landing 'finals' even at the last second, whatever the altitude, on the just-in-case principle. The problem was simply that there is no helicopter on earth yet built that can pull out once committed to a landing at 3800 metres, which was the height of the Weissmies Ridge where Roger and I wanted to take the Duke and where Roger had identified a large landing site.

Stuck up on the top of a mountain in what must be the highest accommodation in Europe, we lived in an atmosphere of great detachment from the world. I did not have the same thought processes as Nietzsche's Zarathustra on the top of his mountain but Douglas's discovery of the telephone gave us the modern equivalent. Without leaving our retreat as Zarathustra had had to do, we were now able metaphorically to swoop down from our eerie on anyone in the world. I used the Carabinieri's emergency telephone to discuss the matter of the royal visit with Tim Spicer. Speaking from the normality of his home in Wandsworth, he was amused to hear where we were, and said other more usual telephone links between England and the Alps were buzzing with the subject of the visit, so far without resolution.

'Duke killed in chopper!' the tabloid headlines might scream. Plainly, everyone was terrified of losing him down a crevasse or in a spectacular helicopter crash on the top of a mountain. With the greatest frivolity, as I proposed to be in the same helicopter with the Duke, and with all due respect to His Royal Highness, I thought this would be sure-fire publicity.

We needed it. Our climbing was being used by a cot-death charity, the Foundation for the Study of Infant Death Syndrome, to publicise their cause and raise money for cot-death research. The Foundation had sent out information about our climbing in their newsletter to bereaved parents, but they had not been able to generate any real publicity at all. This was disappointing and I called Sarah Wollaston, the Foundation's Appeals Secretary, to find out what she was doing. In Belgrave Square, she was suitably surprised to hear that I was in a hut at 4556 metres and assured me she was doing her best. We agreed journalists preferred to report disasters and I began to think wistfully of the Duke's visit again. Maybe it was the altitude.

That evening there was another discussion about cooking the spaghetti for supper. Douglas pointed out morosely that this time we had no minestrone, we had eaten the last of the battered sandwiches from our picnic lunch two days before and he began to develop a practical but revolting suggestion that we make soup out of an ancient-looking packet of Knorr salt-flavouring he had found at the back of the greasy cooker. When Gary produced a tin of jugged hare and put it on the table, his eyes widened in amazement.

'Where on earth did you find that?'

We told him about the hole at the back of the cubicle and the hut next door. There was a larder upstairs from which we had taken some small tins of meat. Supper was still spaghetti-based but a huge improvement for all of us except Simon who got over-excited and spilled all his on the rubber matting on the floor.

I expect there will be some righteous folk who will be outraged that we helped ourselves to food from the hut, so before they work themselves into a life-threatening cardiac lather, let me just say that it is common practice to pay for overnighting even in the winter quarters of an unmanned hut, where there is no warden or cooking provided, and we paid our dues. Before we left, I put 200 SFrs (nearly £100) in the box. I reckon that was generous payment for the nights, the telephone and a few tins, considering we cleaned up their filthy khazi and then set about spring cleaning the kitchen and other rooms as well.

The weather showed no signs of improving and calls to Roger Mathieu, the Geneva met office and Charlie in Brig all confirmed the forecast was grim. After two days shut up with nothing to do, waiting to climb the summits all round which were invisible in the storm, we were now beginning to wonder if we would be able to climb anything at all no matter how long we waited.

Douglas stamped about to keep warm, made several trips outside to fetch snow to melt down and cooked up an unnecessary number of brews. I suspect his frustration had less to do with being cooped up than with thinking of the time he might be spending with our new physiotherapist in Brig. At the start of our trip, I was worried by injuries we might sustain and I had persuaded both the

British Ministry of Defence and the Swiss Army to allow a civilian physiotherapist called Nikki Hatrick to stay with us in our building in Brig. I did not tell them Nikki was a girl's name, and nor, as I discovered when she arrived, that she was extremely attractive, tall, dark-haired and good company. Brigadier Mudry was amazed and delighted when I introduced him one day during a quick visit, but I really did not think it would be fair to mention her to the British officers stuck away in some dusty room in the Ministry of Defence in London.

Friday dawned with a view. I sprang out of bed at five o'clock and saw snow peaks racked out to the south like sharks' teeth tinged with the dawn. Below in the dark valleys, the lights of villages and towns still glowed in the shadows. Level with the hut, clouds scudded past at a huge pace, maybe 80 mph or more.

'A great day ahead!' I said brightly, and began packing my rucksack, thinking at the same time about the wind chill factor. I decided to wear my woolly long-johns and duvet jacket.

None of the others budged, except Douglas who rolled off his bunk and went down the rickety wood stairs for a piss. He came back, looked at me, rubbed his black hair in an off-hand way, glanced out of the window and went straight back to bed.

'Don't fancy these winds on the Liskamm East Ridge,' Gary muttered from beneath a pile of blankets. I could just see his tousled fair hair.

'We could go at the Parrot from the south-west to keep the wind at our back, in the ascent at least,' I suggested lamely. No one stirred so I clambered back onto my bunk above Simon, deliberately lay on my back to snore as loudly as I could and passed out.

An hour later the clouds had surrounded us again and the wind stayed violently strong. We telephoned out for our daily report, to Roger and Charlie in Brig who phoned the met office in Geneva. We learned all Friday would be stormy, with some snow precipitation as well. This was the last thing we wanted. New snow would present us with the same difficulties we had encountered on the Rottalsattel on the Jungfrau. Saturday and Sunday were supposed to be clear.

In spite of this depressing report, the sky cleared somewhat again and at nine o'clock frustration drove us out to try our luck. Excited by the prospect of action after nearly three days cooped up getting on each others' nerves, we donned loads of warm clothing and went out to climb the Zumsteinspitze.

Outside, the weather was breaking up into patches of open sky around the hut but the wind had not abated. We could see the nearby peaks quite clearly but several miles away to the north-east over the Belvedere glacier a huge bank of raging black cumulus reared from the valley to the sky high over the frontier mountains. We resorted to high technology. Sticking our moistened fingers into the wind, we judged this storm would pass us by and skied down from the summit of the Signalkuppe through ten centimetres of fresh snow and glided as far over the Col Gnifetti as we could. The Zumsteinspitze stood out temptingly clear a kilometre away.

We fitted skins and crossed the rest of the flat col. We left our skis topside of the bergschrund, where the slope steepened to the edge of the Macugnaga face, and fitted crampons. No sooner had we started up the ridge to the summit than the black storm hit us. The wind thrashed us and it began to snow fiercely in our faces.

We were so close to the summit, we pulled our cagoule hoods round our faces and carried on. The drop over the edge on the right is impressive, more than 3000 metres down onto the della Sesia Glacier which we glimpsed from moment to moment between the clouds rushing over us like great shreds of grey rag. I climbed as far from the cornice as possible without compromising myself on the slope on the left. Ahead in the lead, Gary reached up through the last easy rock section onto the summit. Suddenly I could hear his shouts even above the noise of the wind, 'I'm alive! I'm alive!'

I thought this was rather quaint. Sort of celebrating the victory of another summit. I squinted up through the blizzard and noticed him backing off the summit at an alarming rate.

He was alive, literally. The storm all round us was electric, charging the summit with static. Two metal statues on the summit were vibrating furiously. The air was singing, his hair crackled on his head as if pounded with hail and his ice axe sizzled.

'Your turn now,' he shouted as he back-stepped at speed down the snow arête towards us. 'Guide book says the Zumstein's one of the easiest.'

We declined the invitation. We all felt our hair standing on end, the skin on our faces twitched with charge and the points on our ice axes vibrated. Without delay, I turned face into the strong winds of the snow-laden front which had overwhelmed the mountain and retreated downhill.

At this point, I saw that visibility below us on the col had closed in to twenty metres or less. This was not a good look-out. The Gnifetti Col is flat, several hundred yards wide and there is plenty of room to go wrong in bad visibility and slide off course either to the steep ground over the top of the Grenz Glacier on the right, or over the edge of the East Face on the left. Happily, there was a meteorological stand in the centre of the col which we just saw through the mist and I had taken a compass bearing earlier. We followed the bearing across the col to the summit slopes of the Signalkuppe.

Skinning up this slope was most disagreeable. By this time the fresh snow was two feet deep, quite unconsolidated, and the top crust broke away under our skis at each step. No one said anything. We had no option in the conditions but to climb to the hut, but we were all sure the whole slope would break away at any moment. For me, anticipatory fear, fuelled by a good imagination, is worse than the fear of something that has happened. Then, if you can screw yourself to the sticking point, I like to think fear gives way to action, to escape or minimise the damage. Keeping our thoughts to ourselves, we each made our way solo up the slope, very slowly, loose step by loose step, in horrid cold winds and blinding snow.

I was last in, and extremely grateful of the brew the others had already put on. A cup of hot chocolate had never tasted so good.

The afternoon had been disappointing. We had been out for four hours, achieved nothing and nearly been electrocuted. We stripped off our wet clothes and hung them up to dry on the beams in the cold room and I wondered if the risks were worth it. Not for the first time, I persuaded myself that we could minimise the dangers inherent in mountains. We took precautions and our decisions were governed by safety and survival, because we had time on our side, but there was still the element of chance.

I could not help thinking of what my body might look like dug out of an avalanche, bruised, torn and stripped-off naked for iden- tification, and I thought of the distress it would cause my wife.

Gary was buried in his guide book and maps again.

'Well,' I said in a bold voice to dispel my gloom. 'Which are the missing six?'

When I first thought of the trip, Gary and I had worked on Richard Goedeke's book *The Alpine 4000m Peaks* which gives sixty-one summits, but somewhere in the previous two years I had discovered another six. The trouble was, in all the research I had done, I could not remember which peaks they were, or even where I had found them. Since we had gone public on trying to climb sixty-seven summits, we had to decide which the extra six would be.

'I don't know,' Gary replied. 'There seems to be no rule governing how to define an independent peak. Some say a true summit should be 100 metres above the nearest col, but the Balmenhorn, for example, is only twelve metres above its nearest col. And there are others like it.'

'So, why don't we choose fifty metres?'

'Same reason. There are eleven summits only fifty metres above cols but we've still got the Balmenhorn, Stecknadelhorn, and Mont Brouillard and Aiguille du Jardin.'

In 1932, the 4000ers had been reclassified and the Aiguille du Jardin 'became' a 4000er. Karl Blodig, then aged seventy-two, climbed it solo up the steep North Couloir to protect his claim to have been the first to have climbed all the 4000ers. He must have been cross about the reclassification. The seemingly arbitrary denomination of what constitutes a 4000er gets in the way of the mountains themselves, presenting committee decisions before the pleasure of the places and their environments. Gary and I came to no conclusion about the extra six, other than to call them 'tops' and left it at that for the time being.

After another plateful of spaghetti and more speculation about the weather, we went to bed and listened to the high winds buffeting the hut. At one moment in the middle of the night, we were all woken by the sound of the front door smashing open and noises just like someone flinging open the passage door into the room downstairs. Although it was inconceivable that anyone could have been outside at that time and in those conditions, this sounded so like a person that Gary and Simon went gingerly down the stairs with head-torches to see who it was. Of course, they found no one, but we all went back to sleep thinking of ghosts, long dead mountaineers visiting their last place of rest, or the place they had wanted to reach when they died in the snowy cold glaciers below.

The storm finally blew over during the night. The sky dawned an exceptional translucent pale blue, utterly clear, ice cold and windless. Even in the distance beyond the Matterhorn twenty-five kilometres away, the Dent Blanche was in crisp focus.

Trouble was there had been more snow and we waded out of the hut for the last time through sixty centimetres of fresh powder which had accumulated during the previous day and night. Gary and Simon had done winter expedition leaders' courses and pointed out that much over forty centimetres of powder on slopes between thirty and forty-five degrees presents a serious danger of avalanches.

All the same, I was reluctant to leave the Zumsteinspitze. We could see no sign of our footprints but we skied off the Signalkuppe, fitted skins on the col, skinned across to the Zumstein, changed to crampons and waded up to the summit in brilliant cold early morning sunshine. Gary's two statues turned out to be a bas-relief plaque and a gold Virgin quite innocent of the charge of trying to electrocute Gary the previous day.

The powder skiing from the Gnifetti Col all the way down the Grenz Glacier was unforgettable. We all had the greatest satisfaction of looking back at long series of neat swinging curves each of us made in the fresh snow and the run lasted for eleven kilometres, past the Monte Rosa Hut where we stopped for hot chocolate, and across the Gorner Glacier to the bottom of the Gornergrat.

After a frustrating four days stuck in a hut waiting out the bad weather, which I swore never to do again, we had at least climbed some more mountains and we were thoroughly acclimatised. Better still, we had had the opportunity to sort out our relationship with the mountains and how we wanted to approach the remainder. Unplanned and frustrating, our five days' time out had none the less been valuable.

We were pleased to get back to Brig and clean up, but when Dave Moore said he had laid on a special Italian spaghetti dinner, four pairs of hands reached out to throttle him!

4

GLACIERS IN THE
BERNESE OBERLAND

Time comes to us in the cadence of music, the rhythm of our
heartbeat and of breathing.

Johann Georg Hamann (1730–88)

A couple of days after coming down from Monte Rosa we returned
to the Bernese Oberland. After another gut-wrenching early breakfast in Brig, Gary announced he was unable to join us, so just Simon,
Douglas and I made the long journey round, through the tunnel,
along the Thunersee to Interlaken, up the Wengen-Alp-Bahn to the
Jungfraujoch, and we climbed the Jungfrau.

This time we had no problems at the Rottalsattel and climbed
straight up the south-east snow slope to the summit. As we
clambered up past the bergschrund, clouds closed in and on the
summit we were denied the wonderful view of the Mönch, the Eiger
and Kleine Scheidegg far below with the Grindelwald valley beyond,
which Hodler painted so beautifully early this century.

Travelling all the way from Brig, we had not started from the
Jungfraujoch till after 10 a.m. and it was nearly 3 p.m. by the time
we arrived back in the middle of the Jungfraufirn Glacier to pick up
our discarded extra gear. By this time ragged shreds of grey clouds
obscured the sun, the snow was tacky in the warm afternoon air and
we could feel spots of rain. There was no wind, but the conditions
did not remotely match the weather forecast we had been given.

'There is a high over the Alps,' the seers in Geneva had

said cheerfully. 'Good weather is guaranteed all Tuesday and Wednesday.'

Rather than slog over the Grünhornlücke to the Finsteraarhorn Hut, which would have taken us an extra two hours or more, we opted to stay at the Konkordia Hut from which we could reach the Grünhorn if the weather stayed reasonable, or exit the glacier system if not.

The Konkordia Hut is among the most remote in the Alps and looks the part. First put up in the middle of the last century, the bleak stone building stands on a rock shelf over 100 metres above Konkordiaplatz which is six square kilometres of open flat snowfield where four big glaciers merge, the Grosser Aletschfirn, the Jungfraufirn, the Ewigschneefeld and the Grüneggfirn. Together, they form the longest glacier in the Alps, the Grosser Aletschgletscher, which flows from there at 200 metres a year for twenty-two kilometres in a great curve to Belalp in the valley above Brig.

Insignificant busy specks, we skied across the edge of this impressive scenery which nature has cunningly hidden right in the centre of Europe, safely remote from human depredation (so far at least) and I allowed full rein to my sense of wonder.

'Looks just like Glencoe,' Douglas announced, bringing me back to earth.

We reached the hut about half past four o'clock and I had to phone Charlie Messervy-Whiting in Brig. Charlie is a remarkably slender young second lieutenant with a shock of boyish fair hair, and his main interest in life, chasing girls, was diligently recorded on the wall chart. When the rest of us were out in the mountains, Charlie was the 'officer in charge' so he took the flak from England. This time there was more panic about the impending visit of HRH The Duke of Kent.

'What's the problem?' I shouted over the radio-telephone which the lady warden of the hut had reluctantly let me use, even though all huts charge enthusiastically for its use, incoming as well as outgoing calls.

'They want a programme,' Charlie's distant voice echoed back.

'What?' Did everyone have to be clairvoyant? 'They haven't yet told us when he's due to arrive on the Queen's Flight, or when he'll leave. Or which airstrip they will use.'

'I know.' The brevity of his reply indicated he was under pressure to produce answers anyhow, as if to say one must be patient dealing with those who run the lives of our royals. So, I reeled a plan off the top of my head which he promised to type up and send on. I was just thinking he would probably delegate Mike Nutter to type it up for him, when the lady warden came back and, without preamble, interrupted our conversation with, 'Get off the telephone. Now!' Then she stuck her hand out and demanded, 'Three francs.'

Shocked, I wagged my finger and corrected her, 'Three francs. *Please!*'

She shrugged carelessly, still with her hand out. I finished off my call to Charlie and as I handed her the phone I fell back on that classic English conversational strategem, the weather. It's a desperate topic really, as we were finding out, our lives on the mountains being ruled by it, but I thought it might reduce tension. I said, 'What happened to the sun today?'

'The weather is not the same as the forecast,' she stated in clipped English. This impressive grip on reality was very Germanic and rather typical of some German-speaking Swiss.

'I know,' I said, wondering how she thought anyone could reach Konkordia without being exposed to every nuance of the prevailing weather. The hut was full of red-faced, wind-swept skiers. I stated the obvious, it seemed the thing to do, 'I'm only here because we were given a good forecast.'

'So am I,' replied our host bluntly and thrust out her hand for the three francs.

Hut wardens fly in and out by helicopter. Long gone are the days when they skied, or walked in, bringing all the food and supplies with them, and if the weather forecast is really bad, they don't come at all. They just leave the 'winter' emergency accommodation open for those foolhardy enough to ignore the gurus in the weather centres.

There must be some meteorological clairvoyants about (but not it seems in the met office), because the wooden dining room in the hut at supper was not as full as it could have been in spite of the good forecast. A group of Italians were shouting and joking at one table, two Austrian couples, young men with girls, sat with us and several pairs of hard-looking Swiss mountain men sat alone at other tables. These men had the brutal uncompromising air of bearded monks, with hard blue eyes and tortured expressions, wild and wind-blown, as if they were out in such a remote place to expiate some terrible sin, to stretch their bodies to the limit, *ski extrême*. They pored over their maps to plan some awful new expedition for the next day. Weather permitting of course.

I noticed that the Austrians at our table looked very weather beaten after their day out, as if they had been sand-blasted. They just sat exhausted, staring at the table waiting for their goulash soup. Their two girls, however, looked fresh and sprite, ready for anything.

Naturally we thought of sex. Men do. Certainly Douglas and Simon. Even married men like me. We decided there was not a lot of sex in these huts. It is not that the bunk-beds are rather hard, just mattresses on boards, for that never stopped anyone and there must be plenty of exciting chances for a couple tucked up under the blankets in a cosy wooden hut in the mountains. In fact, as most bunks take half a dozen in a row, group sex is eminently possible: wife-swap parties take note. No, the problem seems to be statistical, at least for those of us in the heterosexual community, as there simply aren't enough women.

I have seen some very attractive girls in the huts, that is, running them and working hard in the kitchens, and we met a guide or two who claimed romantic successes, but for us ordinary visitors to these remote refuges, without the god-like status of being a UIAGM guide, sex is like a picnic or a Walkman cassette player: you have to bring your own.

'What about the gay mountain community?' I said after a pause.

'There must be one, statistically,' said Douglas who was always very technical.

We looked speculatively around the dining room.

After my run-in with the lady hut-warden, we were not surprised to find her food was not up to scratch. To the Austrians' disgust, the soup was a thin bouillon, with no bread, the main course was another revoltingly mild 'Bernese Oberland' curry and there wasn't enough. As we went upstairs to our bunk-bed, I could hear her shouting at one of the Italians in the kitchen. He was pleading with her to let him use the radio-telephone to call home to talk to his little son Stefano and she flatly refused.

I was woken at 4 a.m. by a person with a very wrinkled face who had been sleeping beside me at the end of our bunk. She turned out to be an elderly woman, so I was inclined at first to be nice to her, but she made a terrible noise getting up, shining a head-torch in my eyes and tossing blankets about while she folded them.

Douglas grinned, 'She's only cross because you ignored her all night.' Muttering uncharitably, I turned over and tried to sleep again.

It was no good. The commotion woke the Italian group on the bunk-bed over our heads. They had to have the room light on. They had to mill about putting on their ski gear, having slept in odd sexless combinations of underwear and shell-suits. They had to gibber endlessly in loud voices and finally they spent half an hour rattling karabiners and buckles like Silas Marley as they put on full body harnesses. They took absolutely no notice of the fact that we were trying to sleep. Well, rest anyway. We watched them, feeling exhausted already. Whatever happened to the 'get up and go' principle?

After an hour and a half, we gave up, got up, and, as we slept in our ski trousers, went straight downstairs. Breakfast was no incentive to rush out of bed: two small slices of hard black bread, two little packet pats of butter, jam and a pot of coffee. We did not feel talkative.

When we left the hut at 6 a.m., the Italian group, nearly two hours after first getting out of bed, were still fooling about outside with their skis and ropes. We passed them on the steel ladders fixed to the cliff which takes you down to Konkordiaplatz below. I counted 305 steps, none of which was necessary when the first Konkordia Hut was built. I cannot say if global warming is responsible, but the snow surface of Konkordiaplatz is 100 metres lower now, melted away. According to seismologists there are still another 800 metres of solid ice in the glacier beneath your feet.

Ahead, as we skinned steadily up the side of the Ewigschneefeld icefall to the Gross-Grünhorn (4044m) we could see two black dots.

'They must have loved each other once,' sang Elton John in my ear. 'But that was a long time ago and now nobody wins.'

Gradually we overhauled the two dots, grateful there was a light cover of cirro-stratus clouds to protect us from the heat of the sun.

We overtook them as we zigzagged up the steeper slopes under the Grünegghorn and the dots resolved themselves into a man, a bronzed young guide with long fair hair, and a woman, none other than the old bird who had woken me up at 4 a.m. In the harsh light of day, she was plainly well over sixty years old, and tired out, plodding on her skis and having to stop to catch her breath every few metres. Her guide looked thoroughly fed up going so slowly. He glowered at us as if to say that were he not tied down by this old bat we would have no chance.

On a treadmill, I thought. 'Like a candle in the wind,' sang the music in my ears as we passed her, but it was not long before we were humbled ourselves. The Italian party we had passed on the stairs, three men and a woman, came bowling uphill going like trains.

They reached the summit a little before us, partly because I fell over just below the bergschrund where we had to leave our skis to climb the summit ridge on foot. I was trying to execute a kick-turn, facing out from the slope, but I did not feel very supple. I lost balance and toppled forward downhill. Fortunately, the snow was soft and I somersaulted once into a heap cursing freely. Steep slopes and hard snow would have been another matter, but we none of us knew anything about that yet.

We passed the old lady again, on the narrow summit ridge, going down as she was coming up. She hung on to my trousers as she edged past, and said something about having to visit certain mountains for personal reasons, to settle the past. I wondered at that, for there is something terribly emotive about places on mountains where friends have gone, and perhaps, who knows, not come back. But there was no time to speak. We moved on down, but not before I noticed the expression on her guide's face as he watched over her carefully, holding the rope between them ready for anything. He was delighted. Contrary to his every expectation, he knew that she was going to reach the summit after all and he was tremendously proud of her.

By 12.30 p.m., we had skied back to Konkordiaplatz again at 2740 metres. We were hot and sweaty as the clouds had burned off in the morning and the skiing had been good but hard work. We fitted skins and began a long tiring three-kilometre haul in blazing afternoon sun up the Grüneggfirn to the Grünhornlücke (3286m). High on the vertical ridges either side of us we heard the continuous sound of rocks breaking away in the warmth and setting off spumes of snow avalanches down the steep gulleys. We were tired when we reached the Grünhornlücke and grateful for the downhill run across the Fiesch Glacier the other side to the Finsteraarhorn Hut. We had covered over 16 km in 9½ hours and climbed 1878 metres, our longest day so far.

I recommend the Finsteraarhorn Hut. A jolly, determined man ran it, speaking nothing but German, or rather Schweizerdeutsch, in the manner of someone who cheerfully assumes everyone can understand him, no matter whether they speak his language or not. This is wonderful optimism and works. He was assisted by a plump young woman, the sort who seems at home in a kitchen and they ran a good show. The hut is pleasant and light, with pale wood inside, well laid out and built on the east side of the Fieschergletscher where it catches all the afternoon and evening sun. We relaxed on the terrace with several cans of beer.

As we guessed, the food was good: a thick broth followed by piles of spaghetti bolognese, and, to our real delight, especially Simon's, there were second helpings.

Our start next morning for the Finsteraarhorn was not elegant. For some reason, none of us thought of fitting our harscheisen ski crampons. We were last out of the hut, at 6 a.m., and watched the others move steadily up the first short slope behind the hut, pull away from us and disappear from view over the first ridge. We set off after them, constantly slipping and falling on the hard early morning ice. There was a lot of shouting. Simon skied off to the left of the gulley, for some privacy I think, while Douglas and I slithered over to the right and took an age to reach that first ridge. As I teetered up the last few metres, cross and hot, Simon was up there already sitting down and looking cool. He said smugly, 'Aren't you wearing harscheisen?'

I stared at him as the penny dropped and I realised how stupid I had been. Then I said, conversationally, 'Sod off.'

Still, when Douglas turned up, we both asked him if he was using harscheisen and then roared with laughter at the furious expression on his face.

The rest of the day was glorious. The sun came up as we skinned up the glacier to the Hugisattel. We swept back and forth in long, sure traverses on excellent snow, utterly confident with our skis and harscheisen, lost in a world of brilliant snow crystals and wonderful clean air.

'Don't go breaking my heart,' sang the Walkman. I confess to enjoying some songs over and over. Maybe the rhythm matched that day, or the heartbeat of the steady skinning action, but we were so fit now that I felt no pain. Like an addict, my endorphin levels were so reduced I enjoyed going up, and up, and felt only intense satisfaction in the achievement of each long sliding pace, in each neat inside kick-turn for the next traverse.

Don't go breaking my heart.

I was absorbed and lifted by the endless repetition of movement, like a mystic repeating the Name of God over and over until there is no longer any trace of the word on his tongue or image of the letters left on his heart. I was no longer a gauche tourist but part of the movement and the mountain itself.

Don't go breaking my heart.

On that ascent, I was gripped for the first time with a powerful, emotive determination to try to finish what we had started. The purity of this thought, turned over and over in time with the pace of our climb, four short hours to the saddle, acted like a drug, firing me with a strength I have not experienced before.

Wondering if this buzz was the real reason people climb mountains, I reached the Hugisattel (4088m) first, with Douglas behind, to find a quite magnificent view of the world all round. There is no freedom like it.

We plunged our skis into the snow at the Hugisattel, a flattish, easy place named, unsurprisingly, after a man called Hugi who, on 10 August 1829, doubtless wearing thick tweeds and stout walking boots fitted with tricouni nails, preferred to sit there rather than make the final ascent of the rock ridge to the summit 200 metres above. He left that to two men called Leuthold and Wahren who claimed to be the first ascensionists. This final ridge was airy and the traverses on snow round various little rock steps were already losing strength in the sun's warmth, so we did not spend long on the summit of the Finsteraarhorn.

My chief memory of this day was the descent on skis from the Hugisattel. The snow slopes at the top of the glacier were softer than on our ascent, but still firm and we swooped down in great curving runs on the top snowfield above the crevasses in the glacier below. We crossed the short rock section at Point 3616 metres without taking off our skis which slowed us for only a few minutes and skied on fast down much softer snow which had been in the sun for hours, with shorter curves, harder work, more turns, exciting to make, especially between the rocks of that first frustrating slope behind the hut, avoiding a new slide of snow over the glacier beneath, till, breathless, sweating and hot we had to stop on the rocks above the hut. It was the most exhilarating twenty-minute ski run I have ever had.

Foolishly, we decided to wait in the hut, drinking beer in the sun, feeling tremendously self-satisfied, till next day when, the theory went, we could ski down the Fiesch Glacier on crisp icy morning snow.

Theory means nothing in the mountains. The weather turned, the morning dawned grey and miserable in thick cloud with sleeting snow and visibility down to a few metres on the glacier. We waited till after eight o'clock, speculating hopelessly about 'what if' and 'what might' before plucking up our courage and setting out into the cloud, roped up, Simon and I taking it in turns to lead the way.

The nineteen-kilometre descent might have taken a couple of hours in good weather. With visibility down to a few metres at times on a glacier a mile wide, moving with exaggerated care to avoid unseen crevasses under the soft snow and needing to use our compasses to find our way for the first time, we took seven and a half hours. We concentrated a lot. We did not listen to our Walkmans. Later, Roger told us not many people descend the Fieschergletscher, especially not in cloud. It was an adventure, Simon said.

Once off the glacier, the walk down the Fieschertal valley was delightful. Douglas, as usual, shot off ahead on long tireless legs, to phone for transport he claimed, while Simon and I proceeded at a more comfortable speed to enjoy the scenery. Spring flowers were out everywhere, especially Alpine dwarf rhododendrons and violas, there was a powerful scent of fresh junipers and pine, and on a rickety old wood bridge over a roaring stream we passed an old Swiss farmer driving his two cows up the valley for the spring pasture now that the snows were retreating.

Spirits high, we finally reached Fiesch and sat in a café drinking beer and waiting for the transport. When Dave Moore turned up with a basket of hot baked potatoes and delicious hot meat pasties straight from the oven, we felt truly at peace with the world.

5

NUMBER THIRTEEN

The principles of this journey . . . should be employed in solitude
and only by men alive to the results.
                                        Muhammad al-Sanusi, d. 1859

When we arrived in Brig at the end of April, the larch trees on the
sides of the valleys were brown, winter-shorn of their needles, the
grass was bruised and old, just recovering from the winter snows
which still capped the low mountains ringing the valley. At the
end of May, by the time we came down from five days in the
Margherita Hut, we noticed how much everything was changed.
The Glishorn above Brig was still white but spring was in full bud,
fresh and green.

On the Bishorn in the north-west Pennine Alps just north of the
Weisshorn, we had this new landscape to ourselves. The low clouds
which had made our descent of the Fiesch Glacier so 'adventurous'
cleared and we were given a forecast for two good days. As usual,
we were suspicious, since the settled spring weather which Roger
kept talking about had not materialised. Sunny days alternated with
awful winds and cloud, more snow and the föhn. The bad weather
was most frustrating when we were stuck in Brig unable to climb but
once we were up on the mountains all irritations slipped away. This
was the beginning of pleasure in the mountains for their own sake.

On our first climbs we had been rather obsessed with the bare
statistics. I knew the routes we would take by heart, from the guides
books which I had studied endlessly at home. I knew the exact height

of each mountain, sometimes to the nearest decimetre and could quote the names of cols and features on each route. Gary and Simon meticulously monitored our progress. Thommen had sponsored us with their excellent Thommen Classic altimeter and the Altitronic, a newer electronic altimeter. Gary set his Altitronic so that every time we reached 4000 metres it made a sharp electronic beep, a truly appalling noise to hear on mountains, whereupon one of us would note down the time. We recorded the altitude and real time of nodal points on our climbs, at the start, at cols, on summits and at the end, using excellent Promaster watches which Citizen had very generously given us.

This bureaucratisation (sic) of our climbing happened partly because we had been given the toys to play with, partly because we were still awed by our self-imposed task of climbing so many big mountains, but arose mainly from the sheer amazement of finding ourselves actually climbing after months and months of frustrations, wishing and planning, so familiar to everyone who sets out to climb anything. Of course, in the early days we were also still getting fit and conscious each painful step we took uphill was but a tiny fraction of the amount we would have achieved by the end.

However, by the time we set out to climb the Bishorn, we had climbed twelve mountains; we had begun to feel confident, if not accumulate some real experience; we were extremely fit, having ascended 11,000 metres, which is more 'up' than required to pass an SAS selection (9380m), and the childish excitement at reaching altitude for its own sake had faded. We continued to use our altimeters as navigational aids to check the time and our location as we climbed, but now we had begun to enjoy the mountains for themselves. The Bishorn, for all that it was graded 'Facile', was delightful, and the start of the realisation that I was on a long journey.

At five thirty in a cool fresh dawn promising a hot day, Simon, Gary, Douglas and I left Brig, half-asleep, and I drove out to the Zinal valley in a Volkswagen Transporter minibus. This was one of two green Swiss Army VWs which Brigadier Jean-Daniel Mudry had just given us for the duration of our stay in Switzerland. I guess a good many people, including myself, have always thought that the Swiss were rather hard-nosed about cash like the Scots, a reputation which may have something to do with mountains, but the Swiss Army was unfailingly generous throughout. They gave us free fuel too, from another, more usual-looking barracks, with a gate, barbed-wire fence and guards on the other side of Brig. The impact of this generosity on our finances may be imagined when I say that by the end we had covered nearly 20,000 kilometres in these two VWs.

As I drove up the open valley on a narrow bumpy track beyond the village of Zinal, I realised the VW had seen almost as much service as our own ancient Land-Rovers, but it did not have four-wheel drive. It had a superb lock, but the steering was loose as a bowl of soup which made the last few miles quite exciting. We edged round some sharp bends above scrub-covered slopes which dropped sharply to the river far below. I thought I was coping with the ruts and potholes rather well, but when we turned a corner and faced a powerful stream tumbling over the track in a mess of boulders and earth, Simon, Gary and Douglas leaped out at once.

Standing well back from the edge, the stream and the VW, they began waving their arms like manic traffic wardens, grinning and shouting useful instructions, 'Left hand down a bit! More to the right. To me!' Ignoring it all, I took the stream at speed.

We parked beside a footbridge at 1908 metres above Le Vichieso. Roger had advised us not to take the path straight up from Zinal village as it was steep, dull and, crucially, started 250 metres lower down the valley. This may not sound much but I had tried to call the Tracuit Hut, where we wanted to stay overnight, without success, so we were carrying our own bivouac gear: tents, food, Epigas cookers and pots. All this, with our heavy Swiss Army mountaineering skis, made an all-up weight of 60+ lb.

In bright sunshine, watched curiously by a large group of hikers cooling their feet in the stream, we changed into our ski-mountaineering boots, strapped the skis to our packs, hoisted our packs to our backs and crossed the wood bridge into the trees. I always think the first hour of any walk carrying a heavy pack is the hardest. Leg and back muscles complain till they settle into the rhythm of the climb. However, this walk was delightful right from the start. Although we started late, at nine o'clock, the first steep section was in the shade of pines, birch and larch with sprouting rosettes of bright green needles. The track climbs fast, winding uphill, and our skis protruding high over our packs kept catching in the branches above our heads. By the time we emerged above the tree-line 300 metres up, the angle seemed to ease off and my attention was taken by a mass of spring flowers.

The open slopes were thick with low Alpine rhododendrons (mostly '*ferrugineum*') and the famous dark shiny-leafed 'Alpenrose' in full flower. In places, they filled the ground in a springy pink and green carpet between the boulders and rocks. On the grass further up, we saw lush yellow *Trollius europaeus*, sulphur-coloured *Senecio* and yellow and purple furry Alpine pulsatillas, or Pasque flowers, clumps of white crocuses, puce violas with pretty yellow streaked faces and tall long-stemmed white asters (*Belliastrum*), but the most eye-catching of all were the brilliant blue gentians.

Fresh and young and bright in the sun, these beautiful plants deserve their fame. I identified the neat perky *Gentiana verna* and the voluptuous bell-shaped flower of the *Gentiana acaulis*. Even a plant with a couple of blooms catches your eye from yards away but there seemed to be hundreds of them everywhere we looked. In the sunlight, they reflected the blue sky and seemed incandescent. Common they may be but only someone very pretentious could claim they do not give pleasure.

We were in no hurry, having all day to reach the Tracuit Hut, and stopped for a brew from our flasks (we still carried them then) at a broken-down stone cow byre at Tsijière de la Vatse (2388m). All round us were flowers, specks of colour in the grass, the deep valley, the stream and the trees were far below now, and beyond the distant grey moraine of the Zinal Glacier we could see a fine line of snow-capped mountains rising to the Dent Blanche in the south.

After two hours we reached the Roc de la Vache, a prominent nose of rock overlooking the Zinal valley. The track leaves the hot grass and flowers on the south-facing slopes behind, and turns east behind the Roc into a long valley, still white with snow, which runs deep into the mountain. With particularly good eyesight you can see the black square shape of the Tracuit Hut nearly four kilometres away and 600 metres up, under the snowy Diablon des Dames. Thankfully we unstrapped our skis from our packs and put them on. We left our heels loose in the uphill mode but without skins so we could slide along the traverse under the north flank of the Pointe d'Ar Pitetta on our right, by the Torrent du Barmé (an appropriately named stream if ever there was one).

The snow was soft and we broke through the surface several times crossing the flat snowfields by the stream before we began the climb up to the hut. Gary and Simon lost patience and opted to walk up the red rocks showing through on the south-facing slopes under the Diablon. Douglas and I followed the stream bed nearly all the way up and emerged on broad open snow banks under the Col Tracuit.

'Blue eyes, my baby's got blue eyes,' sang Elton John in my ears as I slid my skis endlessly forward uphill, sweating and deliciously tired in the hot midday sun.

Skiing, or skinning, uphill is faster than walking because it is smoother, more efficient pace for pace and more economical of effort. Douglas and I stopped for a picnic half-way up. We munched garlic sausage and brown granary bread as we watched the little black figures of Gary and Simon far below struggling through the soggy snow on foot.

This was a place everyone could enjoy. There was nothing remotely dangerous about the route, whereas the sun, the clear air and the mountains ringed round, sharp dark ridges white with snow, combined to produce a delightful feeling of being quite remote from the pettifogging demands of civilisation in the valley far below.

By two o'clock when we reached the Tracuit Hut, we were parched. Not expecting any sign of life, Douglas and I were all set to make our camp and melt-snow on our cooker for a brew when we found the door open. We dumped our packs, discarded our skis and I went inside. The hut is stone-built and old-fashioned, rustic and not modernised like some of the more popular places and this guarantees its charm. Ducking my head under low beams, I passed a dark locker-room full of worn wood clogs which smelled of old leather, and found a small boy, aged nine, in the kitchen. His father was the warden, but the two sons were preparing the evening meal. The older was stacking wood in the cooker and, as we were in French-speaking Switzerland, I was able to persuade the younger to sell us some beer and lemonade.

We sat outside in the sun and slugged down several shandies, shading our eyes to see the gleaming snow summit of the Bishorn way above us to the south-east. As we discussed the route, the small boy staggered manfully back and forth fetching bucketfuls of snow inside to melt down for cooking. This was a scene which would have been quite normal to any of the first climbers who visited the Tracuit Hut at the beginning of this century.

Later, Douglas and I set up our tent on rocks just beneath the hut, and the beer, sun and exercise overwhelmed me. I fell fast asleep in the sunshine, sitting bolt upright in front of a fine potful of curry I was preparing for our supper. The others thought this was very amusing, a sure sign of age and decrepitude.

It was a good thing I did pass out that afternoon in the warmth. Simon and I were testing a new lightweight 'sleep system' by which we had deliberately left behind our conventional but heavy four-season sleeping bags. Instead, we put on every bit of clothing we had and carried anyway for emergencies – long-john Helly Hansens top and bottom, fleece jacket and trousers, a useful lightweight Mountain Equipment duvet jacket and an excellent Calange fleece balaclava – and slept inside just a Gore-Tex bivvy bag. It was not a great success. We both froze during the night and got very little sleep. Maybe, we told each other next morning as we stood by our hoar-frosted tents in the cold dawn trying to warm up with a steaming brew of hot chocolate, the concept might work better later in the summer when ambient temperatures were higher.

We left late, stiff and slow to warm into the rhythm of the climb, far behind a group of three Italians. The long sweeping slopes of the upper Turtmann glacier were icy hard névé, perfect for skis, good enough for anyone to try on foot, and nowhere was there the slightest chance of a serious fall. Even on the last few hundred metres, the slopes are easy and run out, more or less, in safety. We overtook the last two Italians just before the summit, much to their disgust. The one at the back was splendidly overweight, his typically colourful ski-wear bulging under his body harness, and he was delighted when we passed his two fitter friends ahead because they had been ignoring his frantic, breathless calls for them to go more slowly and not leave him behind.

We had to leave our skis just below the summit but there was snow to the top, a flat place with plenty of room to enjoy the fantastic views. The Weisshorn's North Ridge sweeps round from the Bishorn, over the Great Gendarme which was white with snow and ice and looked a decidedly serious proposition, to the magnificent 1000-metre North-East Face of the Weisshorn itself where the huge curtains of hanging glaciers and séracs seem to defy gravity.

In spite of the Italians, the sense of remoteness never left me. The Zinal and Mattertal valleys on either side are miles away, out of sight far below. A couple of mercenary black choughs flying about waiting for titbits of sandwiches and a small very unfortunate spider in a hollow of snow, perhaps brought up by the birds or the wind, seemed to emphasise this detachment.

However, we had to try and contact our base camp using our Swiss Army radio. We had been given the radio 'in case of emergency' but I was fed up carrying it about in my pack. It weighed several pounds and I had not been able to speak to anyone on the mountains yet. As I pulled it out of my pack and fitted the aerial which I stowed separately to avoid breaking it off, I wondered – not for the first time – what good it would be if I was the one to fall with it into a crevasse.

I had arranged some rather unmilitary comms procedures and callsigns with the Scots Guards signallers, 'Gonzo' Martin and 'Death' (because he looked terminally ill) Cowell. I switched on the radio and said, 'Hallo Thunderbird Two, this is Thunderbird One!'

The Italians were just climbing over the cornice onto the summit and gave me a funny look.

I tried again, but raised nothing, so Douglas took over, being our self-appointed technician. He stuffed his pocket computer back in his pack and spent several minutes stalking round the summit shouting into the radio, without any success.

The ski run down from the summit was excellent and fast on the big open, safe slopes. We easily avoided the few big crevasses and any unseen dangers were well covered with hard snow. We were back at the hut again in minutes. While I packed our tent, Douglas employed the fine military principle of 'concurrent activity', combining a call of nature with another attempt to raise base on the radio. He disappeared into an outside khazi which was perched like a wood sentry box over the cliff at the top of the Col Tracuit. Along with the usual noises, we heard muffled shouting, 'Thunderbird One? Hallo Smokey, this is the Bear!' etc, but he still failed to raise any reply. These hut long-drops-over-the-nearest-cliff are not very savoury and perhaps in the circumstances it was not surprising no one wanted to speak to him in there.

We continued on skis down from the hut, edging carefully as we traversed the first steep part from the col before we could let rip on the wide slopes below. We were moving so fast we caught a large marmot unawares a long way from its burrow and chased it on our skis across the snow between rocks until it disappeared breathlessly down a hole. There was something very free about the ski down from the Bishorn summit all the way to the Roc de la Vache, as if the wild open runs were the antithesis of everything that is complicated in life down in the valleys and plains far beneath. I was left thinking that if there was anything lasting to be learned during our stay in the Alps then the freedom of mind necessary to appreciate it began during our two days on the Bishorn.

The walk down from the Roc de la Vache to the valley floor was as sunny as the day before, the flowers the same brilliant colours, the air as clear and filled with the scent of pines and junipers, and the birds really did sing through the dappled sunlight in the trees. Nature, it seemed, approved of us and we returned the compliment. We moved quickly, pleased with our day, with the memories of the summit, the views and the skiing down. The sense of well-being was almost overwhelming, producing in the end, when we reached the bridge over the stream, a sensation of great calm and satisfaction. The Bishorn was one step on our long journey, an easy step, remote and unspoiled, and this was both its greatest charm and a contrast to what came later.

We met the Italians again, red-faced with exertion, their designer clothes dark with sweat. Oddly, though they had left their car in Turtmann village in the main Rhône valley, they had decided to walk down the other side of the mountain on the dull route from the Tracuit Hut directly to Zinal village, thinking it would be shorter. Sitting in the sun on the terrace of a café where we had repaired for a beer or two we observed them tiredly holding their packs, skis and sticks and trying to hitch a lift. We took pity. Turtmann was on our way back to Brig from Sierre. We threw their gear in the back of our ropy old VW and drove them to their car, where, of course, we were obliged to accept their offer of another beer. Our feelings of satisfaction deepened.

In fact, by the time we reached Brig, cleaned up and then enjoyed several Paulaner *Weissbier* in the 'Pirate' later that evening, we were all very self-satisfied indeed. I slept well that night, for I had rented a neat, very Swiss chalet in the meadows above Brig, where the farmers were cutting grass for barn-dried hay, and my wife was coming out the following day with Claudia and Madeleine to join me for a week.

6

FULL MOON OVER THE MATTERHORN

It was the lovely moon that lovelike
Hovered over the wandering, tired
Earth.

John Freeman

'Goodday, sport!'

It was not, but a flamboyant figure materialised through the dense fog above the Längflüh lift station. Dressed with studied outdoor nonchalance, coiffured dark hair, designer stubble, a smile full of white teeth and bronzed for the discos, he continued with, 'They rang up to say you wanted a lift. Last one of the day.'

Closer to, the Australian twang was tinged with a sharper German accent. Born in Saas Fee, he had returned from three seasons as a *Ski-Lehrer* in Australia to drive his home-town *Feechatz*. This snow-cat linked Längflüh with a T-bar lift further up the mountain. The connection is also used by ski mountaineers who want to cross above the Fee glacier to Felskinn to reach the Britannia Hut when the Felskinn lift is closed in the summer season.

Simon, Douglas and I were impressed: the lift man at the bottom station in Saas Fee had bothered to call up the mountain. We did not fancy skiing off uphill in thick cloud and finding our way over the icefalls of the Fee Glacier. We climbed in the snow-cat and hoped it was all going to be worth it. The signs were not encouraging but we had been given a good forecast for the next two days and wanted to get in position to attempt the Strahlhorn and Rimpfischhorn.

We lurched to a stop somewhere up the mountain, still in dense cloud. In his cheerful Aussie accent, the driver pointed into the whiteout and said, 'Ski down the tracks of this piste-basher, then follow a T-bar lift up to the Metro-Allalin railway. You'll see the tunnel leading into it.'

Skiing downhill in whiteout is strange. You feel you are going faster than you are and have no reference how steep the slope is. In a whiteout in Norway years before with the army, I was convinced that the strong wind blowing into my face was due to my speeding downhill, I leaned forward to keep balanced on the slope and fell flat on my face. Squashed by a heavy rucksack, I twisted round to look up and saw a friend roaring with laughter. We had been standing quite still and he had watched me slowly topple face down in the snow.

At the bottom of this slope we fitted our skins and set off up the mountain. There was no difficulty finding the route. Above us, hidden in the mist, we could hear the roaring engines of several JCB diggers grinding back and forth, shouts and all the noises associated with a large, active building-site. They were developing the Felskinn ski-lifts.

There is something very unpleasant about the metal spider's web of ski-lifts on mountains. During a ski holiday people are too busy having a lovely time to think about the machinery whisking them uphill, but at the end of the ski season when the sounds of people enjoying themselves have faded, when the pylons stand idle, when the wires strung across the landscape sway pointless in the wind, then the damage to the environment is starkly depressing. Even then the lifts are used for summer tourism. When we reached the building-site at Felskinn the real impact of this on the mountains struck home.

A wide area by the top of the Felskinn lift had been torn apart by huge metal dinosaurs. Between the lift and the tunnel to the Metro-Allalin mountain railway was a sea of mud and rocks, steel supports were dumped about by the pannier-load beside more stacks of timber, bags of concrete and steel reinforcing rods, torn plastic sheeting flapped in the wind, and the air was thick with the smell of diesel and exhaust fumes. I imagine Konzentrationslager Dora or the worst of Stalin's Russian tin mines looked like this, but it is the reality behind every construction in the mountains. I believe we should encourage people to go into the mountains, but we ought seriously to question whether we can justify the price we pay.

Feeling like trespassers, we passed various tough-looking workmen wearing yellow helmets as we slipped and slid through the mud carrying our skis, and we were grateful to leave the awful sight behind us in the cloud. The noise followed us till we turned a shoulder of the Allalinhorn past the Egginerjoch.

On the other side, the clouds began to break up, giving us a sight of the surrounding mountains. White mist still dragged on the peaks but patches of blue appeared, and by the time we reached the Britannia Hut at five o'clock the gloomy cloudbase was high but visibility was good. We looked across the Hohlaub Glacier up the long Allalin Glacier to the Adlerpass (those eagles again: the first visitors named the pass after finding a golden eagle's feather there), but the route did not look very appetising in the cold wind at that time of the afternoon, so we decided to spend the night by the hut.

The Britannia is a typical Swiss stone mountain hut but it was funded by the Association of British Members of the Swiss Alpine Club, and given to the Swiss Alpine Club, Geneva Section, in 1912. The Union Jack flying from the flag-pole under the usual Swiss flag testifies to the hut's origins. Fixed to the wall outside the entrance is a large brass plaque set up by the Government and People of the Canton Valais, the Swiss Alpine Club and the Swiss National Tourist Office expressing the finest sentiments of the heyday of Alpine mountain exploration, 'On the occasion of the 75th anniversary of the ABMSAC, we take the opportunity to thank our British friends for their continued devotion to our mountains and our country.'

On the other side of the door is a low-relief sculpture on a plaque in memory of Clinton T. Dent, MC, FRCS, a splendid-looking man with a beard, who was once President of the Alpine Club and a 'lover of mountains', born 1850, died 1912.

The hut is perched on a spit of land with steep ground all round so we set up our tents near one corner, unobtrusively, and well out of the way of a snow-mobile parked there. As we had been quite unable to find any Epigas refills for our cooker in Brig, Visp, or Saas on the way up and were a bit short of fuel to melt snow, I went inside and bought two litres of hot water, 1 SFr each, (the going price) and we cooked our main meal, a mess of 'all-in' stew.

After a brew of tea, we went to sleep for an hour to warm up in our sleeping bags, oddly tired though we had not done much that day, and looking forward to nipping into the hut later for a couple of beers before turning in for the night.

'*Was machen Sie hier? Das ist verboten!*'

Someone was shouting at us. I opened an eye and peered out of the tent. A middle-aged woman with blond hair was bending over and bellowing into Simon's tent next door.

'*Raus!*' this harpy shouted. '*Sie können nicht hier bleiben!*'

Simon's face appeared from the tent, bemused, his hair tousled. '*Entschuldigen Sie, bitte?*' he said politely, manfully trying to understand why he was being so ill-treated.

I fixed a 'can-I-help-you' expression on my face and tried some French, '*Qu'est-ce qui se passe, madame? Est-ce qu'il y a un problème?*'

She straightened, spotted my face peering from my tent and rounded on me in good French, '*Certainement! C'est interdit de faire du camping ici, tout près de la cabane!*' Hardly pausing for breath, she shouted that it was against the law to camp within 100 metres of her hut, or any other hut for that matter.

I wriggled out a bit, looked round the side of my tent into the growing darkness and inquired where she thought we could go instead. Except the narrow shelf of flat snow we were on, the ground dropped away sharply from the hut on all sides, or rose equally steeply to the East Shoulder of the Hinter Allalin.

'I don't care,' she snapped rudely. 'You must go!' With that, she turned and stamped off back into the hut leaving us speechless.

'That's put paid to our beer tonight,' said Simon, grinning.

We stayed put. It was plainly out of the question to move. Not only had I been into the hut two hours before, but our tents were right outside the kitchen windows in full view, so the staff had plenty of time to say they wanted us 'off the premises' and need not have waited two hours near darkness when we were settled in. Also, when we had thought of doing the Strahlhorn a couple of weeks before, I had telephoned the warden who had said he was quite happy for us to camp outside the hut.

We shrugged and snuggled back down into our sleeping bags. Simon and I had binned our lightweight 'sleep system' for the time being in favour of nice warm four-season bags. Douglas, showing a fine example, had not stirred throughout this tirade. He turned over in his bag and continued to snore gently.

An hour later, she came back. This time Simon and I were ready for her, awake and making a brew of tea in the darkness.

'You have to go!' she announced in French without preamble, arms aggressively akimbo.

'With the greatest of respect,' I began. 'We're not moving anywhere at this time of night.'

She was obviously miffed we hadn't chosen to stay in her hut and pay her lots of money for the pleasure. I pointed out that a week or so before the warden had said we could camp outside and she flatly denied it. 'What was good then is not necessarily good now,' she declared.

Most SAC huts seem to have a couple or more hut-wardens who run the hut in turns. Obviously I had spoken on the phone to her colleague. I wished he was still there.

In the end she just looked silly. She said we were in the way of her noisy little snow-mobile, which we were not, and even that the smell of the snow-mobile would be bad for us. She was thoroughly spiteful and unwelcoming, and when I pointed out that the hut had been given to the Swiss by the Brits, she said she did not care a fig as that was all in the past anyway.

'You going to stay one night or two?' she demanded.

'Madam,' I replied trying to be as haughty as possible squinting up at her from inside my tent. 'After this charming welcome, we have no intention of coming anywhere near your hut ever again.'

She stormed off at that and I called after her to read the plaque beside the door on her way in. God knows what Clinton T. Dent might have thought of her attitude.

This was an appalling episode, but broadly speaking we noticed that the closer a hut to 'civilisation', especially ski pistes, the less attuned were the hut staff to the spirit of the mountains. The Britannia Hut was built as a last night's stop on the famous ski mountaineers' Haute Route from Zermatt to Saas Fee, but since the advent of lifts the hut has lost this importance as most skiers by-pass it now. Instead, it is easily reached by winter on-piste skiers and summer tourists along the track we had taken from the Felskinn lift via the Egginerjoch.

Thankfully, the following morning dawned clear as predicted, so our commitment of the cost of the Längflüh lift and our moving into position in poor conditions were not wasted. I was particularly relieved as my wife and children were still in the little chalet above Brig. There had been so little settled good weather that I felt we had to take every opportunity, even though she and the girls were only with me for a week. I hoped she understood.

'Lay down Sally,' sang Eric Clapton as we skinned past the Hohlaubgrat of the Allalinhorn. 'You do not need to leave so soon.'

The route up the Allalin Glacier is long but we were in good form and gradually overhauled two other groups who were just little black dots in the white expanse ahead when we started. The first was a clutch of portly Swiss men in loud red-and-black check lumberjack shirts, leather plus-fours and thick woolly socks. They were very disgruntled that we passed them skinning up through the crevasse section just short of, and on the left of, the Adlerpass. Later they bustled roughly past us on the narrow rock ridge of the summit, all shoulders and stomachs, when they found us there enjoying the brilliant warm sunshine.

We ate sausage and bread on the summit and enjoyed the view which is superb. I looked down on the long dark ridge-back of the Gornergrat eight kilometres away. Rebecca had taken the children there on the Gornergrat railway, for lunch, and I told Claudia later that I had been able to see them waving at me quite clearly.

To the south, the imposing bulk of the Monte Rosa rises above everything and we identified 'our' hut, the Margherita, where we had spent so long. I carefully studied the route I planned to take to tackle the Dufourspitze and Nordend. I wanted to do both on skis in the same day, camping high to give ourselves a head start.

'I think I might nip over there with Nikki,' said Douglas between mouthfuls of sausage, gesturing into Italy as if he might just step over the South Face of the Strahlhorn by way of a short cut. 'Take her to Lake Como.'

Simon and I laughed. Smitten by the charms of our physiotherapist, Douglas had been rather obviously preoccupied.

'You asked her yet?' I said.

'No,' Douglas admitted darkly and fell silent, plotting how to put this right.

The descent from the summit was hard work. The snow was

thoroughly warmed in the sun and heavy going. Douglas and I plunged head first into snow at one turn or another, laughing hysterically at our stupidity, while Simon skied smoothly down without mishap, irritatingly balanced as usual. The run down the glacier under the fluted vertical rock face of the Rimpfischhorn was fast and delightfully speed-blown in the glaring snow-reflected heat of the midday glacier.

We set up our tents on the glacier under the Hohlaubgrat of the Allalinhorn, far enough away from the cliff to avoid being shelled by rockfall which was breaking off fairly continuously in the warmth of the afternoon. Our plan was to be well placed to ski round to the Rimpfischhorn the following morning rather than return all the way back to the Britannia Hut, saving 8 kilometres and 200 metres of altitude. Plus, camping saved money.

We stripped off naked, scattering our clothes all round to dry in the sun, hanging everything on our skis stuck in the snow so the place looked like a new-age travellers' doss-site. We sun-bathed, made brews and listened to our Walkmans. I lay naked on my stomach on my neoprene mat with my head in the shade inside my tent and typed up notes on my little Sharp PC3000. And forgot all about the sun. I was so absorbed that the sun burned off my suncream, burned my fair bottom and then some. By the time I realised my mistake, my arse was the colour of a Dutch Edam and I could scarcely sit down.

Next morning, we left earlier than usual, at four o'clock, to take advantage of the full moon. I had asked the Swiss in Brig for a moon chart, which shows the phases of the moon, when it is waxing or waning and when it is visible during the night (or day). In the UK, these charts are available from the RAF and I had always used them in the army; it makes a great difference to know the amount of ambient light at night when planning a covert observation patrol, in, say, Northern Ireland, to gauge whether to take image-intensifying night viewing devices. Blithely, I assumed the Swiss Army would use moon charts too. Instead, a rather genial Gefreiter in the offices on the first floor of our building came up one day with some photocopies which appeared to come straight from an original manuscript of the Prophecies of Nostradamus. In Gothic German script these charming old-fashioned charts predicted the daily weather – months in advance, in fact for every day of the year

– giving the astrological sign and the patron saint, but of the moon's chronological perambulation of the globe there was nothing. So, for Friday, 4 June, I was thus reliably informed that we were protected under the auspices of Saint Franz Taracciolo (who?) in the sign of Sagittarius and that it was going to be cold.

That at least was right. Even working hard, our fingers froze as we skinned 300 metres on ice-hard slopes up to the Allalinpass (3564m), but most memorably, we skied under a soft velvet sky with the translucent pink light of a new day at our backs, then traversed along the west flank of the Rimpfischhorn in the face of a huge silver moon hanging over the Matterhorn.

We had the moon and stars above. 'Lay down Sally,' sang Eric Clapton.

Douglas raced ahead all day, impatiently pulling us along behind, so we reached the Rimpfischsattel by seven o'clock. We left our skis under the lee of a rock cliff, fitted crampons and climbed up a snowy couloir, scrambled over some rocks to a false summit and crossed a narrow corniced snow crest to the final turret of rock. We climbed solo which was unnerving as there was too much snow on the rock scrambles to feel really comfortable with the handholds, but the taste of danger left a feeling of acute personal satisfaction when we stood on the top.

The drops on either side of the Rimpfischhorn are fearsome. Standing on the summit is like flying among the peaks all round. The air was perfectly clear, with the promise of a gloriously hot day, and we could see several black dots struggling through the crevasse section up the massive summit block of the Strahlhorn. That morning, we were well ahead of the world. On the other side to the north, we looked across at the Allalinhorn where the cross on the summit was crisply in focus.

Douglas remarked, 'We should have invested in a 500-metre climb to the Alphubeljoch.'

Douglas had done a business management degree at university and talked like that sometimes. He was also impatient to get back to Brig. He had been trying to persuade Simon and me to bring all our gear up to the Allalinpass so we could climb over the Alphubeljoch after the Rimpfischhorn and ski down to the Längflüh lift station.

Simon snorted and I said, 'Investing 500 metres doesn't appeal to me at all.' Plus, we would have had to get up even earlier to pack away our tents and carry them up to a cache on the Allalinpass. Actually the extra climbing, compared with returning via the Britannia Hut again, would not have added much more than 100 metres, but we were climbing uphill enough without 'investing' any more.

Douglas grunted and when we fitted our skis again he set off in the lead again, hurrying us downhill.

I went very slowly at first. I was terrified of falling. There were some impressive crevasses to ski between but much more pressing was my poor sunburned backside which was agony every time I sat down.

In retrospect I would have preferred to take Douglas's investment recommendation. The route from the Rimpfischhorn over the Alphubeljoch is more stylish, with a lovely run down to the Längflüh station. We had done part of it less than a week before when we skinned up to the summit of the Alphubel; three fast hours up, half an hour on the top in the sun, and twenty-five superb minutes skiing down. Douglas and I had left Gary and Simon way behind, mainly because they were still suffering from a heavy session the night before in the Pirate. After the Rimpfischhorn, I guessed Douglas wanted to do the same again and I should have agreed. We would have completed the climbing before the sun's heat softened the snow and evaporated all our energies.

Unable to persuade us, Douglas shot off ahead muttering about wanting to phone for transport to meet us at the bottom. He ignored our salacious grinning and lewd comments about physiotherapy and skinned athletically into the distance.

Our grins soon faded. In addition to our personal gear, Simon was carrying his own tent and it was my turn to carry the tent Douglas and I shared. We made a real meal of it.

'Underneath the velvet skies, love is all that matters. Will you stay with me?'

But no amount of Eric Clapton helped. After a pleasant glide down to the Britannia Hut, we really struggled up the short climb to the hut boiled by the sun. We glared furiously at the harpy who was sitting outside. She pursed her mouth into a tight line of disapproval as we staggered past, red in the face with strain but trying to look casual.

The final straw was the climb up the snow-cat track over the top

of the Fee Glacier which we had descended in whiteout two days
before. I had to stop every ten paces. By the time we reached
Längflüh just before midday, we had been up hill and down dale
for seven hours, covered more than eighteen kilometres, and I was
whacked.

7

THE GRAND COMBIN

All the mind's activity is easy if it is not subjected to reality.
Marcel Proust, *Remembrance of Things Past*

Peter Copeland and Stewart Barron were desperately frustrated at not being able to ski with us. They had tried to divert themselves with endless walks below the snow line and they became experts on the Simplon Pass area, where by the start of June the snow had melted away. They spent nights out in our third tent, which Peter, always meticulously polite, found tiresome as Stewart's snoring runs half-way up the Richter scale. It was small consolation, but during days of bad weather when none of us could go into the mountains, we all went rock climbing in the valley.

There was good friction climbing on slabs under the main railway line at Gamsen, near Brig, but two- or three-pitch cliffs above a village in the Mattertal called St Niklaus were more typical of what we would find at altitude. The rock was quite brittle in places and after one enjoyable day, I mentioned to Roger that we had been unable to find a route described in the guide book. He said, 'Oh yes, I forgot. That must have been the bit of hillside that broke off last year. It killed two people who were on the route at the time.'

'They obviously weren't using any protection,' I remarked and he gave me a funny look.

Peter wanted to do more, so I introduced him to Russell Brice, the New Zealander I had met on an expedition to Cho Oyu and Shisha Pangma in 1990. He had been a UIAGM qualified guide for years and was living in Chamonix. Very experienced, wiry and supremely fit, Russell was first through the Pinnacles along the North-East Ridge of Everest with Harry Taylor, who had given me so much advice when I was planning our climbs. Peter and Stewart drove to Chamonix in the old blue soft-top Land-Rover (the hard-top was banned from use) and Russell took them up Mont Blanc du Tacul and then later along the Haute Route from the Breithorn, to Pollux, Castor, Liskamm and the Vincent Piramide. I admired their determination, as there were still enormous amounts of snow and they did it all on foot.

Russell took immense trouble, teaching technique all the time. They walked down the Grenz Glacier in the warmth of an afternoon, which I did not envy them, then over the Gornergrat back to Zermatt. Back in Brig, gorging ourselves on another of Dave Moore's excellent suppers, I asked Russell how they had got on.

'Peter kept up well. He was steady with his first bit of exposure on the Liskamm Ridge,' he said. 'But Stewart can't acclimatise.'

After Castor, Russell had wanted to traverse Liskamm from west to east, which they could have done nicely on foot, not having to carry skis, but instead they had to go round the south side, via Il Naso because Stewart had been unable to cope with the altitude. When they reached Liskamm from the east side, Russell had had to leave Stewart at the bottom of the ridge because he was feeling so awful and he took Peter up on his own. Russell agreed that it is unusual to find someone who cannot acclimatise even after spending several days at altitude, but he pointed out the problem was not just Stewart's. Having someone on the team who loses balance, judgement and is sick threatens the safety of the whole group, and can easily turn a perfectly ordinary day into an epic of survival.

'He is fine up to 3600 metres,' Russell explained. 'But regular as clockwork as soon as he goes to 3800 metres he suffers headaches and nausea.'

'Throws his teddy bear in the corner,' said Peter, employing a typical piece of army-speak.

Russell, Peter and Stewart had talked it over quite openly in the Gnifetti Hut the evening before Liskamm, and Stewart was understandably fed up but he understood. There is nothing worse than feeling bloody at altitude and I suspect he was secretly relieved not to have to go back up again.

I felt sorry for him. Stewart had been brought onto the team at short notice and been unable to ski. Now he would have to go back to the 'real' world of the Guards: public duties in the barracks in Windsor where Tim Spicer's battalion had just moved to from Germany. Finding out about his acclimatisation problem was a risk of taking people on high mountains without any previous climbing experience, a risk Tim Spicer and I acknowledged when we started. However, at least Stewart had climbed four big mountains and experienced the pleasures and pain of an environment he might never otherwise have seen.

It is not necessary to travel to the High Andes or the Himalayas. The Alps, central to Europe, are a testing ground big enough for everyone, as we found out in full measure on the Grand Combin.

The Grand Combin massif is the third largest in the Alps after Mont Blanc and Monte Rosa and mid-way between the two, some twenty-four kilometres from the nearest other 4000-metre mountain. Remote and huge, the Grand Combin is worthy of more attention but the approaches are long from all directions and the most popular hut, the Panossière, was destroyed by avalanche in March 1988, which must put off a few people. Roger recommended we ski in from the north, and after listening to his description of the off-the-road track up to our start point by the Cabane Brunet, I decided to take our old blue diesel Land-Rover with four-wheel drive in preference to a VW.

On Tuesday, 8 June, we left Brig at the late hour of six o'clock one morning – this time we politely refused Dave's offer of a greasy breakfast – and drove all the way down the valley to Martigny, soft top rolled back in the sun. We turned south on the road to the Grand St-Bernard Pass. At Sembrancher, we branched left, passed the railway station at Le Chable at the bottom of the steep road to Verbier and continued up the Val de Bagnes, twisting through some most attractive Alpine villages. At Lourtier, we turned off to the right and climbed steeply uphill following signs for the Cabane Brunet.

The four-wheel drive was essential. The single-track road was extremely narrow, wet and muddy and the hairpin bends through the forest were hair-raising. In the tiny hamlet of Plena Dzeu (superb name), where meadows of thick grass seemed to flow downhill around the roofs of the chalets dotted on the slopes, some farmers with faces like wrinkled old prunes were turning sweet-smelling hay. They leaned on their long forks with agricultural deliberation to watch us pass, doubtless amazed by our gentian-blue transport. Above the tree-line the track reduced to rough stone and curled precariously up the bare mountain to the Cabane Brunet at 2103 metres.

The hut was modern, locked tight and characterless, a pristine model of Scandinavian pine and big view windows with none of the charm of an old-fashioned place like the Tracuit Hut. We ignored signs which told us only those with police authority were allowed further up the mountain, and drove on. The desire to gain altitude in the Rover and save walking took us too high.

The four-wheel drive saw us safely through several snow drifts which still covered sections of the track and we ended up at Pindin (2384m), thinking we had been rather clever.

'Where d'we go from here?' asked Simon studying his map. He was dressed casually as usual in a purple T-shirt and his black Ron Hill tracksters.

'Over there,' I gestured vaguely across a deep valley at the snow peaks to our south which looked as if they should be the Grand Combin.

We milled about the Land-Rover unloading our rucksacks, skis and sticks, kicked off our flip-flops and pulled on thick socks to wear inside our plastic ski-mountaineering boots. The sun was hot and debilitating. We had started too late.

'No we don't,' said Douglas examining his map in turn. 'That lump over there is the Petit Combin. The Grand one is out of sight two mountains behind, other side of the Combin de Corbassière.'

'We have to cross a col somewhere,' said Simon searching the mountains in front of us for a sign. With a valley between us and the Combin massif, everything looked an awful long way off.

'I think we should go back down to Martigny and round to the south side,' announced Douglas just to confuse the issue. He had been looking at a different approach to the mountain altogether, the one usually taken by the Haute Route ski mountaineers.

'Another investment plan?' I asked.

Simon grunted. We were committed to the northern approach, if only we could see where to go. Or at least muster the energy to get going. Without a guide to take all decisions out of our hands, whom we could have blindly followed, like sheep, we had to be sure we took the right route. The hot sun was not helping us make up our minds. We were gripped by decisive reluctance.

'There it is,' said Simon finally in a shocked voice. He was pointing at a tiny notch which seemed miles away right the other side of the valley below us. There was a col between the sharp rock triangle of the Becca de Sery on the left and the long ridge which led up to the snows of the Petit Combin. This was the Col des Avouillons which Roger had told us we had to cross, rather in the manner of Allan Quatermain giving away the secret key to finding buried treasure.

Dropping off Pindin to the river 150 metres below was easy, even fun in the sunshine. The long hot slog up to the Col des Avouillons on the other side was not. We put on our skis as soon as we could in preference to carrying the bloody things on top of all our bivvy gear and skinned up on the soft melt-snow to the sharp little col where we sat down for a rest and lunch. Already we were hours away from the nearest village, we had seen no one and the feeling of remoteness was strong. At the col we left behind a spring landscape of soggy snow and black rocks covered with patches of grass thick with spring flowers, mainly gentians, violas and bright yellow Alpine pulsatillas. Ahead was the cold expanse of the Corbassière Glacier under the unfriendly black cliffs of the Grand Tave on the opposite side.

We had to lose height again descending from the col to the glacier. Simon and Douglas fell about in the soft snow and then we began the eight-kilometre haul up the Corbassière Glacier in blazing sun.

There is plenty of time to think on a long ski approach and music helps, 'When I give my heart again, its gonna last for ever.' Simon, who was leading, had lent me a Rod Stewart tape.

The continuous action of the skis sliding forward, rocking the body gently in balance from side to side, induces a pleasant, almost religious euphoria, like Buddhists chanting 'Om!' again and again. For four and a half hours we skinned steadily up the glacier and our three figures must have looked very insignificant on the white snow. The ice curved gently south, rising in easy steps over crevassed icefalls every mile or so, and widened between huge vertical cliffs under the ridge of the Tournelon Blanc on our left and the gentler mixed slopes of the Combin de Corbassière on our right. The sun was burning hot, magnified by the glittering reflections off the snow, and our progress was slow, but I felt enormously relaxed. When we were up on the mountains, nothing else mattered. This is not to say I did not think about the things I had done and the things I ought to have done, but everything assumed its proper level of importance. We had left the bureaucracy of our lives behind, in its rightful place in a mess of towns and cities, and gone up into a high place where nothing or no one could clamour for attention.

After four and a half hours, we stopped at 3270 metres on the Maisons Blanches which is a wide-open undulating snowfield, 3 kilometres by 2 kilometres, surrounded by an amphitheatre of black peaks, a rather secret and unusual place to find at the top of a mountain and which gives a measure of the size of the Combin Massif. On the other side, the west side of the summit block rose up massively above us. We put up our tents and sat in the last of the sun drinking brews of tea and chicken soup and argued about which was the best way up.

The normal route is the 'Corridor', a long sloping approach along the north flank of the mountain which takes you towards the Combin de Tsessette (4141m) before turning right-handed up the Mur de la Côte – rather like the last breathless step to the final summit slopes of Mont Blanc – and then to the summit. However, Roger had suggested we look at the North-West Face. This involves steep ice and snow to fifty degrees but in good conditions offers a swifter way to the summit plateau at Point 3987 metres.

The choice is given a certain piquancy because death is involved, not speculation about bringing on the uncertain event we all face in the future, but the actual mortality of past mountaineers. Five skiers died on the Corridor route in 1959 and a year later another four were killed. The problem is the continuous line of ice séracs which hang over the entire slope, from the Plateau du Déjeuner just above our tent site to the ridge under the Combin de Tsessette. We could see chunks of ice which had fallen off the séracs and while we sat talking we heard endless sharp reports, like artillery, as more pieces broke off and set off small avalanches. We all agreed skiing up the Corridor would be like running along the top of a shooting gallery, not knowing when we would be under fire.

There is no telling when ice will fall. An ice cliff, being the face of a glacier, breaks off as a function of the pressure behind, not as a function of the ambient heat. So, whereas avalanches are less likely on snow slopes in the early morning when still frozen after a cold, starry night, blocks of ice can fall from a hanging glacier at any time of day or night. We could see why skiing up the Corridor has been compared to playing Russian roulette.

We examined the shorter but much steeper North-West Face right in front of us. It rose like a steep ramp to the séracs hanging over the route at the top. I wondered if the route up through them to Point 3987 metres was obvious and Simon remarked, 'I can't see the difference in the danger from the séracs hanging over that face to the ones hanging over the Corridor.' Typically, he expressed the essence of our choice in a nutshell.

'We'll be exposed for less time on the North-West Face,' I volunteered. It was a climb of 700 metres compared to nearly 2 kilometres along the Corridor.

'Well that settles it, don't you think?' he said blandly and went off for a shit clutching his snow shovel.

We woke at 3.30 a.m. Douglas and I made our usual mug of hot chocolate and ate instant porridge, made by pouring boiling water (melted snow ready from the evening before) into a packet of flakes. I peeked outside our tent. Dawn light was beginning to silhouette the dark mass of the summit above us. Stars still glowed in a deep blue sky in the west over the black mountains ringing the Maisons Blanches. It was very cold. Perfect conditions.

I led up the slopes to the snow shelf called the Plateau du Déjeuner about 3400 metres and we angled right up towards rocks at the foot of the ridge on the edge of the North-West Face. The slope was steep and very icy, so we decided to continue on foot using crampons, carrying our skis to use on the summit plateau. We felt quite safe moving solo, sure on crampons with our ice axes handy, but all the way up I could not help looking up at the curtain of séracs hanging over our ascent, wondering what secret pressures were at work out of sight inside the blue ice. I knew perfectly well that the chances of being unlucky were slight, mathematically, but I could not help wondering if it was our turn to be a new Alpine statistic that cold morning.

Far above us, thin skeins of cloud raced wind-blown over the mountain, eerily diffusing the dawn sunlight behind and wreathing the moon which floated over the sharp summit of the Grand Combin de Valsorey high on our right. Climbing on the north side was cold but protected from the wind. We made a final traverse over the slope under the hanging glacier to find the route out through the sérac band at the top.

Here the path wound narrowly up between bulging ice formations, the slope was steeper over long drops on the right side of the North-West Face and the névé underfoot ice hard. We followed an earlier track plainly made by skis when the snow and ice was not so frozen as we found it, and zigzagged up between house-sized blocks of fractured ice to the easier snowfields at Point 3987 metres.

With skis fitted again, we continued quickly across uncomplicated slopes traversing back and forth up the last steeper 300 metres and reached the summit just over three hours after leaving our tents. At 4314 metres on that isolated huge mountain, the views were superb all round, especially of the Aiguille Verte group, the Grandes Jorasses and Mont Blanc behind in the distance, but clouds were washing up from the south-east playing hide and seek with the Matterhorn and we could see nothing of the Gran Paradiso due south right inside Italy.

The wind on top was very parky indeed but we had to wait while Douglas bravely dropped his ski pants on the ridge to answer an urgent call of nature (revealing all the hardy talents of a true Scot). We took off our skins and harscheisen and packed them away in our sacks with our crampons, fitted the heel attachments to our ski-mountaineer boots which hold your legs forward for downhill skiing, clipped the plate down on the ski, and skied from the summit. The run was excellent, reminiscent of the Finsteraarhorn for its altitude but with a greater sense of remoteness. In addition, we were alone. We had seen no one for two days and I doubt there was anyone within miles of us. We swooped side to side on the hard névé to Point 3987 metres again, above the sérac band.

We were all skiing so well, I led on into the sérac band, dipping easily between a couple of ice cliffs. I made a few more turns and then came out over a steep and narrow slope flanked by big blocks of ice. Below was a sharp free-fall over a hanging sérac onto the steep part of the North-West Face and the flat Maisons Blanches snowfield 600 metres beneath.

One look down convinced me we were unwise to go for *ski extrême*, and I called back for Simon and Douglas to put on crampons. I moved further down and across to find a suitable place to remove my skis too, conscious that the ice was so hard I would be unable to jab my skis into the slope.

Something made me look up. Douglas had come down too far after me, found himself facing the wrong way and chosen this moment to make a kick-turn. I distinctly remember thinking that this was really rather sporting. I turned away for a moment, busy with my own situation, but something made me look up a second later. Douglas was falling head first down the steep icy slope, one ski off, out of control. He momentarily slowed somehow, then picked up speed again. I slid across into the path of his fall, braced my ski edges against the ice-hard track I was on and stopped him.

There was no time to stand about chatting. Reaching over my back, he extracted my ice axe from my pack, passed it to me and I jabbed it into the ice for security. We disentangled ourselves. He stuck his axe in too and we changed from skis to crampons. We had to hang everything off the axes, as nothing else would penetrate the hard slope, so we took longer than usual, making certain we dropped nothing. Losing a crampon there would have been the last straw. Crampons fitted, we strapped our skis to our packs and carried on down after Simon, who had passed us once he saw we were all right.

Once through the sérac band, we crossed under the hanging glacier cliff at the top of the slope we had climbed up and put our skis back on. The face was hard and good to ski on. In spite of a near-disaster, perhaps because of it, we all felt confident. Near the bottom, I was probably skiing too fast. As I crossed a section of hard icy, rubbly snow where people had walked down before, disturbing the surface, my skis bounced on the ice and one ski knocked off the foot-binding of the other. In an instant, I lost the ski. I saw it shoot off downhill as I began to cart-wheel down the mountain. I twisted, to put my other ski on the outside leg and get the edge onto the slope, at the same time grabbing the end of a ski stick which I rammed into the slope like a pick.

I remember thinking, 'I'm bloody winning! I am going to stop!' I slowed down. I stopped. I looked downhill. My fall cannot have taken more than short seconds for my loose ski was still accelerating away below me. A long way down, Simon had seen me fall and he was skiing across the slope to intercept my ski. I watched him close on it, knowing how hard it must be to judge the right place to stand on the slope and then stop it. I thought he had missed it for a moment, and cursed the idea of having to walk way out onto the snowfield of Les Maison Blanches to retrieve it, when he picked it up, waved it at me and stabbed it into the snow.

The real impact of Douglas and me tangling in the sérac band did not really sink in until later, when we were skiing back down the Corbassière Glacier after packing up our tents. This was a lovely run, 8 kilometres of easy speed, not exhilarating in the sense of being fast, but relaxed, and pleasurable, giving us the chance to look all round at the mountains either side of us, at the sharp ridges and snow glittering in the bright sun, and we had time to reflect on the huge massif we had just climbed.

I felt a curious delight. We had climbed a splendid remote mountain, in good conditions, in a good time, using a good route, but it was the dramas which added the spice. We had all been aware of the inherent danger of falling among the séracs, aware of the drops over the hanging glacier cliffs and the long slope below, but these are no different to the circumstances to be found on any black run in any ski resort. I had skied in Verbier earlier in the year on the Tortin black run when there had been no snow for weeks, the slopes were dangerously icy and I watched a skier fall in front of me. His body bounced horribly on the moguls and he was seriously injured. Had he been on the Mont Gelé run he would have shot over the cliff below the top section of the run and died.

We were not in any more intrinsic danger on the Grand Combin than I had been in danger on Tortin or Mont Gelé, because we were confident of ourselves. That was the theory. The pleasure came from surviving the reality on a superb, massive and remote mountain.

Our reactions had been swift and instinctive. From the moment Douglas fell, he was trying to preserve himself and I was reacting to a similar urgency, only because I was fortunate enough to be in a position to do something about it. My curious delight was a reaction to that rare cocktail of emotions arising from danger, helping someone else in danger, and surviving.

Danger and survival are the real drugs. Some people, like free-fallers or solo rock climbers, deliberately seek them out for the buzz of survival. Soldiers find the so-called 'thrill of battle' provides a similar combination, though in my experience there is no thrill during a firefight, when I was always terrified, but an immense thrill afterwards, when I realised I was still alive. The pleasure of the climbing on the Grand Combin, the danger and survival, lasted all the way down the glacier, and for days afterwards.

The climb back up to the Col des Avouillons in the blazing sun was exhausting. We sweated, stripped off to the basics and used up plenty of suncream. On the other side, it was a pleasure to put the skis back on even for the soggy snow down to the Sery river, but it was very heavy work. Simon skied into a hole, which filled at once with wet snow, set like concrete, and he had to dig himself out with his shovel, grumbling that we had skied on and left him to it.

We stood on the wood bridge over the river 150 metres below Pindin and drew the short stick for who would have to climb up to where we had left the Land-Rover. Simon lost but Douglas volunteered himself instead. He just felt like driving. He set off at speed uphill and by the time Simon and I had walked along a very attractive path through the narrow gorge of the Torrent de Sery, Douglas had driven round to meet us at the old stable buildings at Sery.

As Simon and I walked up the last slope, we passed a group of Italian day-trippers who were taking pictures of the mountains we had just come from. Tourists are a familiar sight and, like others we had met before, they seemed surprised that we had been so far away. This time, however, I was struck that to them we must have appeared like travellers who had been on an odyssey to strange lands, with our big packs and skis strapped above our heads, and they could have had no idea that our pleasure there had been in taking our future in our hands, in decisions of life and death, and then returning home to find all was familiar again. And that our odyssey was not over.

Douglas drove at a hectic pace down hill, got us lost in the woods talking about 'short cuts', but we reached Le Chable below Verbier in time for a late lunch. We sat in hot sun and celebrated with several beers and a huge plateful of spaghetti bolognese. We felt good.

8

A QUALITY MOUNTAIN DAY

Fools take to themselves the respect that is given to their office.

Aesop, *Fables*

'Who's that woman in the passage?' asked Simon, looking in at the door of our office in the building in Brig. We were all in T-shirts, shorts and flip-flops even though the weather had been unremittingly horrid for a week, with low clouds clinging wetly to the hills around Brig. I was using the time to write up notes for this book.

I joined him in the broad corridor which ran the length of our floor and saw a middle-aged lady in a drab skirt and shirt sitting on one of the benches by a rack full of climbing gear. Her stockinged legs were up on the bench and she was staring idly at her sandals. She looked bothered, dishevelled and rather vacant. 'Does she understand any English?'

'No,' said Simon.

I bent over slightly to avoid appearing aggressive, and employed that vague question so typical of the English even when they are sure someone is in the wrong place. 'Can I help you?' I said, in French.

'Yes,' she replied in French, cheering up at once. 'I'd like a cup of coffee.'

'Fine,' I said matter-of-factly. I peered at her a moment. She peered back smiling vaguely. Round one to her. I straightened up. Simon, grinning, said, 'Shall I fetch some coffee then?'

I sighed and nodded. I saw Charlie lurking about behind us in the door of the TV room and asked him to find out why the Swiss had let her into the building in the first place. The front door was supposed to be locked and we were always being reminded about the importance of security. Then I turned back to the woman and tried again, still in French, but this time in blunt Gallic style straight from the shoulder. I said, 'Who are you?'

Without hesitation, she announced, 'I'm the Burgermeister of Brig.'

'Fine,' I said again. Two–nil to her. I stood up and rubbed my face. There was really nothing to say. There was a ward full of lunatics (psychiatric patients in caring-speak) in the hospital across the grass not a hundred yards from our building and the inmates were a common sight. They sat on the park benches under the plane trees by the river Saltina which ran through town and they always smiled genially as we passed them on our way into town. With us milling round our building by the hospital in shorts and flip-flops, most unmilitary, we reckoned the Swiss who walked past must have thought we were an annex to the main psychiatric ward.

Minutes later, Charlie reappeared on the stone stairs and I asked him to nip over to the hospital. Flattering as it was to have a visit from the 'Burgermeister of Brig', I wanted someone to take her off our hands.

Simon came up from the kitchen with coffee, which she enjoyed. The pleasant Swiss corporal who had given me Nostrodamus's medieval moon chart joined us and she talked happily to him while she sipped her coffee. He persuaded her to come downstairs and all was going well until Werner, the Swiss kitchen orderly appeared. Fat and rude, he bustled self-importantly upstairs from the kitchens, like a Dickensian beadle. He took over, roughly pushed her out of the front door and down the steps outside. At the same moment, she spotted a nurse coming across the grass from the hospital with Charlie and immediately lost her temper. She broke away from Werner and chased the nurse about the grass, shouting and trying to kick her, swinging her leg as she ran. The nurse vanished through the trees screaming for help. I hate to think what treatment merited this sort of reaction, but eventually, another nurse came over and led the 'Burgermeister of Brig' back to her ward.

Our building in Brig, like all Swiss Army installations, held classified documents and rifles, which belonged to the soldiers working there, but the woman had been let in without a word said. The Swiss soldier on duty released the electric door lock and made no effort to ask who she was.

I was rather amused. After suffering twenty-five years of murder and disruption because of Northern Ireland, even members of the British public with no military service have more security awareness. In Switzerland, there is no threat of death and mutilation from indiscriminate bombings in public places and soldiers happily walk around in their uniforms, which British soldiers have not been able to do at home for a quarter of a century and likely enough never will again. I hope the Swiss realise how lucky they are.

I went back to my office and rang Roger. The met office in Geneva and Chamonnix had cautiously forecast a change in the weather for the better. I wanted to hear what he suggested we climb next.

Roger announced, 'I went to the Mountain Warfare School in Andermatt today and gave a report on you all to Brigadier Mudry.'

I listened intrigued.

'I told him,' Roger continued in all seriousness, 'that you are now capable and experienced enough to go on the mountains by yourselves.'

'Really?' I said, trying to sound impressed. We had climbed seventeen mountains but neither Roger nor anyone else had come out with us yet.

'Yes. You have done a lot and plainly understand the best way to behave on the mountains.'

I think he would have had heart failure if he had seen Douglas and me in the séracs on the Grand Combin, but he was right. Being on mountains is a question of behaviour and understanding, not just the sterile business of grades and technique.

'You have done some difficult mountains,' he added. 'Like the Gross-Grünhorn.'

I thought of the sixty-five-year-old woman on the Gross-Grünhorn Summit Ridge, talking nineteen to the dozen as she climbed stoutly to the top. Still, it was nice to know we had been given a tick of approval. We all liked Roger. He shared the same attitudes to mountains and much else, and a bit of praise never goes amiss.

On the other hand, I am sure the British Army's Adventure Training department in the Ministry of Defence in London would have been appalled to hear our conversation. Briefly, when the army is not on operations – like Northern Ireland or Bosnia – or training to fight, or on leave, soldiers are supposed to take part in 'Adventure Training'. This can be any activity with an adventurous element, like diving, parachuting, caving, walking and, obviously, mountaineering. This was the basis of the British Army's support for our expedition. Tim Spicer and I had been to the Adventure Training department in the MOD at the start of the year to meet a Colonel and a Major.

'You must use guides throughout,' said the Colonel emphatically and the Major nodded.

Keeping our thoughts to ourselves, Tim and I agreed. The Swiss had already offered the services of a guide (who turned out to be Roger Mathieu).

The Major added righteously, 'Of course we insist you will still need two Jezmell qualified men as well.' He was referring to Gary and Simon who were both on an army 'outward bound' expedition-leaders' course: pronounced jezmell, this was a JSMEL winter course (Joint Service Mountain Expedition Leaders') which sounded ideally suited to an Alpine trip like ours. However, the sheer idiocy of the system is manifest when I quote from the aim of the final assessment for this course, 'To assess suitable officers and NCOs who wish to lead expeditions in mountainous country under *Scottish* winter and similar *non-Alpine* conditions.'

'But we're going to climb in the Alps,' I said to an Adventure Training officer.

'That's not the point,' he replied tartly.

The insidious mycelia of bureaucracy spread like dry rot across our plans but Tim and I agreed to everything. We had no option. The regulations are God and the functionaries in ministries are the high priests. However, I ignored the Major when he suggested that Gary and Simon might not pass. His Adventure Training department had asked for a very detailed account of their quite extensive climbing experience, which included mountains and rock all over the world, and then studiously refused to accept any of it. Actual experience means nothing: bureaucracy is only concerned with rules and certificates, not the real world. A few poor souls who work in Ministries admit this, and loath the unreality, but not these two.

'What about the Base Camp party?' asked the Colonel, switching ground, presumably to demonstrate he was a practical man at heart. 'Can't have them sitting about doing nothing, eh?'

Cheered by this sudden positivity, I assured him there would be masses of scope to go walking in the mountains, at least up to the snow line as no one in the support party had previous experience of snow conditions.

'Ah!' said the Major, his eyes lighting up like a Customs official finding one packet of cigarettes over the limit. Smugly, he said, 'You can't let them do that unless someone has a UEL!'

I lost patience and snapped, 'Are you seriously telling me that soldiers trained to find their way across any terrain, by day or night, on operations in Northern Ireland, the Gulf or Bosnia, let alone in the jungle, can't be allowed for a casual walk in the woods without a bloody certificate?'

The Major shook his head with absolute certainty. Tim interrupted before I caused a nasty scene and said, 'I can assure you we'll have a UEL-qualified officer in the Base Camp party.'

Both the Colonel and the Major nodded.

I never had any intention of using a guide, but I never told Tim. The pleasure of being in mountains is making your own decisions, not being bossed about by guides, ever aware of insurance implications, with the risk of being sued, which cramps their style even more. Of course, working on your own runs the risk of learning by trial and error, but this is the essence of life and I had every confidence that Simon, Gary and I produced safe decisions. What we lacked in knowledge of the more technical routes we made up for in good common sense and in more experience than most on snow and mountains. Together we had, in Ministry-speak, more than ample 'quality mountain days' under our belt, and after seventeen summits we were steadily improving all the time with actual experience on the big mountains.

The concept of a 'quality mountain day' is sickening. It epitomises the bureaucratisation (sic) of adventure which is the very antithesis of what we seek in the mixture of man and nature. Among the long list of stipulations for a 'quality mountain day' (its very length proves the absurdity of trying to define a good day out) some are restrictive like having to be out for five hours (too short for a decent climbing day) or walk ten miles (normally too long on mountains in the Alps) and some are ludicrously vague, like noting that the weather must 'have an effect on the day'.

This attempt to quantify and control real experience places bureaucracy in importance above reality. I know the problem of insurance claims is serious now, but far from encouraging adventure training the army department was hidebound with negative thinking, like 'quality mountain days', which is the curse of initiative. And why? Because regulations allow security of mind in a nice clean system, from which the tangled delights and sorrows of real life have been kept out. God forbid the civilian climbing world suffers the same fate.

Thankfully, we were a long way from the Ministry of Defence in London but we certainly enjoyed a quality mountain day when we returned to the Monte Rosa group. Our plan was to tackle both Switzerland's highest peaks, Nordend (4609m) and the Dufourspitze (4634m) – still without our intrepid guide Roger – in a day.

On Tuesday, 15 June, Simon, Gary, Douglas and I left Brig early again and drove right up to Zermatt village. The police were about, checking other traffic for their authority to come beyond Täsch on the narrow metalled road to Zermatt, but they ignored us in the Swiss Army VW and we escaped a fine. We were fed up with taking the train from Täsch: it took too long and cost too much for all of us added together. Besides, it rained depressingly all the way in spite of the forecast for a high, and there was the chance that our plan to position ourselves for the next day would be wasted, with the added expense of the Gornergrat train which cost 48 SFrs each.

After leaving the train at Rotenboden (2818m) we walked over the Gornergrat Ridge to find that, in mid-June, the snow had gone from the Gorner and Grenz Glaciers which were now a filthy grey colour all the way up to where they disappeared into cloud about the level of the Monte Rosa Hut (2750m). The debris of rocks and broken ice on a glacier is not attractive and I missed the smooth clean snowfields. Now we had much further to carry our skis along with our tents, cooking and other necessary bivvy gear.

The threat of good weather translated into a swelteringly hot day, mercifully clouded over from time to time, or I think I might have just sat down and cried. Instead, I kept stopping for a breather with, 'Oh, do look at this pretty clump of pink *Primula latifolia*!' or 'Aren't the petals of these Alpine *Soldanella* incredibly delicate?'

With dismissive glances at the little bright purple flowers nodding on their long stems, the others stormed on. They did stop when we saw a couple of ibex casually leaping up a steep gulley half-way along the Gornergrat (we smelled them long before we saw them) and at the bottom by the glacier we watched a mountain sheep give birth to a second lamb and gently lick off the afterbirth.

We stopped for our lunch of sausage and bread at the Monte Rosa Hut, which was closed except for the winter emergency quarters. I thought this was odd as there was still plenty of snow about for skiers and we put ours on just above the hut on the Unter Plattje at 2800 metres.

The first steep slope at the top of the Ober Plattje was awful. The air was unbearably close and warm, the snow was soft and we found the going hard. Bare rocks especially needed a wide berth. There were often large holes under the surface by the rock, where wind or water had carved the snow into a hollow which collapsed if we skied too close. The snow was like blancmange, sinking away under our skis, and I seriously wondered if the whole slope might just sag away in a tired wet avalanche over a steep drop onto the Monte Rosa Glacier. There was a lot of sweating and swearing. Even seeing a lone figure on foot ahead failed to raise much interest.

He was German Swiss and spoke worse French than me, I discovered when we overtook him, and had come from the hut. He stumbled and fell about in the heavy snow at every step, shouting and cursing with frustration.

We had wanted to camp at 4000 metres on a flattish plateau which is also officially designated as a helicopter landing site for heli-skiing, but by 3.30 p.m. we were knackered and slumped opposite a cliff of rotten rock at 3670 metres.

The clouds had closed in again and it began to sleet. I dug out a flat place to put the tent while Douglas made a brew and then we passed out for over an hour, warm and cosy in our sleeping bags. When we woke, Simon called over from his tent, 'Have you got a cooking pot?'

'Er, yes,' replied Douglas frowning as he made delicate adjustments to our evening scoff, another huge mess of all-in stew in an old aluminium cook pot my father had bought in 1968. Watching him, I was thinking that whoever designed dehydrated beef granules for army rations obviously never, ever, had to eat them.

'Well,' continued Simon smiling hopefully, his head stuck out of his tent. 'Can we use it too?' Gary and Simon had no cooking pot. Back in Brig, each of them had thought the other was fooling when they asked if the other had already packed one. What a pair of prunes, eh? So my old Dad's cooking pot did good service for us all.

At five o'clock just before first light, we left the tents in a very clear, perfect morning and began skinning up to Nordend. In the burgeoning dawn, a sickle moon hung over the glaciers on the horizon and the snow squeaked under our skis and harscheisen. About 200 metres above our campsite, we noticed that the chap on foot had slept in a bivvy bag in a trench in the snow, though his pack had been so big he might easily have been carrying a frame tent. We followed his footsteps, this time just neat crampon holes in the crisp névé, and as we turned over the snow shoulder of the Satteltole (4170m) we saw him making his way under the steep West Ridge of the Dufourspitze towards the big crevasses at the top of the Monte Rosa Glacier on his way to Nordend.

Not for the first time, I was relieved to be on skis. He was going very slowly, breaking through the crust of hard snow into deep snow every several paces and he looked thoroughly fed up. We passed him on the next very steep section before a big icefall where we had to cast about to find our way up and through a complicated system of crevasses which cut the glacier near the top. We roped up to cross some snow bridges over these crevasses. They looked as if they might not last the summer and must present quite a problem to cross later in the year.

We reached the Silbersattel (4515m) at 7.30 a.m. and the view to the south was exceptional, over clouds and mountains and valleys so far into the distance it seemed to Rome itself.

We stuck our skis in the snow, put on crampons and began the sharp south-south-west snow crest to Nordend. There were no footprints visible at all, which gives a pleasant feeling of breaking new ground, and we found no cornices to speak of overhanging the Italian side. Apparently this is so unusual the Alpine Club guide book specifically mentions that it also occurred back in 1972. If this was a measure of the peculiar weather Switzerland had been experiencing that year, I was not encouraged for our future climbs.

However, the lack of cornices meant we could see more of the astonishingly steep East, or Macugnaga, Face of Monte Rosa. Standing like a massive frontier wall between Italy and Switzerland, this face is more than 2000 metres high and fully ten kilometres long. Being south-facing, it is shot with stone fall and avalanches. Even top climbers consider it extremely dangerous. After 500 metres along the crest near the last rock scramble under Nordend's summit, I turned back to look at the famous Marinelli Couloir which commemorates the death in 1881 of Damiano Marinelli, Battista Pedranzini and Ferdinand Imseng, who had led the first ascent of the face in 1873. They were swept off the face at 3400 metres by an avalanche which took their bodies 1200 metres down the mountain. Most amazingly, on 7 October 1969, Sylvain Saudan made a ski descent of this same couloir. There were cornices then, which he had to smash through, and he begins his description with a quite exceptional piece of understatement. 'Mistakes are out of the question,' he said. As a skier, I was awed looking down the extraordinary slope he descended thinking how he said he had to ski without exaggerated movements, and allow the dynamics to come from his feet, with his whole body, hips and stick placements perfectly synchronised. Feeling rather sick, I turned away, happy to stay on the nursery slopes.

The crest ends under the summit at a sharp rock scramble. There was still plenty of snow about and we chose a route up a short gulley, which was rather exciting as every time I went to put my fingers in a hold the place was full of snow. Nordend looks sharp from a distance and it is. There was only room for two on the top.

Coming down, Gary found a more exposed but easier route on the outside above the huge drop over the East Face and we made our way back to the Silbersattel. Gary and Simon did not delay as there was a cold wind and soon became small dark figures going up and down the curves of the crest in the distance. By the time Douglas and I started after them, they had reached the Silbersattel and I saw Gary carrying his skis down. He was not too confident about making the final turn on the steep section through the crevasse complex and took the safe option.

I was a bit bothered too, but as usual in practice, the ski down was superbly enjoyable. The going was firm with a covering of downy snow and turns never a problem. We dipped and weaved through the crevasse system, shot over a couple of snow bridges and schussed the long traverse under the Dufourspitze before we had to stop and put on skins again on the top side of the Satteltole (4200m).

We had taken five hours and at this stage Gary announced he was going down. He had been complaining of headaches and the blisters on his foot were serious again. I told him we would be about two hours and he skied down to the tents.

Simon, Douglas and I put on our skins again and set off uphill to climb the West Ridge of the Dufourspitze. At the Sattel (4359m) we pushed our skis into the snow again, put on crampons and set off up a steep snow slope, about fifty degrees. The snow was good after a short very icy section at the start. At the top of this, we saw the rocky broken ridge stretching away up and beyond us. It looked very long. I realised two hours had been optimistic.

With Simon leading, we roped up and climbed on up. With a lot of snow on the rocks, holds were not obvious and we were slow with three on the rope, stopping and starting as Simon led over delicate snow arêtes, teetering as he kicked new steps. There was pleasure in knowing no one had been up there for some while but the narrow sections were unnecessarily slow.

After easily front-pointing up a second steep snow slope we reached another much longer rock ridge section where the heavy covering of snow made life quite tricky at times. As we topped each rise in the ridge, we hoped it was the summit, but the ridge is 600 metres long and there always seemed to be more. Finally, after turning a vertical step by a broad slab on the right, which was exposed and airy to say the least, we topped the last ridge on dodgy snow covering the rocks, dropped down the other side and found a narrow couloir with a fixed rope to the true summit at 4634 metres.

We had been so absorbed in our clambering up the ridge that we only then noticed the world around us. The views were superb, of the whole Monte Rosa group from Nordend to the Zumsteinspitze, 'our' hut on the Signalkuppe, the Parrotspitze beyond, and Liskamm's long, infamously corniced ridge. We were amazed to find we had taken three hours from where we had left our skis on the Sattel.

You can always spot a Brit on the mountains because he will be wearing Ron Hill tracksters – Simon and Douglas swore by them. But that day was sunny, if cold in the bitter wind high on an exposed ridge. We took a few quick photos and turned back down. Descending was quicker, just. You can never move fast with three on a rope. We found the snow sections much easier going down, and we reached our skis at four o'clock.

Fortunately, the cold wind had kept the snow lower down in good condition and our ski down to Gary in the tents was excellent. We felt terribly pleased with ourselves. We had climbed two very good mountains, the second and third highest in the Alps, and they had been the most interesting and testing so far.

Gary was relieved to see us back, four hours overdue. He had packed the tents, so we loaded our rucksacks and skied further down through very slushy snow to the Ober Plattje (3109m) where we found a place to camp out of the wet snow on flat rocks. We had been on the go for over twelve hours and felt deliciously tired, suntanned and blasted by the wind. We stripped off and dried our sweaty socks and T-shirts in the evening sun with a magnificent view down the Grenz Glacier to the Matterhorn in the distance.

My water bottle had frozen on the climbing that day so I had had nothing to drink. Douglas and I melted lots of snow, made numerous brews and more all-in stew, mutton granules this time, and we were asleep in our bags by 8.30 p.m.

Our tactics were that camping on the Ober Plattje put us an hour above the Monte Rosa Hut, which was well below us at 2800 metres, and so cut the time we had to spend skinning up the Grenz glacier to the border. If we had reasonable weather, as forecast, we wanted to climb Liskamm and the other five peaks named in Richard Goedeke's list of 4000ers. Roger had been sure the conditions would be excellent, and waxed on again about, 'the start of the new season's weather'. I should have been suspicious at once.

After sleeping only moderately well, I woke in darkness at 4 a.m. and shouted out to wake Gary and Simon next door. I leaned over Douglas to find the Epigas canister where he kept it warm beside him inside the tent – it worked too sluggishly if we left it outside in the cold – and put the pot of melted water on the cooker for our hot water. We always dug a small hole in the snow in the bell end of the tent, deep enough to take the Epigas and the pot on top, so we did not have to leave our sleeping bags while it boiled. Nor could we knock it over if we were desperate for a pee outside.

We dressed ready to go while it boiled, drank our hot chocolate – with added Maxim energy drink for an old'un like me – and wolfed the rolled oats porridge. Then came the unpleasant part: leaving the cosy tent. Outside was not as cold as I expected. Gary was still unable to join us, so Simon, Douglas and I clipped on our skis, having fitted the skins and harscheisen the night before, and left our campsite in darkness just before 5 a.m.

After an hour the light had improved enough for us to see that there was a ceiling of clouds threatening us from the north. The cloudbase appeared to be high enough. We were making much better speed up the Grenz Glacier than the first time a month before when we had still been getting fit, and we could already see the top of the Parrotspitze, which was our first target. A thin and torn layer of silver-grey clouds skated fast above the summit. The other summits we wanted to do that day en route to the Gnifetti Hut on the Italian side of Monte Rosa – the Ludwigshöhe, Schwarzhorn, Balmenhorn and Vincent Piramide – were all lower so we carried on.

Rod Stewart sang 'Maggie May', 'Ah Maggie, I couldn't have tried any more!' as, quite alone on the vast white expanse of the Grenz Glacier, we skinned steadily uphill. We made good time but all the while clouds scudded over the Gornergrat towards us from the north, lower and lower. By 8.30 a.m. when we reached the pass area we could no longer see the Lisjoch and we disappeared into grey mist at 4150 metres.

The temperature dropped unpleasantly and I froze to death while Simon and Douglas fiddled about zipping Gore-Tex trousers over their Ron Hill tracksters. I switched off my Walkman. Music right inside my head does not help when I am trying to concentrate.

'We should turn back,' said Douglas wisely, bending over and trying to connect two sides of the zip on one leg.

He probably said this to stop me whining about being cold but I was still determined to find the Lisjoch (4246m) somewhere in the cloud above us. I wanted to ski down to the Gnifetti Hut into Italy in the hope of finding that lower summits like the Vincent Piramide (4215m) were clear on the Italian side. We carried on skinning uphill in thick cloud with numerous checks of our compasses, maps, Citizen and Thommen altimeters and tried to remember the look of the s022.003 séracs under the Parrotspitze from the last time we had been up there. The wind was relentless, occasionally tearing the cloud to give us warning glimpses of huge crevasses, then closed round us in conditions frighteningly like whiteout.

The wind worsened, biting cold and blowing loose snow in our faces. Our ski tracks filled up so that after only a few minutes they were difficult to see. We reached a flat place, thought we were on the broad expanse of the Lisjoch, at the right altitude, then found ourselves under another steep slope. Lost. I glanced back at our tracks. If they disappeared we would be in real trouble. There were emergency quarters in the Margherita Hut, but I doubt we could have easily found the hut two kilometres away on top of the Signalkuppe. We turned back.

Our tracks had disappeared. Simon stood still while Douglas went on ahead on a back-bearing of our approach, I followed and when we were almost out of sight of Simon in the cloud Douglas stopped and waited for Simon and me to close up on him. Then we repeated the process. This kept us on course until Douglas picked up our tracks, very faint now in the blowing snow. We descended as quickly as we could and I noticed on my watch altimeter that the cloud had come down still more. I warned the other two. There are two big crevasses which cut deeply across the top of the Grenz Glacier beneath the Parrotspitze, then further down a long thin one, wide enough to 'accept' an unwary skier, which crosses the whole glacier side to side. The visibility was down to about two ski lengths ahead and the crevasses loomed from the white cloud at our feet like dark caverns. After the second crevasse zone, about 3900 metres, we emerged from the cloud.

From there, the ski down somehow made the whole effort worthwhile although we had gone to 4250 metres for nothing. In spite of the tiring day before, I felt on really good form. Far from being exhausted as I had been the first time we all slogged up the Grenz Glacier, I felt fit. We made sweeping curves on the firm snow, some like big pendulums swinging easily from side to side, others small and tight, working hard through short neat turns through the two icefalls until we skated to a halt in front of the tents at 10.30 a.m.

Gary was not surprised to see us back. We sat in the sun which broke through from time to time and had a brew. Then we packed all our gear and found just enough snow between bare rocks in a series of gullies and slopes to ski in ten minutes right down to the Monte Rosa Hut. We got there at the same time as two Brits who had passed us going downhill nearly an hour before while we were packing our tents.

Even in mid-June skis were still essential. Staggering about on foot in soft snow is exhausting. The Swiss on his own the previous day never attempted Nordend. He was so shattered by the time he reached the Silbersattel, he simply turned round and walked down. We overtook him on the way up and also on the way down hours later after we had done the Dufourspitze as well. Must have been very demoralising.

It was frustrating having to leave the mountains this time. The walk across the dry glacier was dull, the long uphill path traversing the Gornergrat to the railway at Rotboden seemed to take for ever, and my skis and pack got heavier and heavier. At least the cloudbase stayed low, justifying our decision to turn back.

Down in Zermatt, we repaired at once to the smoky, old-fashioned but pleasantly unspoiled atmosphere of the railway bar in the station and consumed several plates of *pommes frites*, German mustard and Schneider Hefe Weissbier. Much to Douglas's delight Nikki turned up to collect us – this time he had been more organised when he rang up for transport. As the rest of the Base Camp party were out in both Swiss VWs – they were on a visit to a brewery in Sion where they got lost in the back streets trying to find the place, and got drunk in a bar instead – Nikki had brought the gentian-blue Land-Rover. The sight of this peculiar paintjob, hardly the last word in covert entry, driven by a beautiful dark-haired girl, was too much for the Zermatt constables who stopped her at once on the outskirts of the village. We had been told the fine for driving into the village without proper authority was a 100 SFrs, but with a smile or two she persuaded them to accept 50 SFrs. They invited her to park up anyway and come back to the vehicle when she felt like it. So we enjoyed some more beer. I felt we deserved it. We had had two excellent mountains which made up for having to turn back from the Lisjoch. What was better was being in good shape after the busiest three days so far.

Back in Brig, we found Peter had been in the Bernese Oberland with Russell Brice. Like us, they had climbed the Mönch en route from the Jungfraujoch station to the Mönchsjoch Hut where they waited out for twenty-four hours on their own, freezing to bits in the winter quarters, in thick cloud and buffeted by strong winds. Russell had intended to walk over to the Fiescherhörner but visibility remained impossible the next day so they came down.

Geneva admitted they had not expected the low clouds but as consolation promised the three following days would be sunny. I decided we must go back to the Monte Rosa group, hopefully for the last time. However, skinning up the Grenz Glacier again did not appeal, so we took the old blue Land-Rover into Italy the following morning to try our luck from the Gnifetti Hut.

Simon drove our soft-top 'sports' model with great *élan* through mist and cloud round the tight hairpins on the Simplon Pass. Douglas checked progress on the map and talked a lot. I suffered in the back trying to sleep, rolling about on our rucksacks and all the knobbly bits of our skis. I did not feel too crisp.

> Drink and dance and laugh and lie,
>   Love, the reeling midnight through,
> For tomorrow we shall die!
>   (But, alas, we never do.)
>   Dorothy Parker

I wish I could have. We had done a pub crawl the night before. By this time, several of the Base Camp had made good friends with Heidi, Lisalotte and Vibeke, but there were still lots of Danish girls to go round, so a nightly circuit took place around the bars in Brig which we joined when not on the mountains. We wandered along the river into town, down 'leafy lane' under the plane trees, to check out Johnny's Bar (Annemetta), the Pirate (Lena, Hella, Sos, Christina and Delphine), the 'Brit' (Beatrice, Ula and Linda), and later, when all these bars closed in near-religious Swiss style at midnight, we ended up in the Lötschberg disco where the girls came after clearing up in their bars and where the barmaid was a dark-haired Croat called Emma who was very fizzy indeed in seven languages.

The weather brightened along the shore of Lake Orta, though cloud dogged us through the hills of Vercelli to Alagna, a typically shambolic Italian village in the valley below Monte Rosa where the main hotel was a burnt-out shell (probably an insurance job). We arrived about one o'clock, checked the last lift was at 3.30 p.m., and went back to the pleasantly quaint Ristorante Stollenberg for an agreeable lunch and a skinful of Chianti.

Benign, replete and uncaring of all the petty things in the world, we returned to the lift, changed into our ski gear and stamped up the concrete stairs with our skis and packs.

I am sure that lift was used in *Where Eagles Dare*. If not, it was bought off the set. The whole place looked as if it would fall apart any moment, with rusting pieces of lift and coils of cable lying everywhere. But the Italians were charming. A man with a face like leather and a voice trained on incalculable litres of red vino and decades of pure tobacco took charge of the little eight-man contraption and whisked us off into the clouds which filled the valley. I wish he had not chosen to bring up several gallons of diesel with us. The stench was sickening. A couple of trays of courgettes and lettuces for the restaurant at the top were stacked on them, drooping in the fumes.

'This lift's a shambles,' said Douglas appalled as he looked round the cabin with the critical eye of a Guards officer inspecting troops.

The liftman grinned and coughed on his cigarette. Apart from the air of mechanical disrepair, there was a suspiciously loose trapdoor in the floor which we all avoided standing on.

Simon agreed, 'No one would use a lift like this in Switzerland any more. Far too grand there now.'

'I know it looks bad,' I said hopefully. 'But I'm sure it's just as safe as any Swiss lift.'

I had no sooner spoken than a pylon loomed rapidly out of the mist and the cabin smashed into the buffer guard, making us stagger across the floor. Conversation died and we stared up ahead through the cloud willing our destination lift station to appear PDQ. There were three legs to go to reach Punta Indren.

Twenty-five minutes later, like an ancient rusty submarine coming to the surface, the top cabin finally emerged from the cloud into bright sunshine just short of Punta Indren (3260m).

Things were looking up. Shreds of cloud clung to the pistes which stretch across the Indren Glacier and a few last downhill skiers were coming back to take the lift down to Alagna. By the time we had fitted our skis, even these clouds blew over and we had a very leisurely hour and a quarter's ski in warm sun to the Gnifetti Hut at 3647 metres. Skinning easily and steadily, we overhauled three desperate characters plunging about in the soft snow on foot.

The Gnifetti Hut is excellent. Built of wood as late as 1967, it looks rather chaotic, but the passages and stairs inside have been cunningly designed to take up the minimum space and to accommodate the maximum number of rooms. The hut has nearly 300 bunk-beds, six to a room, stacked three high on each side. Outside, a balcony runs the full length facing south and this soon filled up with Italians who had been walking up behind us. They was a cheerful mix of men and for once plenty of girls come for a weekend in the mountains. As it should be and a complete contrast to the determined, serious and boring atmosphere we so often find in Britain and Switzerland (where the stony old Monte Rosa Hut on the other side of the mountains was still firmly shut). They sat about in the sun on the balcony, chattering, laughing and, as Italians always do, taking the mickey out of each other. The stone was soon strewn with more colourful designer climbing clothes, bright ropes, gleaming karabiners and natty protection devices than you would find in the average kit shop. They all seemed ready to tackle Sylvain Saudan's Marinelli Couloir, or the North Face of Liskamm. Sniff if you like, as I admit we did, but at least they were all up there, in the mountains, enjoying themselves.

The hut-warden was a guide, and charming but totally unsurprised when we asked him about the peaks we wanted to do the following day. He was bored with people coming up to do the easy 4000ers. Still, he generously offered to get up early to make our breakfast at 3.30 a.m. We gave him our water bottles to fill with 'march tea' – a thirst-quenching sugared lemon tea – and asked him to leave them with our breakfast on a table with a thermos of hot water for coffee.

Perhaps inevitably, dinner was good, the best we had eaten, with excellent minestrone, a choice of pasta, followed by stew, peas, mashed potato and a good sauce. And plenty of it. We finished off with a small bowl of apricots and custard, or *sauce anglaise* as the French so rudely call our national delight. The hot chocolate which I drank as a night-time brew beat everything. In a breakfast bowl, it was so rich and thick I really could stand a spoon in it.

Finally, this was the first hut we visited which had real porcelain lavatory fittings, long drop style, inside the building. They were unheated of course – they never are – but the view of the Monte Rosa through the little ice-rimmed window was superb. When I stood there just before I turned in, I stared up long snow slopes to Liskamm's sharp ridge glowing darkly white under the stars and I was excited but apprehensive.

Liskamm (4527m) rises in two hanging summits along a huge three-kilometre long snow crest running east-west and the cornices have a fearsome reputation. In 1861, eight Englishmen (typically in the period of Alpine exploration) and two Swiss first reached the East, main summit (which was our objective), but the mountain has been associated with tragedy since 1877, when on 6 September another two Englishmen, William Lewis and Noel Paterson, and three Swiss brothers, Niklaus, Johann and Peter-Joseph Knubel fell to their deaths. A huge cornice broke away under their feet on the same part of the ridge we were to try the next day. In 1896, three more explorers died the same way and periodic disasters since, including guides, have increased the mountain's awesome reputation.

Next morning, we left the hut under the stars with head-torches, skinning fast up easy crisp glacier slopes under the Vincent Piramide. Inside forty minutes, we overtook a guide with two clients ahead of us and by the time we reached the col at Lisjoch (4200m) just as the pale light of dawn was spreading over the peaks all round they were out of sight way behind us.

Liskamm seemed untouched. The East Ridge rose pristine and clear of any sign of footsteps, the crest sharp as a knife. Simon led and soon had to kick steps, keeping on the south side of the arête, where the fall to the Lis Glacier has something of a run-out, several hundred metres down, it must be admitted. The snow on the north side was not at all well consolidated and drops fatally to the Grenz Glacier far below. As we progressed, I found I was embarked on the next stage of my journey.

I cleared my mind of everything except the next step. I was not concentrating particularly, just sweeping aside extraneous clutter, the usual concerns, thoughts and constraints on our lives. This is not to say I was no longer aware of them, but just that they assumed their proper place in my head while I was busy. Following Simon, my left foot moved first into the socket he had made, spread-eagling my body across the slope, knees against the snow, then I moved my axe over my left foot, plunging the shaft into the snow with both hands, then my right foot across. And repeat. Rhythm and peace. A sort of freedom.

I did not feel I was 'communicating' with the mountain, as some call it. This was more absorption with what I was doing which freed me of worries of the danger. I was happy to look down the precipice below us onto the Lis Glacier, or the steeper drop onto the Grenz Glacier when at times we had to cross the edge to the north side. We passed the place where the first men had lost their lives. I wondered at the terrible effect on the Knubel family of losing three sons and considered my own family so far away in the flat rolling Cotswold countryside, fields yellow now with summer corn. I was so detached and remote from them on the snows high above the glaciers either side of the arête, like flying a narrow course through white clouds of the mind, but that very detachment seemed to distil my feelings for them, painful for the separation, calm in the satisfaction of their existence. I found I was able to observe the drops, the séracs and crevasses below with equanimity, utterly calm about falling, free of fear.

The top slopes were fortunately not too icy, but we could see where they can become difficult later in the summer when there might be less snow covering, and at 8 o'clock we reached the main Liskamm summit (4527m), four hours after leaving the hut. About par time. What we gained moving fast up to the Lisjoch, we lost again having to cut our steps on the ridge.

By 9.30 a.m., we were back at the Lisjoch (4200m) for a grisly breakfast of sausage, granary bread, chocolate and 'march tea'. Then we set about the remaining five summits on the Monte Rosa. There was a viciously cold wind blowing clear air from the north and clouds still filled the valleys far away to the south in Italy. The distant foothills looked like fingers of dark land reaching into a sea of waves rippling white in the sun.

We skinned across the Lisjoch where we had been in thick cloud two days before, left our skis at the bottom of the Parrotspitze (4436m) and nipped up the easy ridge to the summit in forty minutes. On the way down, we met a group of three Italians where we had left our skis in the lee of a rock cliff out of the cold wind. One proved very talkative.

'Allo!' he shouted above the wind. About fifty years old, he was brimming with *bonhomie*, square-jawed, lots of teeth in a wide smile and handsome in a florid, faded way. Speaking someone else's language is the quickest way past the usual barriers to acquaintanceship, even between people who meet in remote places. He declared his personal ambitions at once: 'I am in training. The North Face of Liskamm. This is my ambition. I am wanting to do this all my life!' Having bared his soul, his teeth flashed in a huge smile and he added, 'I am Adriano!'

We introduced ourselves. Adriano looked up at the Parrotspitze and asked, 'How long to the top of this mountain?'

Douglas shrugged and said casually, 'Half an hour.' He loves a yarn.

Adriano looked rather shocked, and said with a hollow laugh, 'Good! Good! Maybe we will meet again!'

We left him looking up the cliff, and by the time we were on the summit of the Ludwigshöhe (4341m) twenty minutes later, at midday, he was still faffing about with his two friends on the initial steepish mixed scramble onto the Parrotspitze snow ridge.

We romped round the last three. At 12.42 we topped the Corno Nero (4322m), a sharp climb to a rock pinnacle over the dizzy southern end of the huge Macugnaga Face. Twenty minutes later we were standing next to the enormous figure of Christ on the Balmenhorn (4167), which people complain about but is unsurprising in a Catholic country. After all, Christ himself went to chew the fat on a mountain, and I have seen a lot worse statues. At two o'clock, we shook hands for the sixth time that day after skinning to the top of the Vincent Piramide (4215m).

We were gasping for a drink as we had finished our waterbottles hours before, so we packed away our skins and headed back to the Gnifetti Hut at speed, passing several exhausted parties still struggling up the glacier on foot in deep, soft snow. They stopped and gawped as we zoomed past them on skis.

Adriano found us drinking beer and lemonade in the bar. We gave him a beer and shared the last of our bread and Emmental cheese with him.

'You like to ski down to Alagna?' he asked, his mouth full and smiling toothsomely. 'I have been coming to this area for years. I know a good way down.'

We should have smelled a rat at once. But Adriano knew every-one, of course, and went to the counter by the door to the kitchen to ask the hut-warden about the snow conditions below the top lift at Punta Indren. He came back impressed, saying, 'The warden, he says you have done six summits today.' Flattered that the hut-warden, a guide, had even bothered to mention this to Adriano, we forgot to press him on the important issue of how much snow there was downside of the lift at Punta Indren.

By the time we left the Gnifetti, the snow was as soggy as I have ever known it. We took a rather gripping direct line down a steep gulley in the cliffs on the west side of the Indren Glacier onto the pistes, expecting the slope to slide any moment, and then ducked under the rope onto the forbidden pistes beyond the Punta Indren top lift station with Adriano in the lead shouting, 'Itsa fine! I know the way.'

The first twenty minutes were fun, even though we were surrounded by thin cloud which spoiled what must be a fantastic view in good weather. We skied down empty pistes on slushy snow, sort of like surf-boarding, but being quite alone on the mountain hidden by cloud somehow made the experience rather intimate. Of course, Simon called it an adventure.

Then Adriano lost his sense of direction. Increasingly desperate, he kept stopping to check what he could see through the poor visibility. Perspiring hotly, his grin faded by the minute.

Then the snow ran out. We unclipped the back binding on our skis to slide along without skins on increasingly scant patches of snow and walked like huge penguins over rocky bits without snow (thank God the Swiss Army could not see us treating their skis this way!). After we had all plunged through the soft surface into hidden pools of water between boulders, we binned our skis, strapped them to our packs and continued on foot.

'The lift station is near,' declared Adriano periodically, a note of desperation in his voice. He was trying to convince himself we might find it in the fog. His face was running with sweat by this time and he took a tumble as we traversed round the mountain on steep scree, hopping from rock to rock and hanging on to heather and Alpine rhododendrons. The final straw was having to put on our skis and skins again to climb out of a gulley because we had seen the lift wires overhead. Sure enough they led to the second lift station at 2396 metres, and sure enough it was utterly silent, wires soughing gently in the damp cloud, stanchions red with rust, so desolate it was hard to believe it was ever used at all. We had missed the last lift down by five minutes.

Pathetic toothy smile from Adriano. He said, 'I ama very sorry, but we musta walk down now. To Alagna.'

'How far is that?' asked Simon.

'Maybe two hours,' said Adriano.

'Good job we haven't climbed any mountains today,' remarked Douglas, looking very fierce with a bandana round his head.

Adriano looked brave and diplomatically went a little distance away from us to remove some of his ski clothes and adjust his skis and pack for the walk down. We did the same. There was a lot of swearing, but quietly so Adriano could not hear. Somehow, we felt sorry for him.

'It's an adventure,' Simon repeated, grinning. Douglas and I just looked at him.

We set a good pace on the path which dropped steeply downhill following a noisy stream through rich meadows of grass spotted with thousands of big yellow Alpine pulsatillas and brilliant blue myosotis.

'Arr you British special commandos?' Adriano gasped on a flatter section of the path. By this time, his direct but charming manner had elicited that we were in the Army and, like so many people I have met around the world, he felt that anyone a bit fitter than usual must be in special forces.

'No,' I said. It was my usual reaction to deny having anything to do with the SAS, because of all the obsessive, phantasmagorical and ludicrous publicity about the regiment, and because so many people pretend they are in the SAS. So much so that when two genuine members of the regiment meet but do not know each other, they are suspicious and cannot immediately enjoy a chat about mutual friends. I have always resented that by-product of the publicity about the SAS.

I said, 'We are all members of the Scots Guards.'

This meant nothing to Adriano who pointed at Simon stepping nimbly from rock to rock on the path ahead in his purple ski-mountaineering boots and said desperately, 'Then, he must be a sergeant major!'

Douglas grinned and I said, 'Of course!' By this time, Simon and I considered ourselves part of the Scots Guards. There was no one in the SAS who was fitter than any of us at that time, and the Base Camp group was the best I have known. All of them were good company, they did their jobs well, they were proud of their Regiment but they treated the big wide world with equanimity. They had none of the arrogant pretensions I have come across too often in the SAS, due in good measure to the effect on behaviour of the endless sickly publicity.

Actually, the SAS had been particularly unhelpful. Only a week before we were due to leave England, and although our expedition had been planned for over a year, the SAS withdrew its support. They ignored the fact that they had actually approved the plan first, followed by a bucket-load of Ministry of Defence departments, the Chief of the General Staff and finally HRH the Duke of Kent. I mean no offence to the Duke or the CGS, let alone the great MoD, but the order is less a question of the 'proper channels' than symptomatic of SAS thinking, for they are an egotistical bunch who look out of Hereford on the rest of the world like Mao Tse-Tung's 'frogs in the well'. So, when a complete rethink on the SAS Reserve started and the SAS ran ragged before an onslaught of suited accountants (who run the army now), I was told the expedition had to conform. We could not go.

Great self-control is required when the rug is pulled at such a late stage! I took a deep breath and explained that military training had nothing to do with adventure training, that our adventure training expedition had been agreed over a year before, and that the expedition would fold up without Gary, Simon and me. Lastly the SAS had only just paid out 630 days (many more than we needed) to other SAS Reserve soldiers to go mountaineering on Everest. They let us go.

However, the issue rumbled on. Perhaps jealousy played a part. There are those in the SAS who believe that the SAS is the only organisation capable of mounting such 'endurance' expeditions, stemming from an attitude that nothing in the army, or very possibly in the world, is as important as what happens in Hereford. Pride, my old father used to say quietly in his pulpit, goeth before a fall. After Gibraltar . . . ?

Adriano was suffering. His pack grew heavier and heavier and his pace slower and slower. Finally, after the Mortara Refuge Hut at 1945 metres, Douglas and Simon could stand the snail's pace no longer and shot ahead, disappearing into the trees, leaving me to bring Adriano down. For a man in training to climb the North Face of Liskamm, he was hardly in good shape, but he was trying and remained unfailingly cheerful.

'You are not angry with me?' he asked in a small voice, looking up at me as he went ungainly backwards down a steep rocky bit.

'No,' I replied and meant it. I enjoyed the walk down. The exercise did not trouble us and it seemed the right thing to do after our day among the snows and peaks on top, to see and be part of the flowers, streams, waterfalls, which Adriano called 'swallows', trees and forests all the way down to the valley floor. This is how they used to climb mountains in days long gone, and we were on exactly the same path Queen Margherita must have descended to Alagna after opening the hut on the Signalkuppe named after her. She must have been a plucky old bat, because the walk down made this our longest day so far; we had been up and down 5500 metres and covered over thirty kilometres.

Adriano was shattered by the time we sank our first beer in a café in Alagna. He tottered to his chair on blistered feet, massaging his shoulders where his pack had been biting into his soft muscles and his clothes were soaked with sweat. He was an insurance salesman, an Italian, a figure of fun perhaps to some arrogant sods, but he never complained and he was still smiling. He even offered to find us a bed in a hotel, owned, naturally, by a friend of his. I think he was quite relieved when we declined.

There is a time to every purpose under heaven, and it was time to leave Alagna. After our success on the mountains, we had not expected the day to end this way, but it had seemed right. We thanked him very much for that, flung our gear in the old blue Land-Rover and drove down the valley.

We stopped in Varallo, about forty kilometres away, ate a quite delicious spaghetti bolognese made with fresh spaghetti in the cheapest coffee-shop café in Varallo, sank several bottles of beer and booked into an hotel appropriately named the Monte Rosa.

The place was old-fashioned and creaked. The highly polished, uneven wood floors creaked as you walked on them, the wrought-iron French Empire-style lift, which we avoided, creaked, and the stairs creaked. The three old people who ran the place looked as if they should creak too as they fluttered round an ancient and very worn black telephone waiting with childish excitement for an international call. Between showing us to our rooms, and supplying us with a nightcap of bottled beer, the eldest lady kept us informed, in poor French, of progress as the Varallo telephone exchange tried to connect a call from someone in Miami. I wondered if the person in Miami had the slightest idea what sort of instrument he or she was trying to call into, or that all the ladies in the Varallo exchange were listening in, but we had been on our feet for over fifteen hours that day and this was too much excitement. We opted for bed.

Our beds were enormous, with curling beechwood headboards rarely seen in modern hotels, great puffy duvets in white linen covers and supremely comfortable. We slept very well indeed.

9

LONG HOT JOURNEYS

I try to forget what happiness was, and when that don't work I
study the stars.

Derek Walcott, b. 1930

The Swiss border police gave us a hard time coming back into
Switzerland. Three tanned 'hippies' wearing sweat-stained T-shirts,
flip-flops, plugged into Eric Clapton Walkmans – 'You can run, you
can run!' – driving a battered old gentian-blue Land-Rover open to
the elements was too much.

'*Was machen Sie in Schweiz?*' demanded one corpulent official.
Why are so many functionaries of the State fat?

'We're in the British Army,' Douglas told him rather pompously.

The official looked sideways at Douglas's bandana, pushed his
peaked hat to the back of his head, stuck his thumbs in his belt,
with difficulty, and stepped ponderously round the Land-Rover to
peer in the back. Simon, sitting on a pile of climbing gear, rucksacks
and skis, grinned benignly.

The fat official shrugged and wandered into his office. I was just
getting cross when he wandered out again and waved us on with an
insolent flick of his wrist. Is there some special school of studied bad
behaviour where Customs officials are trained? Later, Dave, George
and Gabriella, an irrepressibly large Italian girl, were coming back
after a football match in Milan and they were pointlessly held up for
three quarters of an hour at this border crossing.

The rain started as we crossed the Simplon Pass, forcing a very hasty effort climbing like monkeys all over the Land-Rover to fix the canvas back on, and it carried on raining for four days. Brig is normally fairly sunny even when the high mountains are bad. They are twenty kilometres away so the rain is spent by the time it reaches the Rhône valley, which is wide enough to force a break in the clouds. This time we were dogged by low clouds hanging in the trees on the slopes above the town.

As we were pinned down in the office, the 'system' came sweeping in again, like the tide running over sand flats, and the telephones buzzed with chatter about the Duke of Kent's impending visit in a week's time.

'The Weissmies is off,' said Roger on the phone one morning. 'The Swiss pilots of the Super Puma say they are not being allowed to land on the Weissmies Ridge.' The Queen's Flight were still putting up objections about landing on the site Roger had given them at 3800 metres. Our plan to let the Duke walk to the summit at 4023 metres was in tatters.

I rang the British Defence Attaché, Lieutenant Colonel Bill Thatcher to explain that the Duke actually wanted to climb one of the 4000-metre peaks we were climbing. Bill, who was at all times extraordinarily helpful, understood and explained that the Queen's Flight regulations state that any helicopter carrying a member of the Royal Family must have two engines, so it can hover on one engine if the first conks out, and anyway there was an altitude limit of 2800 metres. The Weissmies Ridge was 1000 metres higher than the limit, and apparently no heli on earth yet made can hover in the prescribed Queen's Flight manner at that altitude.

'But the Swiss pilots have been there and they're quite happy everything'll be really safe,' I said. The pilots were among the finest in Switzerland, with extensive experience of mountain rescue in appalling conditions. Bill promised to do what he could.

A day later, just as we were planning to take advantage of another vague suggestion of good weather from our weather gurus in Geneva, Bill called back to say his colleague at the Embassy, the Air Attaché, had been busy on the phone to London. Quite undeterred by regulations, which I must admit is surprising in an RAF officer, this worthy man had pressed the Queen's Flight for a dispensation of the 2800-metre limit and hover rules.

'And he got it,' said Bill. I could hear the triumph in his voice and he had every reason, for the RAF are usually adamant about their rules. Way back in 1946, Air Vice Marshal Bennett, who ran the Pathfinders during the Second War, wrote in his memoirs that the RAF regulations were killing pilot initiative dead as a dodo (Bennett was Australian), so you can imagine what the 'regs' are like now.

Douglas, Simon and I left the field of bureaucratic battle for the mountains on the day Bill Thatcher, Charlie and the Duke's bodyguard, a genial policeman with extraordinarily large feet, drove to Hoh Saas to examine the proposed royal lunch site. The oracle at Geneva had intimated a change in the weather, what they blandly called an 'amelioration' for Thursday and half a day's good weather for Friday. It was just enough for the Piz Bernina.

Piz Bernina (4049m) is one of the outlying 4000ers, six hours' drive from Brig in the east of Switzerland south of St Moritz on the border with Italy. The local guides told Roger the snow conditions were suitable, we flung our gear into one of the Swiss Army VWs and immediately plunged into cloud at the top of the Furka Pass which is only 2431 metres.

However, the further east we drove, the better the weather became. After the Oberalp Pass (2044m), we stopped for a picnic lunch near Sumvitg and stuffed ourselves with dried meat, salami sausage, goat's cheese, Emmental, granary bread and a bottle of Dole. I looked upon the world with a glow of goodwill, and observed a small and beautiful church below us, with smooth perfectly rounded wooden roof. Religion in the mountains always has more substance than in the cities, perhaps because it is face to face with what is real; the pressures of living among mountains cannot be ignored.

Then on to another pass. I refuse to say who drove after lunch but we climbed the Julier Pass (2284m) which went up for ever, before dropping down quite quickly into St Moritz, a place of enormous Disneyland hotels demanding Mickey Mouse prices. We reached the Diavolezza lift at 3.30 p.m. in time for the last lift. The sun shone and, strangely, the car park and wide open slopes by the lift station were seething with nuns in black habits and a few in white. This seemed to be a good omen.

We took the lift to Diavolezza (2973m), which is a modern ski restaurant with enormous view windows which stands on a ridge above the Vadret Pers Glacier, overlooking the Bernina group. Clouds still dragged on Piz Bernina far off in the distance and on Piz

Palü (3905m) close by to the south, but the air seemed more defined. We walked down the steep rock-strewn hillside from Diavolezza to the glacier and set up our tents on a drift of snow under a strip of moraine. The snow had gone from the glacier at this level (2725m) and I wondered how much longer we would be able to use our skis. Sitting on the moraine, I tried to pick out the route we planned to take the next day. This ski expedition involves a lot of up and down, over features with wonderful names like places or people in a Tolkien story, the refuge of Chamuotsch, a climb onto the Fortezza Ridge, the Bellavista terraces, down to the Pass dal Zupo (what strange caravans crossed this in the grey mists of time?), across to the magical Fuorcla Crast'Agüzza, before climbing over La Spalla to the summit.

I got up for a leak at 1 a.m. and was encouraged to see the dark sky clear with not a cloud in sight. I cannot recall seeing so many stars in the sky, like falling snow. I could see the faint white silhouette of Piz Bernina far away on the horizon. It wasn't as cold as I expected for a cloudless night, but cold enough, and I hopped back in my tent for another couple of hours' kip.

I only just heard the electric alarm on my Citizen Promaster watch at 3 a.m. I stuck my head outside the tent. God, it was colder out than I had thought! But ideally crisp and wonderfully clear.

'We're on, Simon!' I called out to wake him up, but as usual he was already ahead of the game, getting dressed inside his tent.

The only antidote to a cold start is business. We whacked on the Epigas stove with the melted snow water we had prepared the night before and set to putting on socks and inner boots while the water boiled. Douglas made the chocolate brews and poured hot water in the Army ration rolled oats. I put two good measures of Maxim in my chocolate and was later glad I did.

Skis, skins, harscheisen and Walkman, Eric Clapton again, a beat to bump-start a long day, 'I've been waiting so long . . . in the sunshine of your love.' The old ones are always the best!

The mushy snow and ice over the glacier was rock hard but there was no difficulty finding a path in the darkness through the crevasse zones. We found an easy route up the left side of the Chamuotsch rocks onto the Fortezza Ridge and soon came to the rock section where we had to take off our skis for the first time. We were going like trains and made short work of the snow and rock ridge, zipping up the short steep snow slope which turned the rock step at the top.

Skis on again and we skinned steadily up and across the Bellavista terraces at about 3700 metres. By this time dawn was on us, glowing all colours of warmth in the east and casting a superb clarity over the mountains. Every rock on Piz Bernina was etched sharp but still a long way off.

At the end of the Bellavista terraces, the slope drops more steeply towards the Pass dal Zupo, losing several hundred metres of altitude, and we stopped to take off our skins to ski down. I rammed my ski sticks into the firm snow, stuck my gloves on the ends and bent over to release my skis. The wind was gusting hard and as I was removing my second ski, a gust caught one ski pole and knocked it over. It fell tantalisingly close, only a metre away below me, but I could do nothing, half on, half off my skis, without crampons, unable to step down for fear of losing a ski or sliding away myself. Furious, I watched the pole and glove slide irritatingly slowly down the slope and disappear over the edge of a glacier cliff at the top of the Morteratsch Glacier.

I closed my eyes for a moment and said flatly, 'What a pisser.'

'That's very controlled of you,' said Simon, amused.

I shrugged. We both knew there was no more to say. No amount of swearing would bring the bloody thing back, and way up on a mountain you just have to get on with what you've got left. I had some spare lightweight inner gloves which I put on to replace my lost Dachstein inner mitt and Gore-Tex outer (an excellent combination).

Earlier the wrist strap had broken on the other ski pole so I was not doing well. Someone, probably my sister-in-law who always bossed me about when we skied together, said, 'Skiing without poles is good practice.' I had no option. I clenched my empty fist and pretended I was holding a pole as we skied down past the crevasses into the topmost snow trough of the glacier below the summit block of Piz Bernina.

We stopped again to put our skins back on. This time I dropped a harscheisen. I stared speechless as it rattled off down the slope gathering speed in the wind and disappeared way below in powder snow blowing along the surface. This was not my day. Losing a harscheisen was more serious. I looked up at the slopes I had to climb on skis, assessing whether I could do them mainly traversing up right to left, on the remaining one harscheisen on the left ski.

As I was thinking about this, Simon's ski pole shot off down the slope after my harscheisen. Swiss Army ski poles are heavy as sin with great baskets on the point, not at all the same neat shape as a small metal harscheisen, so it stopped in a dip two hundred metres down. Expressively silent, Simon skied downhill to retrieve it. Douglas and I bent our heads against the cold wind and traversed above him towards the summit slopes.

We left our skis at 3730 metres, above the Marco e Rosa Huts on the blunt snow slope under La Spalla (4020m). Simon fitted his crampons, pulled out his water bottle for a drink and dropped that too. Lozenge-shaped and smooth, it shot off down the slope at a great pace and disappeared in a flurry of wind-blown snow dust over the edge into Italy, somewhere down on the exotically named glacier called Vedretta di Scerscen Superiore.

'Slide well, those British Army plastic bottles,' I observed, wondering what else could go wrong before the day was out.

The climb to the summit was not as simple as the guide book suggests, which is merely, 'Summit climb 2 hrs from the Marco e Rosa Huts. Head over steepening snow slopes to rocks of the south-east ridge, follow this on fixed ropes to the fore-summit (La Spalla) from whence (sic) one rock section (II) leads to the summit.'

No problems, I thought.

The slope did steepen, to at least fifty degrees, on worryingly unconsolidated snow and then over loose rocks thinly covered with snow. Chunks of rock which looked as though they would provide immovably solid belays suddenly came free from the ice and fell away bouncing and leaping at huge speed into the flat snow slopes of the col below. Fascinating watching them fall, like bodies when they become small and black in the distance. I turned back to concentrate on the climbing.

There was no sign of the promised fixed ropes. Either this is a fiction, or they were covered with rime ice and snow. Simon, leading, decided to turn the summit rocks of La Spalla, traversing on a steep snow slope under poor rock glistening with meltwater. Then he front-pointed steeply up to the ridge above. The snow was rotten, crystalline and too loose and though we were roped up the rock on our left was devoid of spikes or crevices so we could use no protection.

We made the ridge, which is narrow but easy, crossed La Spalla and dropped across the snow crest to the Summit Ridge beyond. There really isn't much room on this arête, with a vertical rock drop on the left and a steep snow slope curving away on the right. I convinced myself I was in good hands. The summit rock slope is, typically, the easiest and safest part, with plenty of spikes to slip the rope over, even allowing for the over-generous snow cover. In summer, this summit climb would be a doddle.

The view was fantastic, and we were out of the wind as long as we didn't stand too close to the west side where the wind streaked up the vertical rock wall behind us. However, it was eleven o'clock and I was worried about deteriorating weather conditions forecast for the afternoon.

'Let's sod off,' we said, and did.

From the summit, we decided that front-pointing down Simon's route behind La Spalla would not be much fun, and we opted instead to traverse the bowl of snow slopes between Piz Bernina and La Spalla to reach a point on the ridge below La Spalla where we could descend casually on gentler slopes to our skis. Also, the snow nearer the summit seemed more consolidated and we decided this would be a safer course. That at any rate was the theory.

The first part went well, including crossing a bergschrund on the shallower slope under the Piz Bernina which gave out a heart-stopping crack as I stepped over it. Leading, I found the slope steepened considerably, a fact which had been concealed from us by perspective when we were sitting on the summit. Plus, the snow worsened, which no one could have guessed. From the summit, we had been unable to see round the corner where the route took us beneath a rock face which dripped melted ice water onto the snow, weakening the structure. As I kicked steps, I wondered if the snow would hold my weight. The alternative to the concept of 'stay' was the certainty of 'go – down a steep fifty-five-degree slope which vanished over a line of oblivion or I-can't-see-anything-below-that-so-it-doesn't-matter.

This was one of those times when you wonder for a brief moment what the fuck you are doing in a place like that. Equally, you realise that fruitless questions of this sort do not help. I looked down, I looked at the awful crystalline snow, I looked up at the icicles dripping water, I kicked another few steps, terribly slowly to make sure each step held, and all the time I kept glancing further to my left where I thought I could see better snow near the target ridge I was traversing towards. I never thought of praying. I was too absorbed in the business of moving. This was not some philosophical abstraction but the real essence of experience, of being, and I found it strangely pleasurable. Like skinning uphill, the steady cadence of my actions seemed to match the rhythms of my heartbeat and my breathing. This time, the sense of danger removed the euphoria, leaving just me and the slope on the mountain. Over an hour of slow, careful moving, ice axe in, kick steps and repeat.

Suddenly a bright spot of moving colour gripped my attention on the periphery of my vision. Simon's purple Gore-Tex jacket. Sliding fast downhill thirty metres across the slope behind me. I snapped my head round. My mind working with absurd logic informed me that Simon was indeed still inside his jacket and on the move, feet first, digging his toes in and fruitlessly trying to slow himself in the soft snow with his ice axe.

This happened so quickly but I remember thinking, 'Oh shit! Douglas is next. Then it'll be up to me to stop us all.'

I stuffed my ice axe into the snow as a brake, or belay, noticing as I did that the snow was so hopelessly brittle my whole arm went in after it, and I wondered how on earth snow as badly consolidated as this would stop anything, let alone two men as large as Simon and Douglas.

Glued to the snow, I glanced back. Simon had stopped. Douglas had held him, ramming his body weight over his ice axe buried like mine deep in the snow, his feet jammed into the foot holes and wishing he had some other things to jab into the slope as anchors too.

Simon had been standing still when the foot steps he was standing on had simply collapsed. I was pleased, to say the least, when after another twenty minutes I reached the ridge. I looked over a small cornice and saw our skis two hundred metres below us across an easy snow slope. I nipped smartly over the ridge, dropping out of sight of Douglas and Simon but safe. Even had they slipped again the friction of our rope over the ridge between us would have held.

We relaxed at our skis, sat on our rucksacks and ate bread and salami sausage. The sun shone, the snow sparkled, still wind-hard for our return, and nothing else mattered. When we looked back at our tracks across the bowl of snow from the summit, we saw we had traversed over a huge hanging glacier. The line I had been looking at below me was the edge of space. Satisfying to see in retrospect, but I was certainly glad I had not known it at the time.

The journey back was tiring. Fortunately, my one remaining harscheisen was on the topside of my ski so I was able to skin back up from the Morteratsch Glacier onto the Bellavista terraces, which is mostly a rising traverse right to left, and the skiing down to the Fortezza Ridge was easy and fun. By this time in the afternoon, when we were lower, the snow was soft and I made a meal of the short descent turning the rock step on the ridge. We abseiled off the insignificant and admittedly easy climb at the bottom end of the rocks, taking far too long, and then thankfully put on our skis again for the final run home. We reached the tents again at a quarter past four.

The joker was that the last lift left the Diavolezza station at five o'clock, but first we faced a balls-aching forty minutes up the steep, rocky 250-metre high hillside above us. Without enthusiasm, we packed our tents and tried our best to reach the top in time. Tired muscles got us there twenty minutes late. Douglas, being young and fit, was rearing to walk down to our vehicle, a mere two hours more, and then blithely talked about driving for six hours back to Brig. I, being older and wiser, opted instead for the bar. I could not walk another step.

Diavolezza is the most luxurious Alpine mountain hut we visited. All polished pine, a dozen or more Italian hotel staff, gleaming stainless steel kitchens, a well-stocked bar and acres of view windows overlooking the pink sunset on the snowy Piz Palü and Piz Bernina range. We drank beer, ate a hearty supper of Wiener schnitzel and chips and decided we had enjoyed ourselves. It was a serious ski expedition and over 2000 metres' climbing in a day was the most we had done. While Simon and I congratulated ourselves on reaching the summit in snow conditions more expected in winter than at the end of July, Douglas scouted round for somewhere to sleep.

'In the ski store,' he whispered conspiratorially when he came back so the staff could not hear. 'It's a sort of bunker, a concrete room with an earth floor in the basement of the lift station where they keep the safety signs and poles for the ski pistes.'

We made ourselves at home. Private, warmer than outside, no

effort wasted putting up the tent, and cheap as air. I stretched out in my sleeping bag on a wonderfully comfortable safety mattress, the sort they tie round pylons on the pistes, and lay in the complete darkness listening to Pavarotti on my Walkman thinking a mixture of pleasurable thoughts, about our success that day, the dangers we had escaped, the pleasure of each other's company, and home. I realised that I had taken another step in my search. It had been a long hard day. It was the best night's sleep for ages.

Two days later Douglas and I drove into Italy again, in the old blue Land-Rover, to climb another outlier, the Gran Paradiso. Confounding the Geneva oracle, the weather turned exceptionally hot. We tied the canvas back, covered ourselves in suncream and took the Grand St-Bernard route from Martigny.

A twelfth-century monk called John de Bremble wrote of the Grand St-Bernard Pass, 'Lord, restore me to my brethren that I may tell them that they come not into this place of torment.' So, we took the tunnel.

The Grand St-Bernard Tunnel is less popular than the Mont Blanc Tunnel, less expensive (27 SFrs compared to 41 SFrs), larger and much better ventilated. The sun was hotter still on the southern side of the mountains, the light shimmering on the bare hillsides as we drove down the L'Artanava river valley to Aosta. Far behind us, beyond and dominating the Valpelline valley the Grand Combin Massif rose majestically over its neighbours. I learned another reason for climbing, for there was something most satisfying about the thought that we had stood on the summit of that sweeping icy white curve so near heaven in the hard blue sky.

Aosta sweltered, the peeling ochre buildings shuttered in painful silence against the Mediterranean heat and the noise of the traffic thundering through from the Mont Blanc and Grand St-Bernard Tunnels. For centuries, the town has made money from trade crossing the Alpine passes, the benefits of which might diminish once the Italians have completed the motorway bypass being built. We drove on, with a careful eye open for a garage as we were running short of diesel, and got off the main road as soon as possible just beyond Sarre.

The Val Savaranche is lovely. In 1922, King Vittorio Emanuele III presented this area, a hunting reserve, to the State and the Gran Paradiso National Park was founded. The valley is unspoilt by horrid ski developments and retains a typical old-fashioned Italian charm. The road curves back and forth between uncultivated hillsides of grass, trees, Alpine flowers and rocks, over rusty metal bridges which look as if they might collapse, and past a few clusters of tatty houses with topsy-turvy red terracotta roofs. This was the Alps before the 'Tourist Industry'.

There is a most useful filling station in Eaux Rousses, open on Sundays, Catholic country or not, where an old lady with a face like a soused olive cheerfully filled our Land-Rover just before we ran out of diesel.

The car park in Pont, a couple of miles further on, was a dust bowl, churned by cars, baked in the heat and whipped into small twisters by the warm wind which was nipping down the valley. We changed into our plastic ski boots and I was grateful that I could unzip my ski pants all the way up the side to cool off. Families were everywhere, lying in the shade among the larch and junipers or playing on the banks of the river. Dressed in shorts and T-shirts, they gave us some weird looks when we passed carrying skis. Several stopped us to ask what we were doing, including an old priest in a black cassock who spoke French. When I told him we wanted to ski to the summit of the Gran Paradiso, he glanced up to the mountains, not in disbelief but with respect, much as he might look up the aisle of his church at the altar, and then he solemnly blessed us on our way.

The path up through the trees to the Vittorio Emanuele Hut is delightful. We took our time, two hours, to enjoy the masses of pink Alpine rhododendrons which were carpeted thickly among the rocks under the dappled shadows of the sweet-smelling pines and pale green larch. The rhododendrons gave way to blue violas, some white ones which I had not seen before, tiny mounds of saxifrage between the rocks, white daisy-like asters (*Aster bellidiastrum*) and then above the tree-line, yellow Alpine pulsatillas, startling pale blue forget-me-nots (*Myosotis alpestris*) and finally highest of all the fluorescent blue gentians, *verna*, *bavarica* and the stately bell gentian (*acaulis*, *clusii* or *kochiana*?). Douglas was very patient when I insisted on stopping to photograph them (I had an excellent 100 mm Macro lens) and talked encouragingly about his mother's enthusiasm for gardening when I got wildly excited at finding a double Alpine pulsatilla.

Later, I sent the photograph to the Royal Horticultural Society, who promptly lost it. I rang up.

'We've not heard of a double,' said the man at Wisley.

Botanical fame, I thought, a flower named after me!

'But the pulsatilla is very difficult to propagate true to its parent,' he continued dismissively. 'Whether by division or seed.'

Tempting to try all the same, for the double yellow flower looked superb.

The Vittorio Emanuele Hut (2730m) looks like an upturned boat, curving to a ridge, and it was very full. The warden asked, 'Are you guides?'

I guess he made this flattering presumption because we were very tanned, but I shook my head and he put us in a tiny room with bunk-beds for six on the top floor.

We sat about in the sun and Douglas amused himself watching me stalk a couple of ibex close to the hut munching grass in a carpet of forget-me-nots. These big-chested beasts with their ribbed flared horns could not give a damn about the humans who lurk after them for a few brief moments in their National Park. We easily came within a short step of them and they ignored us with beady-eyed disdain.

The dining room was full, everyone laughing and talking, the dinner was good, which we had come to expect as this was an Italian hut, and we repaired to bed fairly early filled with minestrone, meat stew and mixed vegetables (option on spag' bol').

We overslept. Too much shooting has left me rather deaf, or maybe it was the nightcap beers we had, and my alarm simply had no chance. Instead, the noise of other people stamping about on the wood floors in the hut at 4 a.m. – it is quite impossible to sleep on in these mountain huts – woke us. We dressed fast, grabbed a quick breakfast from the lady of the house, the warden's wife I think, who gave us a large jug of hot coffee and another of hot milk which was excellent, good bread, butter and peach jam (her march tea was the best I had), went out to our gear which we had prepared the night before, and we were off into the darkness behind the hut by half past four.

The guide books tell you to recce the route up the moraine boulders in daylight as route-finding is not easy at night. The guide book is right, for once. In the darkness, we could see a group far ahead, their pinprick head torches dipping and flashing weakly, and several others set off from the hut at the same time as us.

Within minutes, Douglas had gone up one steep scree slope and I chose another. Separated, we stumbled about on the boulders, fell into soft snow up to our bollocks and the air grew blue with our swearing. I thought we should traverse left as we went up the slope, Douglas as usual was busy 'investing' height-gain to the right, all the time yelling at me from the night that he was traversing too.

'For Christ's sake!' I hollered back through the dark at his faint shadow which I could see scrambling up the scree ridge parallel to mine. 'You'll get bloody lost that way.'

'No, I bloody well won't!' his voice floated back. 'You're going too far round.'

'Fuckwit!' I shouted, exasperated, and promptly fell cursing in a hole of soft snow between several huge stones.

I could hear him muttering to himself and then loudly, 'Stupid bastard!'

Startled ibex scampered away in the darkness and the other climbers kept their distance. Douglas and I reached the top of this awful slope at the same time about fifty yards apart, both of us exactly where we wanted to be, just as the dawn lightened the sky. When I saw the expression of shock on the faces of the group coming up behind us, I cringed with embarrassment.

However, feigning unconcern, we put on our skis, skins ready fitted. The snow was poor, melted by day into deep runnels, like fluted mud flats on the coast, and frozen hard by night, but we both reckoned we were better off on skis than stumbling about in old, rubbly frozen snow tracks.

We left the other walkers behind and several hundred metres up the narrow snow-covered Gran Paradiso Glacier, we came across a Frenchman waiting impatiently by a tent while his girlfriend, an attractive blonde, was fitting her crampons. Slim, fit-looking with his hair cut down to the wood, this charmless Gallic person stared at us rudely and remarked in a tone of derisive astonishment, '*Qu'est-ce que vous faites avec des skis!*'

I replied, '*On va voir, mon vieux!*'

'Nice bird,' said Douglas who had been eyeing up the girl as we skinned uncomfortably past on the unforgiving knobbly snow.

'I'm a married man,' I retorted righteously, actually pleased with my status.

The Frenchman forced the pace with his girlfriend, trying to beat us up the slope, taking a direct line while Douglas and I traversed back and forth on our skis. We slowly overhauled them until at about 3000 metres we found the slope steep and hard enough to fit harscheisen. On all our previous early starts we had fitted them as routine the night before, but at 2730 metres in the hut the temperature had been +19 degrees C in the afternoon when we arrived and was still not less than +7 C at 4 a.m., so we hadn't bothered.

By this time there were a dozen other people coming up behind us on foot, including the Frenchman and his pretty blonde girlfriend, but once we set off again with the harscheisen, we left them standing.

'Stay by me,' sang Annie Lennox so aptly. Even if the stars have made us blind. A good beat for skinning when you feel really fit and strong.

The wind picked up unpleasantly as we came over the first steep slope and we stopped to put on balaclavas, gloves and hoods. The normal ski route goes up in big steps separated by broad snowfields and we were soon over the next and out of sight of everyone behind and on our own in the clear morning light with the peaks of the Graian Alps emerging all round us.

We left our skis at the summit bergschrund and walked the last hundred metres or so on crampons, turning the narrow rocky summit block on the left on frozen melt-snow, which would be impossible later in the day when it softened in the sun. As the whole ascent is in shadow and bloody cold, we sat about on the summit warming up for the first time in three and a half hours.

The sky was clear and the view spectacular. All the big Alpine peaks along the French and Swiss-Italian border werc lined up to our north, the Mont Blanc massif, the Grand Combin, the Matterhorn and the Monte Rosa group. The East Face of the Gran Paradiso is very sheer, but looked interesting, warmer and more enticing than some of the vertical cliffs we have seen from the mountains we've done (AD+ and five hours from Bivacco Pol).

As I set up the camera for a run-round summit photo, Douglas looked down the slope we had skinned up and counted sixty or more people tramping upwards. Time to go. We didn't want to get bogged down with trying to pass hordes on the narrow path to the summit. We nipped back down our iced snow track round the summit block and climbed up the rock buttress to the Madonna Summit, (4058m). The Madonna is rather plain, placid and appealing, and covered with gifts of rosaries, flowers, coins stuck in gaps between metal and stone and bits of cloth tied to the frame which blew in the wind like Tibetan prayer flags.

The Madonna Summit is hardly independent, only about eleven metres from the small snow col between it and the Gran Paradiso itself, but having declared six peaks over Richard Goedeke's sixty-one summits and been unable to trace the names of these extra six, Gary Parker and I had picked six 'tops' at random. The Madonna Summit was one of these. The others later turned out much more difficult to reach.

Our interest from the beginning was to raise money for charity on a money for each peak basis, so the more peaks the better. I had contacted the Foundation through Anne Diamond, who was involved in the publicity for my second book, *Child at War*, and had lost her son Sebastian through cot-death. In December 1992, the Foundation's professional staff had agreed to make our climbing their big charity-raising event for 1993. By July, very little money had been raised and I had set the Base Camp to writing letters to everyone they could think of to improve the tally. Perhaps we chose to climb during a year when the reality of the recession was at its worst, but the Foundation's charity effort was disappointing. Meantime, we were pressing on with our job.

We scrambled down the rocks from the Madonna Summit and found several men sitting on the little snow col, who doggedly refused to look at us. I realised that although they had climbed uphill for over four hours, they were too frightened to nip up the last rocky bit to the summit. Nowt so queer as folk.

There was no time to bother with them. The hordes had increased to nearly 100 and were drawing close, plodding up the slopes below. The Gran Paradiso is a long haul up, 1300-metre height gain in a par time of five hours, yet it attracts people of all ages, sizes, shapes and skills, like Mont Blanc, and so, I believe, it serves a fine purpose of drawing people into the pleasures of the mountains.

During May and early June, most use skis but the day we went up, Douglas and I were the only ones on skis on the mountain. We fitted our skis and pushed off. The snow was hard and easy and I cannot adequately describe the exhilaration as we whizzed past all the people plodding up on foot. They literally stopped and stared at us weaving back and forth down the slopes towards them, their faces a mixture of amazement and jealous fury as they realised the advantage of being on skis. They faced a two or three-hour walk down, while we took only twenty minutes to reach the bottom of the Gran Paradiso Glacier where, to our surprise, we saw the French couple again.

He must have seen us swishing down the steep slope because he began running downhill over the rubbly snow after his girlfriend. I swept up to him, and, knowing perfectly well what the answer was, I said very deliberately in French, '*Alors, mon gars, vous avez été au sommet?*'

He shook his head, obviously impressed to see us back so soon, and then spent the next five minutes explaining that his girlfriend had been sick because of the altitude (probably because he had forced the pace), and he waxed on trying to prove that he was a jolly experienced mountaineer really.

Seeking to belittle us, he fired questions at me like, 'Have you been on the Grand Combin?'

'Yes.'

'The skiing is '*très agréable*' in the Bernese Oberland, is it not?'

'*Génial*,' I agreed, too well disposed with our day to be annoyed by this all too typical piece of French hubris. I was pleased to think that we had actually been to these places and moreover that we had had a great deal of pleasure doing so.

Tiring of his inquisition, we turned away and he set off again running at a great pace down the hard snow, determined to show us being on foot was quicker. Douglas grinned at me. I grinned back. We gave him a couple of minutes to exhaust himself and then skied past him, just to rub it in. Some French just ask for it, don't they?

Worse, for him, when he topped the last rise of snow, he saw us chatting up his girlfriend who was looking very sorry for herself. No fun being on mountains when you are feeling sick and ghastly.

The walk down to the car park at Pont was most enjoyable. Douglas and I took only an easy hour and a quarter and talked all the way, about women mostly, and the theory of life.

And so on.

10

A ROYAL VISIT

Great mental excitement which causes a hypnosis that forces out pain sensations.

Albert von St Gallen Heim, SAC 1892

Gonzo Martin, looking more than ever like a gypsy with his reddish hair, bent hooked nose and wearing a garish T-shirt and shorts, slipped out of the dining room where we were having a salad bar lunch. Nikki, slim and, after hours at the pool in Brig, exceptionally brown, glanced up the long table and wandered out too with a secret smile on her face. I was suspicious.

Dave bustled round from the kitchen. True to his army training he never ate before everyone had been served, even though our lives were highly unmilitary. He was grinning too.

Mike Nutter, straightforward, enthusiastic, loud and amusing, never noticed and continued to chat up his girlfriend Lisalotte, or Fatal as we called her because she never let him alone. She had joined us for lunch.

Nikki came back in, stopped behind Mike and, with one slender hand on his shoulder, she said in a low husky voice, 'There's a bird on the phone for you.'

Mike snapped a quick glance at Fatal, hoping she did not understand English that well, but she did, and he said rather too quickly, 'For me? Upstairs in the office?' He laughed nervously and we were hugely entertained to see him wheel a very suspicious Lisa through the open French windows of the dining room into the sunshine outside and quickly say goodbye. Then he came back inside and said, 'I'd better go and answer it, eh lads?' He had a reputation to keep up with the women in Brig.

Gonzo slid back into the dining room and primed us on the scam. We all stopped talking and waited, listening.

An explosion of raucous laughter echoed down the stone corridors from the office upstairs and set us all off again. Mike had found a full-sized, boned turkey astride the phone in the office. We ate the bird that night, roast with all the trimmings.

Dave Moore and Nigel Taylor were brilliant cooks. Well, they were qualified chefs really, as Dave kept reminding me in his snappy London manner, and they excelled themselves for the visit of HRH the Duke of Kent. With a coterie of Swiss policemen, army officers from the Mountain Warfare School in Andermatt, pilots, diplomatic representatives, a protocol officer, a doctor, the Duke's equerry and his bodyguard, there were more visitors than us and we wanted to put on a good show. Our principle was that the Duke was coming to see us on a mountain, so he should eat as if he were on a mountain. Double-damask napkins, regimental silver and cut glass were out, which would have been old hat for him anyway. Equally we wanted to produce something rather more gripping than our usual fare of granary bread and garlic sausage. I wanted a Swiss peasant's lunch fit for royalty. I left Dave to the details, confident everything would be prepared to the highest possible standards and we went to tackle the Lagginhorn and Weissmies.

For the first time, Peter joined us though we took our skis. After the rubbly snow on the Gran Paradiso, I was not sure how much longer we would be able to use them – certainly not on the Lagginhorn. Gary was still unable to join us so we paired Simon and Peter, Douglas and me, and took the lift through grey cloud to Hoh Saas where we set up our Vaude Hogan tents by the little restaurant at the top.

As usual, we had been promised good weather, but we flung up the tents in drizzling rain and nipped inside the Hoh Saas restaurant. This place deserves a better mention in the guide books. At 3098 metres and therefore closer to the mountains than the traditional SAC Weissmies Hut way down at 2726 metres, the place is privately run, which gives it an immediate advantage in our experience, with a small restaurant and bunk-beds for twelve and more. A most attractive girl looked after us, not at all snooty as some wardens had been, she was helpful about the area and willingly supplied us with an unhealthy mix of soup, hot chocolate and beer.

The weather was not encouraging. I peered out of our tent at four o'clock next morning and could see nothing but damp mist.

'Lie-in time,' I said. Douglas grunted in the depths of his sleeping bag, hardly stirring.

The clouds sort of cleared about seven o'clock and we set out shortly afterwards. There is something awful about bump-starting yourself on a damp horrid day and we felt no enthusiasm at all. It was strange not being on skis too. We slid on our backsides downhill into the basin of the Lagginhorn Glacier and stumbled about in deep soft snow. Breaking through the crust into an icy stream hidden below the surface did not improve my sense of humour. I stopped to empty out my plastic boots, wring out my socks and then tried to warm up again, moving fast to catch up the others.

Like the weather, the Lagginhorn was dull. In thick cloud, we clambered alone up the easy rocks of the West Ridge, the normal route. No one else was stupid enough to be out on a day like this. The ridge seemed to go on and on. At the top, the clouds, the warmth and lateness of the day all combined to make the steepening snow slope feel most insecure, though we were probably being over-sensitive. We did not spend long on the summit and returned to our tents damp and dispirited. The Duke's visit next day needed better weather than this.

The girl in the restaurant cheered us up with more excellent soup and Alastair Bruce, an ex-Scots Guards officer who was working on our PR for us, arrived with Gary to say that the forecast for the following day was good.

'What, in Tunis, Turkey or Tenerife?'

We grumbled on over some more beer. Two Germans, who had all the gear, including fine mountaineers' beards and lumberjack shirts, had decided to go down. They had tried the Weissmies that day and turned back, unable to find their way between the crevasses on the Trift Glacier in cloud. The ridge of the Lagginhorn may have been boring, but at least there were no route-finding problems and we had achieved our aim.

For once that summer, the weather men were right. The clouds blew over at midnight and the snow was still freezing under a clear starry night when we left our tents before four o'clock. Something told me we would have a good day for the Weissmies, even though Peter, who was using skis for the first time, had to go back for his harscheisen. Douglas and I forged on ahead across the gentle lower slopes of the glacier, feeling good in the crisp night air, zigzagging on our skis as the slope sharpened towards the top of the Trift Glacier under the mass of the mountain which loomed darkly over us. We stopped below a series of huge crevasses and watched the faint shadows of Simon, Gary and Peter skinning across the ice bowl below us.

Peter was doing well. Kick-turns in the dark on steep gradients when you are not very practised are gripping to say the least. Simon stayed downhill of him at each turn but Peter was ready for crampons when they reached us. I had chosen to stop in the frozen rubble of an old avalanche which cut the smoother snows on one side of the mountain because it was easier to put things down and not lose them sliding downhill.

On crampons, we found a way through a series of deep crevasses, turned left-handed into the icefall, then right past another great sérac onto the shoulder of the South-West Ridge. From here, the route is straightforward up broad slopes to Point 3820 metres on the ridge. Left of this we found the wide open flat place Roger Mathieu had selected to land the Duke in the Super Puma helicopter. We stuck our skis in the snow, put on more clothes because the wind had turned very cold, left a rude message drawn in the snow for Roger who was making a last recce in a helicopter that morning and carried on to the summit (4023m).

This was really an exhilarating three-hour push in perfect conditions, the first and only time Simon, Douglas, Gary, Peter and I climbed together, and we were lucky to see a fine clear dawn break over the snow-topped mountains all round: the Bernese Oberland far off to the north, and a splendid panorama of the whole of the Mischabel chain in the west, the Allalinhorn, Alphubel, Täschhorn, Dom, Lenzspitze, Nadelhorn, Stecknadelhorn, Hohberghorn and Dürrenhorn.

The first man on the Weissmies, in 1855, was a local solicitor called Joseph Zurbriggen, but guides were as conceited then as too many of them are now and they did not believe him. Pity the guides. They retraced his steps and found he had indeed been to the top. There is a lesson in there for all of us. The mountain does not need guides now any more than it did then and several groups were plodding up on foot behind us. The normal route is not hard, has interest in passing the crevasse zone and gives climbers the satisfaction of being on a big 4000er, with sufficient dangers to heighten the senses. We had our fair share during our descent.

As usual, I had been trying to understand the nature of the mountain on the way up and I had noticed that while the ridge was broad and easy, there was no safe run-out. All the slopes disappeared over bulging séracs into the crevasses of the Trift Glacier hundreds of feet below on one side, or into the Mälliga Glacier on the other. If you fall when the snow is soft there is little danger of sliding, as I knew from the Gross-Grünhorn, but the snow was hard névé that morning and when we put on our skis at the heli landing site, I suggested we all carry an ice axe instead of one ski stick. There is no way a skier can stop himself with ski poles alone when he falls on a steep, icy slope.

Setting off on a good run down is very exciting, with the speed, the concentration needed to keep balance and make turns, and the privileged thrill of skiing so high on a big mountain above the valleys which we could see in green early morning haze so far below. We passed a couple of other groups coming up, and Gary and Peter who were walking down on crampons.

Suddenly, as Douglas was slicing across the slope just below me, his skis vibrating over the crisp hard snow, one ski knocked the heel fitting of the other, just as had happened to me on the Grand Combin. The ski came off, tumbling him at once down the steep slope.

I watched the loose ski shoot away and disappear into space over the crevasses of the Trift Glacier. Detachedly, I observed Douglas pick up speed as he fought to twist round and ram his ice axe into the snow. When a skier falls below you, everything happens so fast there is nothing you can do. Except watch in silence. There is no point shouting. Self-absorbed, Douglas would never have heard, and he was falling away fast on a steepening slope to the edge. It was up to him.

I saw his axe bite into the slope while images flashed through my mind – of the helicopter rescue we would need; or, cynically, what I would do when the radio I was carrying proved not to work; what awful injuries we would find when we located his body in the huge crevasses under the ridge; and the telephoning and the letters I would have to write to his mother and father in Scone in Scotland.

I willed him to stop. His face was grim with strain as he lunged his full weight over his axe which was ripping a track through the snow. I stared, fascinated by the utter reality of it all, searching for the slightest sign of him slowing down.

Time lost all scale and he seemed to slide for ever. His axe dragged a twenty-five-metre furrow down the steep slope. Then quite quickly it seemed to me, though it probably felt more like several years to Douglas, the axe suddenly held fast and he stopped.

I skied down and helped him sort himself out. Glued to the ice axe, he stared down the slope into space, taking in the reality, how close he had come to dying. Danger is the absence of safety as surely as death is the absence of life.

There is no time for the luxury of reflection, indulgent self-pity or congratulation at 3700 metres. It is not like a car accident, or a near-miss, when you can step to one side, to safety, and sit down with a cigarette or a drink to recover. You are still on the mountain, still faced with decisions, of weather, slope, time, distance, safety and condition of mind. These decisions are the stuff of mountaineering, and rendered all the more acute and peculiarly delightful in moments of danger, for there is a very special thrill in survival. Douglas had been as close to the edge of life as anyone ever wants to go, but the sun was shining, the snow sparkled and the world continued all around him. He was still alive.

There was still a long way down. I flicked off the heel binding of his remaining ski which sped off into space after its mate. Douglas watched it go, then shook himself like a man waking from a dream and became a mountaineer again. Quickly, he kicked safe steps into the snow to fit his crampons and hoisted his pack to his shoulders. I skied off. The walk down would take him much longer, but wearing crampons was quite safe.

Simon and I skied back through the séracs, dipping over a bridge and edging along a snow ridge on a steep outside slope beside a deep crevasse. The incident with Douglas had left me supremely confident, filled with an exquisite and unashamedly self-satisfied flood of pleasure at the recollection of my suggestion that we all carry our axes. It was the only time we did it; but there was no safe run-out on the Weissmies.

Douglas was saved buying another round of beers, for by the time we arrived back at Hoh Saas, it was time to pack our tents and take the lift down to Chrizbode (2397m) where we were meeting HRH the Duke of Kent.

Simon and I reached the Chrizbode lift station at the same time as the Base Camp party arrived from the valleys. They had more or less commandeered the entire lift system. One bubble cabin after another popped into sight in the lift station filled with trays, boxes and plates of food, tenting, display boards of maps, photographs and of course crates of drink. We selected a picnic site by a rocky stream and spent a hectic hour putting up an enormous frame tent kindly supplied to us by Relum Tents Ltd. Dave and Nigel donned chefs' whites and spread out the food.

As we worked, clouds thickened from the west, so that by the time the Duke of Kent joined us in a Swiss Super Puma from Sion airport, the Weissmies Ridge was out of sight under a cap of dark cloud. The Swiss pilots agreed to fly up to see if a landing was possible but I was not optimistic as I fitted the Duke with a climbing harness and checked his crampons and the other climbers kitted out Tim Spicer and the other visitors.

The pilots took us up as far as they could but the cloudbase had dropped to 3300 metres and a walk up the ridge to the summit was impossible. Realising the Duke was keen to salvage something of the trip, I shouted over the noise of the rotors in Roger's ear and we hatched a quick alternative plan. Flying skilfully under the cloudbase, the pilots landed us as high as they could on the Trift Glacier, among the crevasses we had crossed in darkness early that morning (and well above the RAF Queen's Flight limit of 2800 metres).

The Duke, keen to experience what he could, jumped out and fitted crampons to his plastic mountaineering boots.

'Remember to keep your feet apart when you walk, sir,' said Roger who was nattily turned out in Swiss Army uniform.

'Why is that?' asked the Duke. He was over-warmly dressed in plus-fours, a thick Aran sweater and an anorak.

'In case you stick the front points of one crampon into the back of the other leg,' explained Roger.

Rashly, I added, 'Just like one of the Base Camp group last week.' Gonzo, typically, had ripped his leg open within minutes of starting out across the Rhône Glacier to do some ice climbing with Gary. George the medic had set about him with grisly enthusiasm. I said, 'He bled like a pig and needed five stitches.'

The Duke looked rather shocked but set off roped up between Roger and me and settled into the necessary gait quickly, lifting his legs rather wide to make quite sure he avoided tripping. Walking on ice in crampons is a strange experience. The ice creaks and crunches noisily beneath the steel points which catch on lumps of hard ice or rock debris and the crampons play a game of trying to throw you off balance.

Under lowering clouds, we progressed well across the broad sloping glacier but the surface of the ice changed lower down, where it was free of melting snow and became very lumpy. One of the Duke's crampon points caught the other foot, he slipped and fell, sliding towards a narrow crevasse. I yanked the rope behind him and Roger nipped back up to help him to his feet again. Unconcerned, he adjusted his crampons more comfortably and we continued on down the glacier.

Our route took us over some crevasses several feet wide which we all jumped easily. The Duke, who is a keen skier, expressed his delight and interest at seeing a deep, blue, empty crevasse close to after skiing over them so often on pistes during the winter when they are covered with snow.

I thought everything was going very smoothly.

Near the bottom of the glacier, one of Roger's fellow mountain guides, Colonel Hans Immer, cut a series of demonstration ice steps for the Duke along a thin ridge of crumbly ice, walked down and jumped a narrow band of snow below onto more ice. I was leading at that point, with the Duke and Roger behind.

'You have to be careful of snow bridges, sir,' I advised the Duke wisely, pointing at the band of snow. 'Especially at this late stage in the season when the snow is melted thin.'

He nodded and watched me step cautiously onto the band of snow, my foot went straight through and I promptly vanished up to my waist in a narrow crevasse hidden under the snow. Hans Immer roared with laughter and it was the Duke's turn to pull on the rope connecting us.

'Just a practical demo,' I muttered to myself, struggling out of the hole, bridging the crevasse with my crampons. The Duke and Roger followed more efficiently, jumping the gap in turn.

From the glacier we walked downhill over moraine for an hour back to Chrizbode and the Duke chatted to various people on the way. He was appalled to hear Douglas's account of that morning's drama. I had foreseen a couple of pitfalls and briefed Roger beforehand about the Army's assumption of his attendance upon our every quality mountain day.

Roger was not impressed with the attitude of the British Army Adventure Training department but when the Duke asked, 'I expect you've had some wonderful outings, guiding the climbers?'

Roger tried to avoid my look and lied manfully, 'Oh yes, sir!'

Few of us, including the Duke, so he said, had seen a picnic lunch as exotic as the one laid out in the frame tent at Chrizbode. Dave and Nigel had prepared glazed hams with a picture of mountains on one and the Scots Guards lion rampant on another, endless small meat and pork pies, with individual pastry designs on each, delicious patterned quiches, a wide variety of locally made dried beef, chicken and pork, small fruit flans, each differently decorated, and two large ones, beautifully made, one showing the Union Jack and the other the Swiss flag. They had baked various types of bread in shapes as if for harvest festival, carved pictures in the butter, made baskets of caramel for cream and sweets and found an excellent selection of cheeses. To drink, there was beer and wine. We had deliberately chosen a cheap local Dole and Gamay, rough and thick on the tongue, because that was the wine of the mountains, drunk after a good day such as we had had on the Weissmies.

The Duke chatted easily to all the people in the Base Camp. 'I expect you've been very busy?' he asked and they happily told him about white-water rafting, bungy jumping, rock and ice climbing. But they never mentioned the Danish girls in Brig.

He plainly enjoyed talking to Nikki who looked tanned and athletic after weeks in the sun at the pool. 'Have you had much to do?' he asked, and she happily told him no physiotherapy had been needed as we had all kept very fit and free from injuries. But she never mentioned Douglas, his Honda CBR1000 or trips to Como and Berne.

There were speeches.

'I am sorry the weather prevented us all reaching the top of the Weissmies,' said Brigadier Mudry, using the doctor as translator. 'Because Roger Mathieu and Hans Immer buried a bottle of champagne up there this morning, during their heli recce on the ridge.'

The Swiss were most put out they had been unable to conjure this bottle from the snows on the summit to impress their royal visitor. I guess it is still there.

Brigadier Mudry reminded everyone that it was the British who started alpinism and that we were trying to do something no Swiss had ever done. The basis of his extraordinarily generous support for our climbing seemed quite simply that the Swiss were delighted that soldiers like themselves, without any special training, climbing without guides, from an old established British regiment like the Scots Guards, showed such an interest in all their mountains.

To mark this occasion, Lieutenant Colonel Tim Spicer and I were each given an old-fashioned wood-and-canvas snow-shoe, with an Andermatt school badge on it. Both for the left foot.

'Wait till the right leg gets blown off,' said Tim.

Much more impressive was the news that the Swiss would pay for our telephone bill. All expenses inside Switzerland, said Brigadier Mudry, would be paid for by the Swiss Army.

Sadly, Tim and I doubted the British Government would ever be so generous to a small group of foreign visitors.

The Duke left by helicopter after three o'clock, tied to a dinner appointment in London that evening. We turned back to the mountains.

11

WATERSHED

Nothing of him that doth fade,
but doth suffer a sea-change
into something rich and strange.
William Shakespeare, Ariel in *The Tempest*

By this time, Simon, Douglas and I had reached the top of thirty mountains and climbed up more than 30,000 metres, four times as high as the cruising altitude of the average plane. Our next, the Aletschhorn (4195m) marked a change in tempo for all of us.

Bad weather each time we had been to the Bernese Oberland had prevented us trying the Aletschhorn from the Aletschfirn Glacier via the Hasler Rib, so we had to commit two days, one in approach, the second for the summit and the walk out again. The mountain is very remote, being some ten kilometres as the chough flies from the nearest road-head or lift in any direction. After more long telephone conversations with Roger, I decided to approach from the south, up the Mittelaletsch Glacier, and take skis. After a short drive from Brig, Mike Nutter dropped us off at the Bettmeralp lift station rather late in the morning. In Bettmeralp, which is a village spread across a most attractive Alpine plateau, summer tourists gave us some odd stares as we wandered past carrying skis. We took the lift to the Bettmerhorn (2643m) and then traversed the mountain to the enormous Grosser Aletsch Glacier, losing nearly 400 metres in height. We had skied this glacier weeks before, above Konkordia, but now the snow had gone, the ice was dirty grey with two dark lines of central moraine running down the middle, where the Grosser Aletschfirn, Jungfraufirn and Ewigschneefeld came together. From high above, the ice looked deceptively smooth.

The glacier is not smooth. There is a trick to crossing the Aletsch ice stream, more than two kilometres wide at this point, which we were to learn to our cost. We dropped off the path below Roti Chumma under the Eggishorn and started onto the ice at 2250 metres. Once among the crevasses and bulging ice formations, you cannot see very far at all. The only comparable experience for those who have not been on a big glacier are high sand dunes, where you can only see a short distance when you are on the top of a rise. As soon as you drop into a dip, you see nothing. In addition, on a glacier, you have to avoid the crevasses. Some you can jump, but the big chasms must be detoured which upsets your sense of direction.

We made a meal of the Aletsch Glacier. We went too far to the right, or north, and found ourselves committed to some intriguing ice climbing up and down some fearsome chunks of ice tens of metres high, jumping deep-blue bottomless crevasses and swearing at each other a lot.

'We should go this way,' I said bossily.

'No we shouldn't,' contradicted Simon quietly, standing above me in his purple Gore-Tex and black Ron Hills on top of yet another sharp ridge of crumbly ice. 'I can see the mountains the other side quite clearly from here.'

'It's what's between us and the side which counts,' interjected Douglas, savagely front-pointing up to join Simon.

Peter kept his counsel and just followed along behind. He was not enjoying walking in his ski-mountaineering boots.

Simon carried on in one direction, I explored in another, cursing, and the icefall echoed with our shouts. Finally, after two hours, we dropped away left-handed from the fierce, impossible ice formations of the icefall and reached the chaos of moraine on the north bank.

Annoyed at wasting so much time, Douglas and I set off at an angry pace up the Mittelaletsch Glacier. The endless rubble of moraine which rolls on steep slopes and thin greasy layer of snow over the ice was tiring, but child's play compared to its bigger brother we had just crossed. We reached the Mittelaletsch bivouac hut (3013m) rather later than I had planned, at nearly seven o'clock, leaving Simon and Peter miles behind long out of sight.

This is a very pleasant little bivvy hut, well designed, octagonal and fairly new. There are bunk places for nineteen, which would be bedlam, but fortunately we found only a German couple in residence, a father aged about sixty years and his daughter. They let us use a fire they had going outside, which produced a wonderful smell of sweet burning wood, I fetched water from a stream running out of the melt-snow on rocks near by, and Douglas and I soon had hot water. We settled down in the warm evening light to cook brews and prepare our supper. We made our usual all-in-the-pot concoction of beef granules, veg soup, mashed potato, dried peas (which are like bullets, they take forever to soften and use far too much Epigas fuel), nuts and raisins and of course 'Biscuits Brown' to taste. We made this awful mixture really quite palatable (believe it or not) by adding a packet of bouillabaisse sauce, a tin of salmon and, naturally, curry powder. The SAS always take curry powder to stir in to every meal in the bush. It can disguise the nastiest ingredients.

Sitting in the last of the sun looking down the valley, Douglas and I had nearly finished our supper before the other two arrived. Peter's ski-mountaineering boots were giving him bad blisters and the extra weight of his skis did not help. Carrying a heavy rucksack is not easy until you build up the necessary back muscles, probably the real physical reason for most people failing SAS selection, and it hurts, but Peter never complained.

Skiing up the glacier, they had reached the bottom of the final gulley leading up to the hut when Peter had fallen on a steep slope and nearly slid into a big crevasse. Irritated by the snow which was very soft in the late afternoon, they had taken their skis off and climbed the rocks on the right which appeared to offer a direct route to the hut. This was a mistake. The best way to the hut is to carry on up the gulley on the snow to the same altitude as the hut and then sweep back right-handed on the hut across the rocks.

We all woke at 3 a.m., and I rolled out of bed for a pee outside. The conditions were perfect, though not as cold as I had hoped. A full moon was slowly going down over the dark bulk of the long South Ridge of the Aletschhorn and the starry sky was crystal clear. Delighted, I nipped back in to tell the others and put on the hot water.

'I can't go,' said Douglas from the shadows on his bunk.

'What?'

'Look,' he said and showed us his leg. He had an angry red swelling on the front of his right shinbone. Even in torchlight it looked tender and painful.

'It must be something to do with when I was kicked playing football,' he said with commendable phlegm. I would have been speechless with rage at coming so far, after a real sweaty effort the day before, only to find I could not put on my boot to complete the summit. 'It must have flared up after the front-pointing we did on the glacier.'

'Agony, eh?' said Simon, kneeling down and gently feeling the bruise.

Douglas winced. I realized he had been awake most of the night and had plenty of time to work over his predicament. After being on every climb so far, he had to pull out.

The cause of this injury was a most bizarre football match which Dave Moore had set up between us, the British, and a motley collection of students from the Brig International College of Hotel Administration, one of the better Swiss hotel catering and management training centres. Dave, Mike, Tim, and the others had played several games of seven-a-side (or thereabouts) with the students and they decided to have a full blown match. They booked the Naters municipal football pitch, borrowed a proper strip and battle was joined on a rainy afternoon, weeks before, in June.

It was the definition of Babel. The students' team comprised a Spaniard, two Italians, a Frenchman, a German, a Japanese, a Turk, two Koreans, and an Israeli playing happily with a Palestinian who was very fat but moved with surprising speed. The only common language was English, but in mist, mud and rain play was fierce and the air rang with a range of cosmopolitan expletives which would have delighted Professor Henry Higgins. I watched from the touchline under an umbrella with Nikki, who was official team physiotherapist and in charge of the oranges at half-time.

The game was declared a draw in the end, as nobody could remember how many goals had been scored on each side, and everyone celebrated in the bars in Brig later that evening. However, the damage had been done. Douglas's injury festered until front-pointing across the Aletsch Glacier, his shin banging the front of his plastic boots. Simon and I were thankful we had refused to play – neither of us could remember playing football without coming

All the tschapps and Nikki Hatrick on our gentian blue transport outside our building in Brig. L to r: Daryl 'George' Roper, 'Gonzo' Martin, Charles Messervy-Whiting, Graham Messervy-Whiting, Simon Whittaker, Nigel Taylor, Tom Boyle, Peter Copeland, Dave Moore, Mark 'Death' Cowell, Mark Bles, Nikki Hatrick, Douglas Glen, Benjie Merton, Tim Spicer. (Mike Nutter is absent.) *Photo: Peter Copeland*

The only time we were all together. Simon, Douglas, Mark, Peter, Gary, on the summit of the Weissmies with the Mischabel chain in the background. I wonder if the Duke's bottle of champagne is still up there? *Photo: Simon Whittaker*

Gary setting out from the Breithorn pass, determined to catch up Douglas who was, as usual, racing ahead en route to Pollux (centre foreground), Castor on the right, and the twin humps of Liskamm towering above in the distance. *Photo: Mark Bles*

Glacier travel when you run out of snow: massive chunks of ice, filthy moraine, high ridges and deep blue holes. Douglas and Mark try abseiling to find a way through an icefall on the Fieschgletscher after climbing the Finsteraarhorn. *Photo: Simon Whittaker*

The summit of Castor in thick mist. Yes, we knew it was down, but on skis, how? *Photo: Mark Bles*

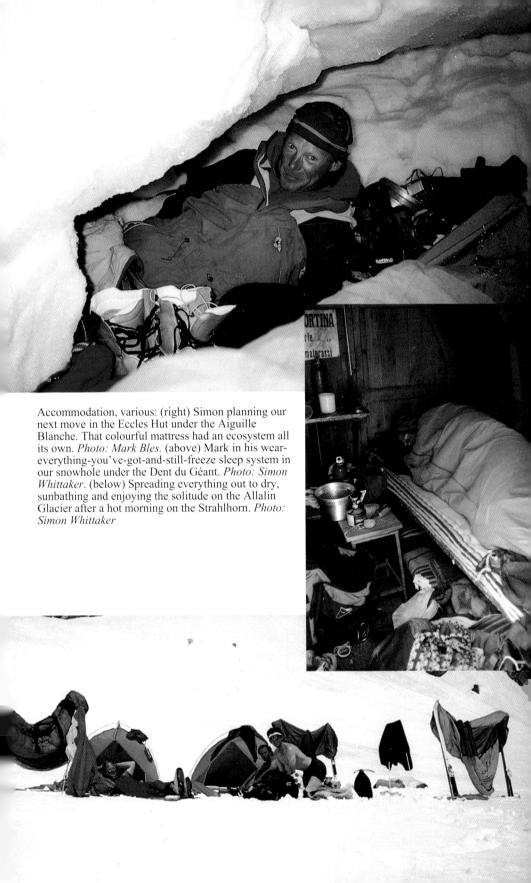

Accommodation, various: (right) Simon planning our next move in the Eccles Hut under the Aiguille Blanche. That colourful mattress had an ecosystem all its own. *Photo: Mark Bles.* (above) Mark in his wear-everything-you've-got-and-still-freeze sleep system in our snowhole under the Dent du Géant. *Photo: Simon Whittaker.* (below) Spreading everything out to dry, sunbathing and enjoying the solitude on the Allalin Glacier after a hot morning on the Strahlhorn. *Photo: Simon Whittaker*

Mark and Douglas (behind) on the summit ridge of the Finsteraarhorn. The ski descent (tracks bottom left) was one of the best. *Photo: Simon Whittaker*

Simon and Gary on the long ridge to Nordend. The lack of cornices was unusual. *Photo: Mark Bles*

Peter, followed by Mark, on the West Ridge of the Dent d'Hérens with black storm clouds threatening above right. *Photo: Simon Whittaker*

The Täschhorn-Dom ridge traverse, three kilometres all above 4000 metres. You can't see where Peter fell through the cornice but you can just see our tracks and we were the first of the season. *Photo: Mark Bles*

Author, leg in crevasse, having moments earlier warned HRH the Duke of Kent that with soft late morning snow he should watch out for hidden crevasses. Roger Mathieu our Swiss guide, crisply uniformed for the occasion, looked in control. *Photo: Household Division*

A memorable morning on the summit of the Zinalrothorn, Mark on a pinnacle in the foreground, with beyond the white dome of the Breithorn, far left, the Matterhorn, centre, the Obergabelhorn and the Dent d'Hérens. *Photo: Simon Whittaker*

Peter traversing dodgy snow on the last section to the Canzio Hut, with Mark behind him on the rocks and the Aiguille du Midi beyond. *Photo: Simon Whittaker*

Mark on the summit of the Grand Combin, a magic and remote massif. *Photo: Simon Whittaker*

Party time on the summit of Mont Blanc. On a nice day like this you will see 200-300 people of all ages and experience, some fit, most not. Anyone can do it! *Photo: Peter Copeland*

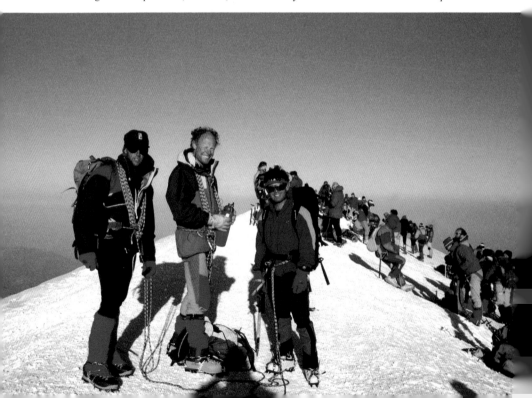

away injured – and Peter had been rock climbing in Chamonix with Russell Brice.

Simon gave Douglas painkillers from a comprehensive First Aid pack he always carried. We left him to walk slowly downhill when it got light and set off ourselves for the summit.

The guide book was not very clear but the route goes north up a quite steep slope behind the hut, left through a dip under the rocks of Point 3482 metres and then traverses upwards to the obvious Aletschjoch (3629m). The snow was hard enough for harscheisen but deeply ridged from melting in the sun, like the Gran Paradiso, and I had to concentrate to make sure I placed the ski with its harscheisen right on the top of a ridge at each step or the ski slipped away beneath me. These melt-ridges smoothed out the further up I went, fortunately, as the snow slopes towards the Aletschjoch become really quite steep.

The view from the Aletschjoch at dawn on a fine clear day must be one of the finest in Switzerland. In the centre of one of the remotest parts of Europe, we had fantastic views across the Bernese Oberland. Not a cloud in sight, the eastern sky swelled with orange and pink translucence, silhouetting the sail-like Finsteraarhorn and tinting the snowy peaks of the Gross-Grünhorn, the Jungfrau, and the mountains all round. Directly below the ridge, the Grosser Aletschfirn Glacier was just visible in deep blue shadow 600 metres down and Konkordia a vast dark cauldron further off. I experienced a sensation of great privilege and lightness of spirit looking round these mountains. Lots of people do climb here, but there are still so many who could but do not, and they have no idea what they are missing. Of all the places and excitements I have experienced all over the world, none quite matches the euphoria of being high among the mountains on such a morning.

I took off my skis, fitted crampons, sat on my rucksack and absorbed the atmosphere. When Simon and Peter joined me, we continued along the narrow North-East Ridge to the broad summit slopes. The snow to Point 4086 metres is fairly steep, forty degrees, and then there is a flat easy section before the final summit ridge which is narrow and quite exposed. We reached the summit, which is big enough for tennis, in just over three hours (guide time four and a half hours) and felt strong enough to fly.

On the way down, we passed the two Germans slogging up the

steep slope to Point 4086 metres. They were making very heavy weather of this indeed and I did not envy them. In just a short hour since dawn, the snow had begun to soften appreciably and was balling badly on my crampons. The Germans were moving terribly slowly and must have found the downward journey awful. We passed two more climbers at the top of the Hasler Rib, one a very pretty girl, who said they were going for the summit. They were welcome. We thought the North-East Ridge was dodgy enough when we went down, not at all consolidated under the surface layer, let alone a couple of hours later.

I put on my skis again at the Aletschjoch, left Simon and Peter to walk down, and had a wonderful ski run back to the bivvy hut. Douglas had already left but I shaded my eyes to look down the valley and thought I could see movement far away on the snow and rock of the Mittelaletsch Glacier. I re-packed my rucksack and skied easily down the increasingly soft snow gulley beneath the hut, shooting the narrow snow bridge over the bergschrund which had nearly claimed Peter the day before, onto the broad expanse of the glacier. Keeping a wary eye for crevasses hidden under the soggy thin snow layer, I kept an airy pace all the way until the snow gave out at about 2500 metres.

Skis strapped to my sack, I walked fast and at the top of the next ice fall, far down, I could just make out a tiny figure. I hurried on and caught him on the edge of the Aletsch Glacier, moving painfully slowly on the broken rocks. I whistled a hundred metres away and he stopped, thankfully dropping his Bergen on the ice for a rest.

Together we walked more slowly across the Aletsch Glacier and this time we worked out the trick of how to see where we were inside the crevasses. You look at the mountain peaks.

The day before, from the southern bank under the Eggishorn, we should have aimed for the Rothorn first, crossing the first central moraine before turning half-right to aim for the Olmenhorn. Then we should have curved left, away from the icefall, and aimed finally for the open valley of the Mittelaletsch Glacier.

From the northern bank, Douglas and I got it right. Douglas was in a lot of pain and had spent hours walking slowly downhill looking at the glacier ahead and deciding how to cross it with the minimum trouble. We started at the southernmost point under the Olmenhorn South-East Shoulder and aimed first for the Eggishorn.

Once in the glacier, we came up against the chaos of the icefall and turned half-right, up and down the ice, across blue streams, crevasses and narrow ice bridges. We aimed for the Bettmerhorn till we passed the second central moraine and nearly reached the other side when we veered off left again to the side of the glacier. This time, we crossed in only an hour, in spite of Douglas's injury, less than half the time we spent on the way over.

The 400-metre climb from the ice to the Bettmerhorn lift station was ghastly. First we plodded up scree, rocks and tufts of grass to the path by Roti Chumma and then turned right for the monotonous rising traverse to the lift. We had agreed to meet Simon and Peter in the restaurant there but in retrospect I would have preferred to walk out via the Mäjela valley and Fieschertal, where there is very little height gain to face. We had a splendid view of the Aletschhorn all the way up this exhausting path, which cheered me if not Douglas, but I was bushed when we reached the restaurant about one o'clock. After a beer I fell fast asleep, propped up on the floor against the sloping view window, and began to snore loudly.

A waiter came along.

'*Was ist das Höllenlärm?*' he asked looking round, unable to see me under the table.

'I'd like another beer,' said Douglas firmly, giving me a kick. I stopped snoring.

Puzzled, the waiter went off. I started whistling between my teeth.

'I told him you were very old and needed your tonsils out,' said Douglas when I woke up.

'Thanks, Douglas.' Bastard probably did too.

Simon turned up two hours later on his own. Peter's blisters were terrible and he was moving very slowly somewhere far behind. Simon had crossed the glacier with him and then left him at Roti Chumma at the bottom of the long path up the side of the Bettmerhorn. We waited till 4.45 p.m. then took the last lift down without him.

He finally telephoned the office in Brig at 8 p.m., when I was bathed, fed and beginning to worry about him. He had walked down from the Bettmerhorn but got the lift down to the main road. Charlie drove out to pick him up.

If Peter developed deep loathing for ski-mountaineering boots and skis in general on the Aletschhorn, the expedition was a watershed for all of us. This was the last time we used skis. We all carried those heavy Swiss Army mountaineering skis thirty-two kilometres all the way there and back, but only I used them. There was simply not enough snow any more. After this, we were on our feet, in Koflachs.

But the mountain struck at Douglas the hardest. That same evening, he went to the hospital opposite our building (home of the 'Burgermeister of Brig'). A Swiss doctor lanced the swelling, drew off large quantities of pus and announced he must rest for at least a week; there was a haematoma which had gone septic and blown up during the long hike over the glacier and rocky moraine. He was put on a course of antibiotics. Climbing was out.

This was not welcome news when the weather pattern appeared settled at last. We still had plenty of mountains to climb, Douglas and I were climbing partners, he had climbed them all until then, and I wanted him to climb the remainder. I decided to wait for a few days to see if his leg improved and deferred the decision to go on climbing without him for three days till his next appointment with the doctor.

In the meantime, Simon and Peter went off to the Gran Paradiso. They took Simon's girlfriend Rebecca and another friend from Cardiff called Jed in our old gentian-blue Land-Rover. British Army regulations are famed the world over, so it will come as no surprise to learn that although this splendid old military vehicle was 'civilianised' for use in Switzerland, a neutral country, although it carried civilian registration plates and although it was insured as a civilian vehicle, no civilians were allowed to travel in it. British Army logic. I turned a blind, half-civilian eye to the rule and let them go. I had complete faith in Peter and Simon but prayed no lunatic Italian with dreams of competing in the Mille Miglia would smash into them on some narrow mountain road.

'If there's an accident,' I told Peter, 'just drag Rebecca and Jed onto the verge and say you've never seen them before.'

Jed was a genial, well-rounded personality but I doubt Peter mentioned this to Rebecca.

On Wednesday morning, after three brilliantly sunny days, when I was busy typing in our office, Douglas came back from the hospital and said, 'Bad news. They want to operate.'

His leg was still badly swollen and the Swiss doctor thought there was a real danger of further infection of the bone, or even gangrene. Before the invention of penicillin when these mountains were first climbed, Douglas would have lost his leg, if not his life. The doctor wanted to slice him open, scrub the wound clean and keep him in hospital for a week. At once, I agreed he should go back to the Woolwich in England. Swiss hospitals are not exactly cheap and he hardly wanted to be loitering about sick in Brig watching us getting on with the climbing.

Jeremy Orwin, Tim's Adjutant in Windsor, sparked quickly, arranged for a flight back to England, and Douglas was rapidly admitted to the Queen Elizabeth Military Hospital in Woolwich. This sudden retreat from the mountains and the boredom of lying in bed all day after so much activity must have been galling enough, but all he could see from his bed in Ward 10 was a large picture on the opposite wall – of the Jungfraujoch train under the Mönch and the Eiger! And the damn thing was screwed to the wall.

Douglas was due to be away for a minimum of two weeks, which was too long to wait. We had to start again. The weather and snow conditions were perfect. I wanted to join Simon and Peter in Italy and tackle the Dent d'Hérens. Trouble was, when Peter tried to phone from the little village of Pont under the Gran Paradiso, having climbed the mountain, the Italian telephone system cut him off every time. Unaware of my plans, Simon went to Milan with Rebecca by train, and Peter drove the old blue Land-Rover back to Brig that evening in time for supper, on his own. Mike Nutter saw him arrive as he went out into the car park to chat up the girl who always passed the building on her way home from work as we sat down to eat.

I was frustrated. My support team was hale and hearty (disgustingly so) with a surfeit of good food and beer (especially so) but my climbing team seemed to have fallen apart, scattered to the winds, in sickness or in health. And we still had a long way to go.

12

WORST JULY WEATHER
FOR DECADES

And bending down beside the glowing bars
Murmur a little sadly, how love fled,
And paced upon the mountains overhead,
And hid his face amid a crown of stars.
                                        W.B. Yeats

The games were over, the skis left standing in their racks in the corridor outside our rooms and the pressure to climb all the mountains
racked up a notch or two in various ways.

First, I wanted to take advantage of the good weather and climb the
Dent d'Hérens with Peter, on our own as Simon was still away. Peter
was keen, but as always he was the voice of quiet reason, offering up
the infuriatingly correct view that as Simon and I were by that time
the only two who had climbed all the mountains it did not make
much sense putting him out by one mountain. Especially as the Dent
d'Hérens needed a long walk in and out over two days, and Simon
might not be able to get back to the mountain another time. Peter
was right, so we kicked our heels for a couple of days and waited for
Simon to come back.

The day he came back, on Friday, 9 July, the weather broke in
a fearsome storm over all the Alps. Clouds, thunder, lightning and
heavy rain even upset the nightly routine of the Base Camp party
in Brig. Being good, determined Brits, they went out all the same
under garish yellow Thommen umbrellas but got drenched on the

way back, in particular Gonzo whom George photographed 'fast asleep' on one of the riverside benches normally used by lunatics from the hospital.

'It's a miracle he never fell into the river,' I said.

'Oh, he's done that before,' said Dave laughing and flip-flopped off into his kitchen.

Up on the big mountains, there was sixty centimetres of fresh snow. I called the Chamonix weather office to find the situation was the same on the Mont Blanc massif. The weather stayed foul for a week.

During this frustrating period, Douglas underwent surgery on his shinbone in Woolwich. They opened him up and discovered a ruptured vein which was busy going septic. They sewed off the vein and left the wound open for several days to dry out. When they were sure there was no further chance of infection, they zipped him up, put stitches in for ten days and advised several weeks 'excused boots'. Douglas was furious and I had lost my climbing partner.

So much fresh snow meant there was a serious danger of avalanches. The rule of thumb is that you should avoid climbing on avalanche-prone slopes for a minimum of two days, to allow the new snow to consolidate. Hardly a day after the storms a party of three Germans went up on the Italian side of Monte Rosa and were killed in an avalanche, paying the penalty maybe for being up there so soon after the new snow, grabbing a couple of days in the mountains at the weekend, and giving it a go rather than turning back 'just' because of the conditions. I wondered how many people die in the Alps at the weekend. They were not the first that year, and certainly not the last.

Finally the following Thursday, the high priests of Geneva and Chamonix forecast a good weekend, including *'une chaleur torride'*! Simon, Peter and I drove to Chamonix, to see Russell Brice and buy some gear we needed. There is so much seductive stuff in so many shops, all state of the art, ultra lightweight, magic-looking protection (titanium just sounds so good!), that you are advised to make special overdraft arrangements with your bank manager before entering the town precincts. We found nowhere in Switzerland remotely comparable, except one small shop in Sion which had sensible user-useful gear.

In Chamonix, I bought a pair of Koflachs. They were bright green, deliberately chosen to match my Dynafit ski-mountaineering boots, and to cock a snook at the bores who harp on about colour affecting the harmony of the mountains.

Haven't we had enough of this fundamentalist nonsense? What makes anyone think that humans wearing plus-fours, tweeds and last century leather gear are any less intrusive in the mountains? Humans are intrusive by definition, their very presence at altitude is unnatural, a pleasure only to the individual concerned. As for all that Victorian equipment, what makes tricouni nails more righteous than crampons?

I am thankful fashion and practical outdoor clothes design have joined forces to produce gear which is both efficient and good humoured, with an element of safety consciousness, a celebration of being human and enjoying it, so that we can get away from the old misery-guts (yet suspiciously arrogant) British attitudes of the past.

We also supplied ourselves with various delicacies in our endless search to make army granules taste of something. Emmental cheese, black olives, sardines (because they are calory-weight efficient) and good French bread. Then we quit the town as fast as possible. Chamonix was bulging with tourists, and we wanted to get on to Italy. We had a long walk in to the Dent d'Hérens according to the guide books.

The Mont Blanc Tunnel is dirty, claustrophobic, fume-filled and expensive (170 FFrs). We were pleased to reach Italy and breathe fresh air again. As before, the temperature was appreciably hotter on the south side of the mountains. Peter drove the old blue Land-Rover through Aosta, turned north towards the gleaming white bulk of the Grand Combin far away on the horizon and streaming with clouds, and turned left off the main Grand St-Bernard road up the Valpelline valley.

The road down this long valley is bendy and narrow and I noticed Peter giving the oncoming traffic very little room. Several times on tight hairpin bends, large construction vehicles swept past us so close I could read the headlines on the driver's folded newspaper hat (remember our old Rover was right-hand drive!).

'Could give these chaps a fraction more room,' I said to Peter as casually as I could, half out of my seat.

'Righto!' said Peter happily, peering through the windscreen. Simon, in the back, wisely pretended to sleep.

The tarmac road runs out at the dam of the reservoir, the Lago di Place Moulin. There are no signs but we had no intention of walking all along the lakeside if we could help it. Peter drove up a short hill, past a *buvette* where the woman waved at us cheerfully, and then followed a very narrow track towards the edge of the steep ground bordering the lake on our right. Keen to avoid going near the edge, Peter nearly overturned the Land-Rover up a bank on the left.

'Probably a good thing to use four-wheel drive,' I suggested, hoping I had not offended him by stating the obvious. Peter looked carefully at the knobs on the floor between us and experimentally moved them about. Simon had woken up. After looking at the drop over the edge into the lake, he was now taking a keen interest in what was happening in the front.

'Driven these things off-road much before, Pete, old chap?' I enquired.

'Never,' said Peter candidly. He yanked the yellow knob backwards.

'Mind if I take the wheel?'

'Not at all.'

The route along the lake is gripping. The track is rough and extremely narrow. On one side right at the edge of the track, a very steep bank drops straight to the water below. On the other, a sheer rock face runs the whole length of the lake and actually overhangs the track in places. There are no passing places. At times I had to go backwards and forwards to ease the Land-Rover round a tight corner, with Simon and Peter outside guiding my offside wheels to the edge. I must admit scratching the side once or twice on the rock wall on my left. Creeping along this four-kilometre track from the dam to Prarayer took an hour, much the same as by foot! Thank goodness we never met a vehicle coming the other way.

'*C'est défendu*,' said an old man wagging his finger at us as we parked against the broken-down wall of an old farm building in Prarayer. '*Il faut avoir un carnet d'autorité de la police pour conduire jusqu'ici.*'

'*Je sais, m'sieur, mais il n'y a aucune possibilité de retourner maintenant*,' I assured him. I was not much looking forward to the return journey anyway, and certainly not before climbing the Dent d'Hérens.

He shrugged, Italian style, and left us. No one cares much at all for authority in Italy. Bureaucracy is tolerated because all other so-called civilised countries have it, and the EC pays the Italians vast amounts to keep it going, but in practice they ignore it. I wished our own dear Ministry of Defence could take a lesson or two off the Italians.

We changed, hid the Land-Rover key under a stone and set off. The guide books give four hours from Prarayer to the Aosta bivouac hut and describes the route as complicated. We took an easy two and a half hours, particularly enjoying the first part through the pine and larch woods alongside the noisy Torrent Buthier, and there are no route-finding troubles. Just be careful not to cross the first enticing wooden footbridge over the river. Instead turn to the left and follow the path up through the trees. The track is quite well marked until the valley broadens out into a maze of moraine. Then keep relatively close to the river and follow the paint marks on stones, or cairns, and you end up a gentle snow gulley on the left side of the Tsa de Tsan Glacier, at about 2700 metres, before making a curving traverse across the ice above the lower icefall to the last short rise of moraine beside the hut.

Leading, I topped this rise and was confronted by a roughly painted sign, which announced in French, 'No Entry! Work in Progress since September 1991!'

Curious, we walked round the corner and burst out laughing. The Aosta bivouac hut looked as if it had been blown up by terrorists. The old hut was gone and a half-built new hut stood on the side of the mountain in the middle of a derelict building site, surrounded by planks, blobs of concrete, cement bags, rusted machinery, and bits of wind-blown scaffolding hanging precariously by the odd nail. Tools – nails, a lump-hammer, long-handled shovels, and a pick – lay abandoned everywhere. On one side, there were two very tatty caravans and an old hut which looked like an outsized packing case. The packing case showed signs of being occupied by three people so we made ourselves at home in one of the workmen's caravans.

The caravan was minging. However, there is always an upside to most things in my experience. As we tidied up, we uncovered cooking herbs and spices, oregano and red cayenne pepper (which we used to improve the jolly old granules) and best of all some rosé wine in cartons. I know, the moralists will say we shouldn't have drunk it, but we did tidy their place up and the wine was well past its run-out date.

Outside, the weather was drizzly, warm, and the snow soft. Not at all what we needed for the following day. Three Swiss geologists came down the glacier from the Tiefmattenjoch Col (3565m) where they had been chipping bits of rock off the West Ridge of the Dent d'Hérens, exactly where we wanted to go. They dumped their sodden clothes back inside their packing-case hut and morosely reported soft gungy snow all the way. Still hopeful, we told them about the '*chaleur torride*' promised by the Chamonix weather gurus.

The blankets and pillows we found in the caravan were utterly filthy. My pillow was dark with hair grease and when I opened a blanket to shake it out full size, a cloud of flaky whiteness filled the air. God alone knows what the Italian workmen have been up to in these beds! We were thankful for our own sleeping bags and the oblivion of several mugfuls of rotten rosé, on which we slept soundly. It was just as well.

We rolled out of these pits at 3.30 a.m. and left half an hour later in the dark. We dropped under the shoulder of rock that runs down from the Tête de Valpelline beside the hut and began a rather tiring sharp scramble up moraine to the first plateau of snow on the western branch of the Grandes Murailles Glacier.

Grey cirrus hid the stars in an empty black sky and Rod Stewart played softly in my ear, 'I don't want to talk about it, how you broke my heart.'

We all thought the guide book a little vague about where to climb onto the West Ridge. Just for the record, we found a way onto it 800 metres past Point 3337 metres, beyond the Tiefmattenjoch and a bulging high point, at a place where the ridge reaches another low point, like a col. A prominent gendarme rises like a huge menhir directly from the bergschrund of the glacier to a point high over the ridge. On the right of this is a narrow, steep, mixed couloir which we scrambled up solo as the snow was quite well frozen. Half-way up, we noted a bolt set in the smooth rock slab on the left, useful for abseiling when the snow is soft later in the day and the couloir becomes a greased tube.

So far, we had made good time, arriving on the West Ridge (AD-, II and III+) at six o'clock in daylight, ready for the rock climb. However, with three of us on a rope our paced slowed dramatically.

Nor did the promised '*chaleur torride*' materialise. In fact, the weather deteriorated. An icy west wind blew fronts of rain, sleet and snow over us continually, temporarily blotting out the sky as the bitter clouds rushed past us along the huge frontier mountains.

The ridge is not hard but has some exposed sections at times, across airy gaps above vertical cliffs and the glacier far below, and would have been much more enjoyable in better conditions. Recent heavy snowfall filled every crevice and the snow had still not consolidated properly because there had not been enough sun. Instead of climbing the grade III+ up a gendarme, Simon took us on a thoroughly alarming flanking route across rotten snow and slippery rocks on the northern side over the long drop to the impressive crevasses of the Tiefmatten Glacier. Of course a front came through as we were negotiating this, thrashing us with a quick shower of sleet and snow.

The snow slopes between the end of the rocky West Ridge and the topmost mixed summit slopes were easy but the snow was heavy. I was pleased I had bought Charlet Moser crampons with the Koflachs. On our last ski outings in the warmer weather my Grivel 2Fs balled up very easily. The boot sits on the edge of a strip of metal which is bent round to form the 2F crampon and the spikes simply point down in the plane of the strip of metal. This design is all right in winter but forms a 'box' which holds gungy snow rather too well. Descending from the Aletschhorn, I had found it very irritating having to tap my boots every other pace to knock off wads of snow. However, the metal strip of the Charlet Moser 'Black Ice' crampons lies flat against the sole of the boot and the spikes are bent down from it, so the snow has nowhere to 'box' inside so easily.

The sun was riding bleakly through clouds racing across the summit above us. I looked up at the steep triangle of mixed climbing to the final ridge. A few rocks poked out of what appeared to be rotten snow.

'I don't like the look of that too much,' I muttered.

Simon shrugged, optimistically smearing himself with suncream, and then led up the slope, for which I was extremely grateful. The conditions were exactly as I had guessed. There was too much loose snow and the rocks we could see slanted down, offering no placement for slings, and precious few cracks for any other protection. In fact, there was nothing till quite near the top when I found a slender crack in which I wedged my ice axe. There was one other placement half a pitch further up, on which meagre belay we all depended. The snow was loose and slippy as grease. We eased over rocks we could not see or delicately pushed our front-points through this same hopeless white mix onto a thin glazing of ice over rocks below. The unusual snowfall late in the year when the temperatures had been warm meant the ice was detached from the rocks underneath, melted off them, so there was often that awful hollow sound as the crampon hit the ice. It did not pay to kick too hard or the ice shattered.

The slope is not particularly steep, but there was an increasingly long drop to the crevasses of the west flank far below, and we were buffeted all the time by winds, cold snow or rain. Streamers of cloud moved fast across the mountains in black ranks from the west and we could see the gusting snow flurries racing up the slopes towards us, turning our heads away as they hit us.

I was looking forward to the 'fine' rock advertised in the guide book on the summit ridge, but we found it covered with more unconsolidated snow. We reached the top about midday in cloud. We stripped off in freezing winds huddled behind a slab to change into all our warm gear, and turned straight down. I had long before given up the idea of getting back to Brig that evening in time to meet my family, who were flying out that day for another week to stay in a chalet in Greich. First, get off the mountain.

We used the few cracks I had found on the way up as belay points and followed each other through, one after the other on the rope, Simon and I taking it in turns to lead and set up a belay for the other two. Descending the triangle this way took an unnerving three hours, slow but safe, and we front-pointed all the way down to the cleaner snow slopes below the triangle.

We stopped for a drink and a bite of bread and sausage, and started talking more freely again. We considered the options. We could either go down the rocky West Ridge again, or look for the normal route up the glacier. The trouble was finding the right place to leave the West Ridge to descend by the normal route on the south-west flank. By this time the snow was even less encouraging than it had been all day. I did not like the idea of having to find a way down to the glacier far below on this steep flank, 'scrambling', as the guide book describes it, in soft unconsolidated snow like we had experienced on the triangle. By this time, the steep snow slopes on the north side of the Tiefmattenjoch were streaked with avalanches, all fresh that day, and we did not want to start the same thing on the south-west flank route off the Dent d'Hérens itself, with us part of the slide. Besides, once committed there would be no turning back, whereas we knew the rock ridge. We would be slow but we could not get lost, a serious problem on the wide open south-west flank, and we knew we could make it safely back.

This is a quick summary of the thinking behind this decision, but we had been assessing all the factors all through the climb hour after hour, and I discovered an interesting new sensation. The seriousness of our position at different moments, as I perceived it, produced a feeling of detachment. My panic over a particular moye which I thought was dangerous had to be brushed aside. My mind needed to be free to cope with the wider implications of what we were doing, where we were and where we wanted to go. This produced some detachment, but that was not the end of it because it was then necessary to refocus very carefully on the actual physical actions necessary to complete the move. This refocusing seemed to strengthen the feeling of detachment, producing a circle of mental and physical effort, constantly renewed each time, like hardening steel with fire and water.

We descended the West Ridge. We were faster but still not quick with three on the rope. We abseiled to avoid the exposed loose traverse Simon had led on the way up. We were rained on, snowed on, hailed on, and blown constantly by high winds, and hardly saw the sun at all. At least, the weather pundits in Geneva and Chamonix had the good manners to admit later that their forecast had been quite wrong for the weekend. By way of justification, they added that the Alps were experiencing the worst July weather for decades. I was pleased I had chosen winter Koflachs with extra insulation.

We recovered our sense of humour on the glacier, sliding on our bums down the steeper snow slopes, and reached the Aosta bivvy demolition site at a quarter to nine, just as it got dark. We were tired. My big toes ached from front-pointing in my new Koflachs. I had been lucky and not suffered any blisters so far but a seventeen-hour-day is probably not the best way to wear in a new pair of boots, especially not plastic ones.

We had a brew, re-packed our kit and set out again to walk back to our Land-Rover at Prarayer. In the darkness, unable to see the snow, I was reminded of Dhofar. There was a war there in the seventies, quite secret really, as no one knew the SAS were involved till after it was all over, and the only way to approach the enemy was by long night marches up dry wadis. The harsh glacial moraine was similar to the rocks of the desert, the sharp silhouette of the mountains above us could have been bare rock rather than ice, the silence between Peter and me as we walked one in front of the other could have been for tactical reasons rather than because we were both too tired to speak, but the smell of the air was the most powerful memory. Sheltered from the bitter wind on the summit, the air had baked all day in the bottom of the wide valley, warming the rocks which exuded a delicate sweet aroma exactly the same as the rocks warmed by the desert sun. From time to time, the roar of the river in the darkness on our left, a sound not heard in Dhofar's wadis for millennia, brought me back to Switzerland.

Simon has infra-red eyes. He strode off leaving Peter and me stumbling about in the dark using head-torches. We took two hours to walk down and we found him waiting for us at Prarayer, a dark shadow sitting silently on a fence by the farm buildings.

'Time for a tincture,' I announced. Sweating on a night march is being both cool and hot at the same time. Peter and I were gasping.

'I think that place is open,' Simon said, pointing at the lighted windows in a building behind, which I had been staring at hopefully for the last mile.

The hostel was open. Although it was half past eleven at night, the staff were only just clearing up and served us cold beer. We hoovered down a couple of cans while I tried to telephone our base in Brig. I fondly imagined they would be worried about us, but needless to say on a Friday night the bastards were all out on the town. More irritating, I was unable to find out if Rebecca and the children had arrived and to let her know we were all right.

We were thankful to have our transport at Prarayer. We had been on our feet for nineteen hours and the idea of walking any further at that time of night was out of the question. The drive back along the reservoir was not easy in the dark and I scraped the old blue Land-Rover again.

Simon took over the driving the other side of the Grand St Bernard Tunnel and we reached our base camp building in Brig at 3.30 a.m. We had been on the go for twenty-four hours. Simon and Peter went straight to bed, but I wanted to see my family, so I sadistically woke Dave, who was comatose in bed, and a blurred interrogation revealed they had gone up to the tiny mountain hamlet of Greich on the last lift.

I took the Land-Rover and flung Simon's mountain bike in the back. After a much-needed shower, shave and change of clothes, I drove up the twisting tarmac road and I cycled under the fir trees in the darkness, past the silent black wooden chalets, like a veteran of the Second World War returning home to his family.

Madeleine was fast asleep next to her mother, just three and a half, her mouth a soft 'O' as she breathed, and she hardly woke when I carried her upstairs to Claudia, who opened her eyes and then went straight back to sleep. Far from being surprised to see me arrive in the middle of the night, they simply accepted that Daddy was back, in the straightforward way children absorb facts. There is something very satisfying and comforting in that. There are no questions, worries, reflections or histrionics. At that moment, after the Dent d'Hérens, I was glad to be alive, glad to be with my family, glad to be home.

14

ONE OF THE FINEST
EXPEDITIONS IN THE ALPS

Man should devote himself to exhausting possibilities of the
finite.

Pindar, 522–442 BC

I am not superstitious (well, no more than anyone else) but carrying
my PC3000 computer around the huts on the mountains, I deliberately missed out Chapter 13, bearing in mind all the mountains we
had yet to climb, and it would be illogical to put it back in. Since life's
cause is not given up till the end, nor is it lost or ineffective till death
(if then) the principle still stands good.

If not superstition, clairvoyance is part of this story. When we
came back from the Dent d'Hérens we could not have imagined
that the weather would be so bad that we would not be climbing
for ten days in the middle of an Alpine summer. I would have gone
home had I known. Maybe I should have gone home. But I was not
clairvoyant.

'Where are you going?' said a buxom dark-haired woman at the
Dom Hut next time we went out, on spec because the forecast was
still bad but we were desperately bored and went anyway.

Mike Nutter and George Roper had volunteered, typically, to
drive Simon, Peter and me in the VW and drop us at a small bridge
on a track through the pine trees just above Randa village.

'"You know how it is, Perkins, in a game of football when ten
men often play better than eleven?"' I rambled on parrot-style with

what seemed to me an appropriate skit from *Beyond the Fringe* as we changed into Koflachs and loaded our rucksacks by the track.

'"Yes, sir!"

'"Well, Perkins. We're asking you to be that one man."'

For some reason best known to himself, Peter was still laughing quietly to himself when we reached the Dom Hut after a sharp three-hour climb out of the thin clouds hanging round the valley. I think the delicate balance of his mind was still wobbling from a heavy night in the Lötschberg disco till 4 a.m.

'There's an awful lot of "up" in these mountains,' complained Simon, who had been in the disco too. The path up to the Dom Hut gives striking views of the Weisshorn and Bishorn but is certainly abrupt. I told the buxom hut-warden, 'We're going to do the Nadelgrat.'

She hefted our rucksacks and whistled, 'You camping?'

We nodded. She told us where we would find a suitable site further up the Festi Glacier.

She told us about the snow conditions. Although the weather had been bad and was forecast bad, people were on the Dom that day and the snow conditions were fine, which was good news.

She asked what route we were going to do and whether we would be coming back to the Dom Hut.

'We plan to traverse from the Dürrenhorn to the Nadelhorn,' I said. 'And if the weather holds to continue over the Dom and Täschhorn. We'll descend via the Täsch Hut.'

'D'you have friends in the valley?' she wanted to know. If we were not going to pass by the Dom Hut again on the way down, she wanted to be sure someone would give the alarm if we did not turn up. I explained about our backup and radio and she smiled.

What a refreshing change! All her questions were specifically asked with safety in mind, because she was a hut-warden, but she showed a genuine interest in our climbing plans.

'The Britannia Hut warden should come up here for a lesson,' said Simon as we sat out in the sun enjoying the view of the Matterhorn and tucking away vegetable soup with an enormous brown sausage lurking in its depths.

We walked for another hour up a steep path on a ridge of moraine, cut across left onto the glacier and plodded up the snowfields to 3400 metres. We found a flat rocky outcrop near a stream which the lady hut-warden had mentioned. She knew the running water would save our Epigas instead of melting snow. We emptied our rucksacks all over the rocks and relaxed in the sun with a brew to enjoy the views.

I looked at all our kit scattered about and remarked to Peter, 'You're going to find it awfully hard to go back to the Army.' One of the delights of climbing is being free to spread your stuff, the antithesis of precious military tactics, being neat and 'ready to move' all the time in case the 'enemy' creeps up on you by surprise! Here, our only 'enemy' was a single chough floating and hopping round our campsite with a beady eye on our food.

Without Douglas, I cooked supper for myself. Peter cooked for Simon who had pulled a muscle in his back walking up the last steep, slippery snow slope. He stiffened up badly after a sleep in the sun. We did not talk about it much, but we both knew that he risked being unable to climb again if the injury was severe. All he said was, 'Bloody Murphy's Law to hurt myself like this when Nikki's just gone home.'

Snug in our bivvy bags under a roof of stars and white mountain peaks, we were late to start the following morning. A couple of groups had passed below our outcrop before we had packed up. Simon's back was still awkward but thankfully not as bad as he feared. He said the mere idea of having to walk all the way down to Randa again having achieved nothing was the best tonic.

The snow was still deep enough on the Festi Glacier, and crisp, so we made easy progress to a point below the Festijoch where you have to scramble up the rock wall on the left. The mud, patches of snow and loose rock were frozen in the early morning and easy in crampons. There is a sort of path, but coming down later in the day is slippy and subject to rockfall. From the ridge, we clambered down better rock guarding the snowy col, which did not seem hard, but I noticed a small memorial bolted into the rock to remind me that danger on big mountains is never far behind the thin safety curtain of a few careful decisions. And luck.

The other groups continued up the North-West Ridge to the Dom, but we dropped away left, down onto the Hohberg Glacier which we crossed on smooth curving snow slopes to the north side. We walked below the first icefall but shied away from losing any more height. We crossed the bergschrund onto the West Spur of the Hohberghorn at about 3620 metres. The slope above us looked loose and was (a good place to wear helmets), but it was not difficult. We removed our crampons and I led an easy route up the flank to the ridge.

Aware we were off the guide-book route, we worked our way up the ridge, then across a steep snow couloir (crampons on again). From here, I chose an obvious fault line in the rock marked by snow lying on the ledge rising at what seemed like a reasonable angle from the couloir to the ridge on our left. Beyond, I hoped we would find the small glacier between the Dürrenhorn and the Hohberghorn.

The fault line began along a ledge which narrowed (crampons off again), then the rock bulged into my chest, obscuring everything the other side, and ran out of holds. I searched experimentally beyond the bulge with my left hand and found nothing. A heavy pack hanging off your back is not a good look-out for this sort of stretching act. After a lot of puffing and terrifying myself, I thought, 'There's no way back, so we've just got to keep going forward!' Warning Peter and Simon behind me, I swung round the bulge anyway and my outstretched scrabbling fingers found a huge comforting jug. The rest of the traverse was a pleasant scramble. We came out high above the little glacier, crossing it above a steep icefall and ended up on the West-North-West Ridge of the Hohberghorn at 3960 metres, higher than we had planned but well placed all the same.

We left our rucksacks secured with slings to spikes of rock, descended the ridge quickly in light order to the Dürrenjoch (3916m), and then up the easy, chaotic but good rock the other side to the summit of the Dürrenhorn (4035m).

It was ten o'clock but the hot day promised by the starry clear night never materialised. A high layer of metal-blue stratus clouds hid the sun and we were cold. The visibility had been good so far, or we would have been very stuck on our traverse of the West Spur, but as we left the summit of the Dürrenhorn, the clouds thickened and the wind increased from the west. By the time we had dropped back to the Dürrenjoch and climbed up to our rucksacks again, the summit of the Hohberghorn was swathed in icy white clouds.

I imagine the Nadelgrat in fine weather is superb, the views unforgettable. Sadly, the cloudbase settled about 4000 metres and the wind blew fiercely. We clambered up the direct mixed climb (II+) to the summit of the Hohberghorn (4219m) in typical Scottish winter conditions. In fact, the wind worsened, whipping snow and ice across the exposed ridge from our right. Heads bent, legs buffeted, we followed the snow arêtes and rock over the Stecknadelhorn (4241m) and stopped at the steep rock step beneath the Nadelhorn.

We stood on a narrow snow ridge and squinted sideways up at the dark rocks rising above us, coming and going in the poor visibility. On our left a track disappeared into cloud across the steep North Face. By nearly four o'clock in the afternoon, the snow was soft, slippery on the hard ice below it and not encouraging.

'Let's stay here,' said Simon.

'Here?' said Peter glancing round the narrow arête.

'Yeah,' I said, acting the old hand. 'In that cornice of snow.'

Peter, who had only heard talk about snowholes, looked where I was pointing, at a small peak in the snow ridge behind us, and nodded politely.

'Room for a snowhole there, no problem,' said Simon already stripping off his pack and pulling out his shovel.

'Spot of digging then?' said Peter in a bright metallic voice, plainly convinced he was in the company of the mentally deficient. We belayed ourselves and set to with picks and shovels, sending chunks of snow tumbling out of sight down the slope into cloud.

There was not enough snow in the bank for a full snowhole, but we cut out an open trench for the three of us to lie side by side. We roofed it with Simon's shelter sheet, leaving our feet sticking out of the entrance hanging over the slope outside. As with every bivvy site, no matter how inhospitable they look to start with, whether in snow, jungle, desert or the awful wet ditches of South Armagh, we felt quite at home as soon as we were installed in warm sleeping bags on our neoprene mats and cooking up a steaming brew.

Just at last light, the clouds blew ragged around the rocks on the ridge, like steam, giving a fantastic glimpse of where we had come and the valleys far away below. We were perched at 4220 metres, high above the glaciers on either side of the Nadelgrat, like swinging in the roof of a vast white cathedral. Though the clouds closed in again fast, thrashing the ridge with particles of ice, I felt we were well placed for the next day.

We were slow to start next morning, telling ourselves we had no height to gain. The real reason was that we were still in cloud, the wind was still unpleasantly fierce and the rocks of the Nadelgrat were now covered with an inch or more of rime ice which made them even less appealing than the night before.

All the same, when we finally got going at ten o'clock, we tried for two hours to climb the rock steps onto the Nadelhorn. While Simon led, terrifying himself on smooth icy slabs, I watched other parties below us having a hard time crossing the iced-up snow slope of the North Face. They were traversing too high and finding themselves on hard unpleasant ice close under the rocks.

Finally, we gave up on the North-West Ridge, abseiled forty metres down the North Face and traversed across to the North-East Ridge. This is the trade route from the Mischabel Huts and from there we took only twenty minutes to reach the summit.

Clouds surged round, tantalising us with glimpses of the Lenzspitze, the snow-capped Dom, and the views of the valleys on both sides. The South Ridge to the Lenzspitze was not inviting. The rocks were heavily rimed, the strong winds raked the ridge and there was no signs of anyone else having been foolhardy enough to try their luck. Plus, Simon's back was playing up again. The day before had been long, with more rock climbing than we had done for a while, and he needed to rest it or he might put it out for good. Disappointed, we turned down.

We enjoyed a beer in the Mischabel Hut, where the warden was intrigued by our tale (and helpful, like the Dom Hut lady). We glissaded down a snow couloir to the bottom of the Fall Glacier (3020m) and continued on the well-worn path to Saas. After the long session on the Dent d'Hérens, I had not quite come to terms with my new Koflachs. Going downhill on rocks, my big toes felt as if they were on fire! I traversed the mountain to the lift at Mällig above Saas Fee and arrived in our Saas Fee rendezvous, the Café Central, only a few minutes after the other two who had walked all the way down.

Two weeks later, on 10 August, we went back to the Mischabel chain, this time starting at the other end. Ignoring the signs in Täsch which warn 'no one beyond this point without Cantonal authority', we drove the old blue Land-Rover into the mountains past Ottavan (2214m) which is a small and attractive summer holiday walking village in the Täschalpen, or flat alp meadows either side of the Mellichbach stream. We got some curious looks in our bright blue Land-Rover as we drove past groups of people in shorts, stout walking boots, small rucksacks and carrying the now ubiquitous telescopic ski-walking sticks. Leaving the tarmac road, we climbed in four-wheel drive up the steep and narrow rocky track which leads to the Täsch Huts.

I turned off at a dodgy hairpin at 2400 metres but a heavy stone fall blocked the track and we had to turn back. Simon turned the Land-Rover and got it stuck, teetering on two wheels over the edge of the hillside below. Peter and I leaped out at once.

I really thought we might lose the Land-Rover, not to say Simon, but he managed to turn it eventually and parked against a rock wall right to the side of the track. We stuffed rocks under the wheels, and left the keys on the front tyre.

Douglas was going to come up with a foolhardy volunteer, Dave, on the back of his Honda CBR1000 to fetch the Land-Rover the following day. He was back after his operation, his wound still sore, and trying to get fit again by thrashing the poor unfortunate Base Camp party up the Glishorn above Brig. They were in training for Mont Blanc, whether they liked it or not!

The soothsayers had given us three days' good weather and we had decided to go for the Täschhorn–Dom traverse. I was apprehensive as there is so much daunting material written about the Täschhorn and I wondered how we would get on. Or if we could do it at all. Two Swiss passed us coming down the moraine ridge beside the Weingarten Glacier. They said they had turned back on the Täschhorn's upper snow shoulder, crux of the South-East Ridge, because of too much unconsolidated snow.

Gloomy, we carried on. Our walk up to the Mischabel Bivvy Hut was pleasant and not too hot. Cool damp billowed up from the fast waters of the Rotbach stream, smelling delicious, like woodsmoke, and above 3000 metres clouds rushed past, drenching us with fine mist.

The route takes you up a narrow glacier south of a rock rib to one side of the Weingarten Glacier, to avoid the steep chaotic icefall, and then up a narrow couloir to Point 3481 which is a deep gash in the rock spur. The climb is about 100 metres and looks easy but the rock is horribly loose and quite steep enough to cause a serious headache if you fell. The guide book gives fifteen minutes for this, but we took ages, roping up and scrabbling about on the shale. It didn't help having large rucksacks, and the rocks were very damp. At the top, where you step out onto the glacier, we saw fresh footprints in the snow (probably made by the two Swiss we had seen earlier) leading down past the entrance to this nasty little gulley and we all felt sure that there was a better and quicker route along the side of the icefall.

We followed the tracks easily (but the route is not hard to see) to the top regions of the Weingarten Glacier, broadly making for the centre of the ice, then over to the left and finally back to the centre to reach the Mischabeljoch at 3851 metres.

Typically, the Mischabel Bivvy Hut was going to be rebuilt, in 1994 they said. However, we found the old one full of character, literally. A rounded metal box perched on the edge of the rocks at the bottom of the Täschhorn Ridge on the north side of the Mischabeljoch, it was similar to Italian bivvy huts we had been in. Two four-mattress bunk-beds filled one half. The other half was occupied by a table and two benches, with shelves on the end-wall by the door. The guide book said, '10 places maximum. No warden.'

We found two women in residence, Swiss, in their fifties, who spoke excellent English. We all wanted to climb the Täschhorn, but the wind shook the hut all night and continued without let-up through the morning. Us strong lads chickened out and decided to wait another day. The two ladies set off up the slope and we promised to keep their places for them.

About lunchtime two Londoners appeared, called Dave and Ian, who had crossed the Alphubel to reach the Mischabeljoch. Then two Italians joined us in the early afternoon from the same route. A clutch of six grumpy Swiss turned up at four o'clock, all in their fifties wearing red lumberjack shirts and Edward Whymper corduroy plus-fours. They were furious that we were there before them. We were now fifteen in the ten-man hut. However, there was still room on the floor and plenty of clean blankets (by complete contrast to the Italian Aosta bivouac).

They kept coming. I imagine the good weather forecast brought them out. By nightfall, we were twenty-four inside the tiny hut. The two Italians, Simon, Peter and I retreated into the bottom bunk bed and looked out at a forest of legs and bodies seething round the table which occupied the other half of the hut. The Italians were from Lugano and most agreeable company and typical of all the Italians we met on the mountains. As was usually the case, we communicated in French, theirs very much better than mine.

Our two Swiss ladies returned at last light, just as we were about to set out to look for them, and were appalled to find the hut jammed with people. With considerable ill grace, two of the men in the Swiss party of six gave up their places on the top bunk for the two women who were exhausted. Depressingly, they too had turned back on the upper snow shoulder.

There was a lot of milling that night. God knows how the others slept, for we only managed a few hours' kip ourselves, interrupted all the time by snoring and people shuffling about. There were bodies lying all over the floor, sitting upright on the benches, on the table and propped against the wall. We reckoned ourselves fortunate tucked away in the shadows inside the bottom bunk. The two Londoners who had installed themselves above were convinced a party of ten Spaniards wearing sombreros would arrive any minute to complete the chaos.

There was no question of deciding when to get up in the morning. The noise of milling started about three o'clock, waking everyone, with stoves being lit, people going out for a pee, people stamping about dressing for the day, rattling harnesses and carabiners. A couple of Austrian boys who had climbed the Lenzspitze North Wall two days before were first off, mainly because they were last into the hut and had slept crushed up by the door. They more or less fell out of the place when everyone else inside began shoving and pushing about behind them.

By four o'clock, we gave up and put on our brew for breakfast on the boards inside our lower bunk. The two Italians next to us lay still, muttering, '*C'est une folie, tout ça!*' They didn't need to get an early start as they were planning to walk down the Weingarten Glacier and wanted to let the crowd out of the hut before making a move.

At 4.55 a.m., we left the hut in the last hour of darkness and found a perfect morning. To my relief, the route was not difficult to find. It starts steeply on the right just behind the hut entrance, reaches the crest of the ridge and continues obviously along the ridge, rising through steps and past gendarmes, easy to follow the crampon marks even in the darkness by a head-torch. Ahead were the Austrian lads and the grumpy Swiss party which we overtook on the traverse of a gendarme rated as three metres of II+. This made them grumpier still, as we quite reasonably cut across above them as they fiddled about with belays on loose rock further down the traverse.

The ridge was excellent, not as difficult as I had imagined and when the sun came up we enjoyed the most superb views of Saas Fee and the Saas valley 2400 metres below us. Even the snow shoulder was not hard and we made good time to the summit block in three hours. There was more milling here. After a not very steep snow arête, the Austrians, leading, put in belays, took a wrong route, came back, put in more belays, then traversed slowly right while a queue built up behind us. After waiting half an hour, we followed on moving together, as did the other groups behind us and there was soon a dangerous scramble as we all climbed the unpleasantly loose rocks to the summit.

Rockfall plummeted down. I was hit on the back of the neck as I crouched for shelter during one shower and Peter took a bang on the helmet. Fortunately neither of us was hurt, but the sun was quickly softening the ice which binds loose stones on that eastern face and we were pleased to reach the summit. It was nine o'clock. We had taken four hours and fifteen minutes, about par for the route, but we had only covered a third of the ridge and there was still a long way to go.

There wasn't much room on the top, so we asked the two Austrians to take a photo of us and turned to go as Dave and Ian appeared through the cornice onto the summit. They wished us well and we set off down the North Ridge towards the Dom.

The guide book describes the Domgrat as 'one of the finest expeditions in the Pennine Alps', but we noticed the Austrians did not follow, as they had said they would, and we soon saw why. There was no sign of anyone being there before us, the rocks were covered with crusty wind-slab snow and big brittle cornices overhung the right, or eastern side.

We edged our way down the delicate snow on this high ridge, everywhere above 4200 metres, with fantastic views on both sides, of the Zermatt valley on our left and Saas Fee on our right. At first, we descended on the edge of the ridge, but then opted to traverse the 'rock knoll' on the right flank. We abseiled off, the rope refused to budge round a spike, I climbed back up, dropped the rope and down-climbed, all of which lost us more time. The rock was loose on the face, but we were warm in the sun, out of the west wind and off the dodgy unconsolidated snow on the ridge. I was glad we never tried the route the day before, when the wind was really strong.

After the 'rock knoll' (4404m), we came back to the ridge and I took over the lead for a while from Simon, with Peter in the centre. I was very conscious of the cornices and stepped down carefully away from the fracture line, looping our rope over spikes of rock which protruded through the crust.

Suddenly, I felt a tug at the rope and looked back. Peter had gone through a cornice right behind me. Simon, behind him, reacted very fast and pulled the rope tight, checking his fall. I pulled on my end, and Peter came to a jarring halt five metres down the East Face with hundreds of metres of emptiness below him.

His fall was terrifyingly quick, but as the cornice collapsed beneath his feet and he started dropping over the edge, he said, the only thought which flashed through his mind was that he just knew I would write it up in the book! He was exhausted. Breathless with such a massive loss of nervous energy, he started to climb back. As ever thinking of others and conscious that I was impatient we were taking so long on the ridge, he glanced over at me. I signalled him to relax, if it were possible hanging in such a place. He spent five minutes or more absorbing the fact of his continued existence before his breathing steadied and he clambered up through the cornice to rejoin us on the ridge.

We still had a long way to go. The snow did not improve, testing our self-control at every step, and we took nearly six hours to reach the Domjoch, the col between the two mountains. There is no way off this ridge, which runs for three kilometres over 4000 metres to the summit of the Dom, so after a brief stop out of the wind for a drink and some chocolate, we carried on up the ridge towards the Dom.

This section of the Domgrat is mostly steep rock, rising in impressively harsh-looking steps, teeth and gendarmes to the summit at 4545 metres, with the occasional short snow arêtes. The climbing was nowhere terribly hard, just relentless, hour after hour. The snow ridges were narrow and hollow. I have to admit that we crossed several with our legs either side, like riding a horse, waiting for the centre to collapse, which happened several times.

The weather deteriorated through the afternoon. About the time I looked down on the last summer skiers leaving the slopes above the Längflüh lift station above Saas Fee, the clouds which had been filling the Zermatt valley on our left spilled over and obliterated our view of the Dom summit. We reached the horizontal snow ridge before the summit block in poor visibility and feeling unpleasantly cold. Simon, who was leading, found an excellent traverse to the right, ignoring the guide-book directions to 'take the summit block direct up the ridge' which looked awful. This route took us up steep, easy rock which was loose as ever and nowhere gave great confidence but meant we could keep climbing together on our rope.

The clouds came in at speed and swirled round us. We stopped once more, in the lee of the wind, to put on overtrousers and a fleece under our jackets and Simon lost an old friend. He dropped his black hat which rolled slowly out of sight down a steep gulley.

By this time, even though we were three on a rope, we were moving together quite well, and we reached the summit of the Dom in four and a half hours from the Domjoch, at 7.30 p.m. I must admit that as I pulled myself over the last step of rock, the sight of the cross on the top was an enormous relief. To our great disappointment, we were in thick cloud and saw nothing.

'Let's sod off,' I said, shivering, and we did.

The light was fading fast in the gloom inside the clouds and we had a long way to go. In view of the clouds and wind which did not match the forecast at all, and because we were tired after fourteen and a half hours, we decided to go down to the Dom Hut (2940m) rather than stay up, bivvy out another night and try the Lenzspitze by the South Ridge the next day. We dropped off the Dom on the trade route North-West Ridge and reached the hut at 10.30 p.m. All the snow had melted off the Festi Glacier since our last visit. It was filthy, muddy, very slippery and not easy to see the crevasses in the dark. We passed two German lads moving very slowly (one had lost his crampons, dropping them on the mountain) but I never saw them arrive in the hut, which was in complete darkness and not easy to see until we stumbled across the wood bridge beside it.

I collapsed in a corner of the dormitory under a delicious hot layer of smelly old blankets and warm clothes, blocked out the snoring with Rod Stewart, 'When I give my heart again, it's gonna last for ever,' and crunched up two packets-worth of Dextrosol tablets till I had relaxed enough for sleep. The long day was a success but the feeling of achievement didn't really sink in until the following morning.

I slept through the usual milling and noise of the early risers. Simon and Peter were less fortunate. Hardier than I, they had curled up in their sleeping bags under the stars on the little terrace outside the hut and were woken by curious parties peering at them as they quit the hut at dawn.

At seven o'clock, I came down to breakfast feeling like an old campaigner. There is something most satisfying about being in a hut where you have done what everyone else there wants to do. The warden, a man this time, his skin wrinkled and brown with the elements, gave us coffee and brown bread.

'What were you doing?' he asked in broken English.

'We were on the Täschhorn–Dom traverse,' I replied, feeling rather pleased with our performance.

'Yes, I know,' he replied impatiently. 'I got reports from others here who saw you on the ridge. But why did you take so long?'

Our balloon of self-satisfaction burst.

'Well, we were three on a rope,' I said lamely. 'And there was a lot of snow.' It seemed a pathetic excuse. We had taken fourteen and a half hours over a par time of eight.

He laughed then, his eyes twinkling, and said, 'I know. You are the first party to make the traverse this year.'

For the first time, we felt like real mountaineers.

The feeling of achievement lasted all the way down to Randa. We bounced down the steep path, overtaking various other people who had left earlier, and ran the last part through meadows to our rendezvous on the track where George met us in a VW van.

Our success on the Domgrat was part of a much bigger whole. The great French routes on the Mont Blanc Massif lay ahead, the Rochefort Ridge, the Grandes Jorasses, the Aiguille Verte and the Aiguille Blanche. The more I learned about the mountains, the more I realised how little I know.

15

'TIME'

I need no weapon against death, because there is no death. What
does exist (in life) is the fear of death. That can be cured.
                            Hermann Hesse, *Klingsor's Last Summer*

My climbing nearly came to grief when Simon and I bicycled into
town to do some quick shopping before our next trip. He cycled
ahead along the footpath by the river on his mountain bike, bronzed
in T-shirt and shorts, athletic and balanced as ever, and twisted neatly
down a steep slope through an S-bend into 'leafy lane', the quiet
sunny road lined with plane trees which was our short cut to the
centre. I followed on my old road racer, which Tim Boyle, our vehicle
mechanic, had tried to update with new tyres, but as I turned down
the S-bend I discovered I had no brakes. The rubber pads, shrivelled
with age, had fallen out. Frantically squeezing the grips to no effect,
I accelerated down the short slope, shot off at the bend and plunged
into the bushes under the trees where I parted company with the bike
and nearly did myself permanent damage to certain soft parts of my
anatomy.

'What kept you?' asked Simon later, lounging in the sun outside
the Britannia with a beer and peering at my dishevelled appearance.

I scowled at him and asked Ula for a Coupe Danemark ice-
cream, which were superb there and, in my view, the panacea
for all ills.

With the rich taste of chocolate and vanilla on my tongue, my
humour restored, I asked him, 'Where d'we go next?' Peter had

been ordered back to London to see his next boss for a week and Simon and I were left on our own.

'Let's try the Aiguille Blanche.' It is arguably the most complex of the mountains we wanted to climb and we both recognised that we would be better equipped to do it as a pair.

That Sunday, 1 August, we drove the old blue Land-Rover through the Mont Blanc Tunnel from Chamonix to Entrèves in Italy and turned right-handed up the Val Veni to La Visaille. The mountains on the south side of Mont Blanc rise sharply from the valley floor, fierce walls and pinnacles of rock rearing up at the sides of the chaotic tumbling icefalls of the Brenva and Frêney Glaciers. We passed a couple of campsites where corpulent Italians in garish shorts lay about under the pine trees among bottles of Chianti and the remains of their Sunday lunch picnics, oblivious of the huge mountains above them, but the area has an undeveloped and pleasantly remote feel.

On the map, we had noticed a lift from La Visaille to the Monzino Hut at 2590 metres. On the ground, we found the lift was for kit only, a small wooden tray suspended from pulley wheels on an alarmingly rusty wire stretched across the valley. The lift operator, called Pino, was drunk. Very cheerful, talkative and helpful, but definitely suffering the effects of a long sunny weekend. He put our rucksacks in the wood tray, shambled into the machinery shed followed by a dusty black Alsatian, sat in an old tractor seat behind an oily diesel engine and started up. Wheezing, he pulled several levers, and our sacks, filled with all our most precious climbing gear, lurched out over the valley to the cliffs on the opposite side where we could just make out the square shape of the Monzino Hut.

As soon as I mentioned the word 'café', Pino and his Alsatian perked up. For a free drink in the restaurant, he revealed he was a guide, or ex-guide, and suggested we cross the Doire river further down, at Freiney where there is a bridge, because the path above La Visaille can be flooded. Tapping his nose conspiratorially, he also warned us about 'slap' avalanches. We all laughed.

We parked by a bridge over an impressive torrent between huge rocks and set out on foot in light order, stripped to the waist to enjoy the afternoon sun. Once we emerged from the larch trees onto the moraine at the bottom of the Frêney Glacier, we kept glancing up at the lift wire swaying far over our heads. We could see the little wood box but no sacks inside and all the way up looked about for our kit which we were convinced we would find scattered across the valley.

The fixed chains up the cliffs beneath the hut are quite fun, especially as we were not carrying heavy rucksacks (which made a pleasant change), and we reached the hut at half past five after an hour and a half.

The Monzino Hut is very well built of stone and well finished inside in a sixties style, rather old-fashioned but made to last, with good hardwood doors and bunks, probably beech. Light and airy, the rooms were immaculately clean and it even boasted showers and proper flushing lavatories. We had a long talk with Marco, the warden, who laid out a very old map of the mountains on the stone balustrade and pointed the way we had to take the following morning: up the Châtelet Glacier, over the Frêney Glacier to the Schneider Couloir which he recommended, and round the back of the fearsome-looking Pointe Gugliermina.

Two very nice English climbers, Les Swindin and Peter Kemp, were also helpful about the climb. In their fifties, Les edited the Collomb guide books and both men had climbed all the 4000ers. With them was Les's wife Barbara for whom the Blanche was the last on her list of 4000ers, making her, so she claimed, the first British woman to achieve this feat. With all the talking we never noticed that as the warm evening sun faded, clouds had crept up from the west to cap the peaks behind the hut.

After a very good dinner of thick minestrone (thinking of my father who adored Italian soup), Wiener schnitzel and spinach washed down with a couple of nightcap beers, we slept well. The warden gave us an alarm clock and Simon and I were first out next morning at 1.30 a.m. We slugged down some good coffee, bread and jam and set off uphill trying to see a path by the light of a weak moon which kept disappearing behind a threatening skein of dark clouds.

The snow had not frozen at all, the temperature was too warm, we were carrying too much, more than 50 lb of bivvy gear and protection, and found ourselves moving terribly slowly. The moraine above the hut was irritatingly loose, like walking over builders' rubble in the dark.

As we reached the bottom of the Châtelet Glacier, clouds washed up under the sharp points of the Peuterey Ridge on our right and filled the Frêney Glacier. We stopped, breathless, pretending we needed to discuss the situation. We sniffed the warm air, checked the clouds above us which had thickened, and decided we did not fancy crossing the broken Frêney Glacier in cloud. Instead, we branched left up the Glacier du Brouillard to the Eccles Bivouac Hut (3900m). Once at altitude, we would have the option of seeing what happened. Either the snow would be hard enough for us to go on to the summit later that morning or we would wait till the next day, hoping for a freeze that night.

The route up to the Eccles Hut is steep at times but easily found up the right side of the Glacier du Brouillard, but the snow was soft and deep and we took five and a half hours. We were exhausted by the time we reached the hut, which was in thick, damp, unpleasantly icy cloud.

The guide books don't tell you there are two bivvy huts here, one for nine people and one for six above it, nor that they are extremely grotty. Like the old bivvy hut at the Mischabeljoch, they are small round-roofed metal boxes tied onto the rocks protruding from the snow on the steep slope to the Col Eccles, actually quite hard to see from below until you stumble on them, and they are held down by dubious-looking hawsers. We chose the smaller, higher one, which seemed cosier inside with a wood lining, and settled in hoping no one else would want to join us.

We were thankful we had brought our own lightweight sleeping bags as the blankets were leaping with wildlife, like the ones in the caravan at the Aosta Hut below the Dent d'Hérens. In fact, we did not care. By eight o'clock in the morning we were tucked up and fast asleep.

Noises outside woke us near midday. The Swindins and Peter Kemp had arrived. After a lot of shouting down the steep snow between us and the lower hut, and an exploratory visit by Peter and Les to see our hut, which involved lots of abseiling in the wet snow, they settled in the larger hut. Two Dutch lads appeared next and joined them. Above them all in our little hut, we fondly imagined that we would be left alone.

French voices woke us again. Three professional-looking men wanted to come inside. We reorganised ourselves. We fitted plank shelves so we could stack the five of us and our gear in the two-metre-long by two-metre-wide hut. Our companions were good company: Pierre Beuscard, a guide from Pau who was born in New Zealand

and spoke good English (plus French, Spanish and Italian), and two nuclear physicists called Michel Dourthe and Jean-Pierre Lamblin who worked in the French Atomic Programme in Bordeaux, all of whom made us Brits feel very insular and stupid.

In between Pierre's appalling tales of frost-bite in the Pyrenees, we talked about the weather. We all wanted a freeze that night but the clouds hung round us all day, the temperature warmed up and none of us really thought there was any chance of achieving much the next day. Pierre, who had been there several times before, said he had never seen so much snow at that time of year and agreed with Simon and me that to consider crossing the steep bowl at the top of the Frêney Glacier to reach the Col de Peuterey in soft snow conditions would be insane.

During the afternoon, Les Swindin took the trouble to clamber up the horrid snow slope from his lower hut and he put us all in a sombre mood.

'There has been a terrible avalanche on the Grandes Jorasses,' he said. He had a small FM radio and had heard that fifteen people had been swept away. Only a few kilometres away on the same south-facing side of the Mont Blanc range, the warm conditions (the föhn again) had weakened the big cornices. Huge pieces had fallen off near Pointe Croz, avalanched the soft snow on the steep Glacier des Grandes Jorasses and washed out onto the Glacier de Planpincieux, right across the normal route to the Grandes Jorasses summit. Eight had died and seven were seriously injured.

I recalled Pino's warning about 'slap' snow conditions. He may have been drunk, but he still had an experienced eye for the conditions. Considering how we had holed up in the filthy Eccles Hut just because we thought the snow too soft and too deep for safety, we all wondered why those poor people had been climbing at all that day.

The cloud did not clear. The föhn always seems to last several days and the conditions next morning were, if possible, even wetter, damper and more unpleasant than the day before. We heard the two Dutch lads shouting at each other in the mist behind our hut as they passed going uphill at seven o'clock, then back down again half an hour later. The three Frenchmen set out to try the Brouillard pillars and returned in half an hour too, soaked and depressed. Simon and I left the Swindins and Peter Kemp to wait out the weather (Barbara was single-minded about climbing her last 4000er) and followed the Frenchmen all the way down to the Monzino Hut.

We had wasted a lot of energy for nothing, but we made the right decision. We could so easily have 'gone for it', just because we had made the effort to climb so high and put ourselves in a good position to reach the summit. We could so easily have suffered the same fate.

Simon and I cheered ourselves up with a cold beer in Purtud, half-way down the Veni valley to the tunnel, in a calm hostelry covered with peeling orange stucco and wistaria. We sat in the sunny courtyard and the owner, a comfortable but attractive woman in her forties, stood by our table, hands on hips, and talked volubly in French about her delight in cooking and her visits to France to find the best cuisine.

'They eat well in Switzerland,' she said when I explained we were living in Brig. 'But apart from *fondue* and *raclette* there is no taste in Swiss food.'

I translated for Simon and we all smiled. I recalled a poem by an early alpinist, A.D. Godley, who wrote in 1899, 'They will dine on mule and marmot and on mutton made from goats, they will face the various horrors of Helvetian tables d'hôte . . .'

After a pause, she looked carefully at the two of us and then asked me straight out, 'Are you his father?'

'No,' I said, my smile turning to steel.

'What did she say?' asked Simon suddenly leaning forward and taking a great interest. I am sure the bastard knows more French than he admits.

With the lady of the house smiling charmingly at us both, I told him. Ignoring his laughter, I peremptorily asked the woman to fetch more beer. She talked too much.

We left the family fussing round an elderly priest who had to be carried from the car that brought him, to a chair at another table. Impressed by such determination to drink, we repaired to Chamonix for a very agreeable lunch in the Bar National by the Post Office (known to all the fluent French-speaking British climbers as the Bar 'Nash') where we decided to go for the Zinalrothorn next, weather permitting.

The föhn cleared in three days but not before more climbers died because of the bad conditions. The freezing altitude was high at 4500 metres so the snow had softened even more. One man slipped off the Italian Ridge of the Matterhorn, two more were lost in an avalanche on the Rimpfischhorn and another in the Bernese Oberland.

In Brig, clouds, storms and rain spoiled the sunbathing at the swimming pool all week but nothing upset the usual evening round of the bars. In the Britannia, I developed my plan for the Zinalrothorn with Mike and George, who agreed to walk up to the Rothorn Hut with us and set up a tent Base Camp. I wanted all the support group to experience what they could of the mountains and Mike and George showed the most interest. Mike, a red-haired Guardsman from Preston, Lancashire, and George, a well-built medic from Worcester, were both fit and enthusiastic, which is all you need. Douglas's wound was right beneath the laces on the front of his shinbone and still too painful to wear plastic boots. He wanted to join us but he dared not risk anything too soon or the cuts beneath might become septic again. Instead, he worked off his frustration and recovered his fitness by bullying the support group.

'Too many people suffering DTs!' he announced with a puritanical and faraway glaze in his eyes, like a tall black-haired kirkman fulminating against the iniquities of the world. He was right, though. I hate to think how many litres of beer were drunk in the Brit, the Pirate, the Napoleon and the Lötschberg, or how many cigarettes were smoked, but I felt sorry for them as Douglas outlined his plan. 'Less of this pumping iron in the bloody gym to look good at the pool, and more walking up hills with a heavy Bergen is what's required to climb Mont Blanc.'

I am not sure the idea of climbing Mont Blanc appealed to any of them at that point but Douglas forged on. He had been poring over the maps and worked out that the height gain necessary to climb Mont Blanc was 1400 metres. To match this he planned a fast Bergen march up to the Simplon Pass.

Simon and I, with Mike and George, left them to it. Finally, the meteorological luminaries in Geneva had promised that the skies would clear at the weekend. Dave Moore rapidly volunteered himself to drive us into Zermatt and I remarked that his fellow chef, Nigel, had also avoided Douglas's route march. Somehow he had got himself appointed to remain behind manning the telephone in Brig in case of emergency.

'Just as well,' said Dave grinning as he yanked the wobbly VW transporter round a hairpin bend at terrifying speed.

We all recognised a good story. Nigel, sporting a fresh pudding-basin haircut which made him look like Henry V, had been joined by his English girlfriend who was staying in the Brig campsite for two weeks.

'They went to the Brit the first evening,' Dave explained, his grin widening. 'Nigel bought her a drink, leaned over and came straight out with, "I've got to tell you I've been shagging someone else behind your back before you came out, and when this two weeks is up, I'll be shagging her again."'

The VW rocked with laughter. What honesty! What a sod! He was, after all, a British soldier, the sort of whom Wellington said, 'I don't know what effect they will have on the enemy, but by God, they terrify me.'

'Did she tell him to sod off then?' asked Mike Nutter, another Lothario taking a professional interest in technique, especially as he was still being chased by 'Fatal'.

'Not at all,' said Dave. He negotiated another bend at speed, grinning widely with the thought of what he was going to say. He went on, 'The young lady merely replied "Well, Nigel, we better make the most of the two weeks then!"'

Ah, the course of true love. This explained why I had noticed Nigel sitting in the Brit, a half-litre of beer in one hand (because he knew his limits under pressure) and a fag in the other, his English bird on one side, his Swiss bird on the other, and a third, a fifteen-year-old, prowling round at his back.

'I find it embarrassing sometimes,' he said shrugging apologetically.

Still laughing, Dave left us in Zermatt and pushed off again quickly before the police noticed we had no authority to drive into the village. Simon, Mike, George and I walked up the main street feeling very rustic with our large rucksacks and boots among the Zermatt holiday folk sauntering in and out of expensive shops in designer sun-wear. The path to the Trift valley leaves the village by a shoe shop in the main street and climbs steeply into the mountains. The views are stunning, and we took our time. The Trift gorge is attractive, with pine trees, shade, tumbling waters and grassy slopes. It is also equipped for essential refreshment with a café at the bottom end, the Edelweiss (1961m), which has a fine panorama of Zermatt and the Matter valley, and the old-fashioned, shabby but rather charming Trift Hotel (2337m) at the top end, half-way to the Rothorn Hut.

Naturally, as it was a hot day, we were obliged to stop at the Trift Hotel for a couple of shandies, called *panaché*, before wandering on to the Rothorn Hut, which we could see far off across a wide bowl of grass, broad streams and stony moraine circled by big snowy mountains and glaciers: the Untergabelhorn, the Gabel Glacier, the Obergabelhorn, the Trift Glacier, the Zinalrothorn, the Unter Äschhorn and the Platthorn.

Most of the day-trippers seem to go no further than the Trift Hotel so we were on our own and enjoyed the feeling of remoteness in this wide-open valley in the heart of the Pennine Alps. The sun burned down and Mike and George puffed a bit on the last haul up the moraine as the hut is at a useful 3198 metres and they were not fully acclimatised. We set up our two tents on the rocks above the hut, warmed ourselves in the last of the sun, made our evening meal, and passed out at nine o'clock after a post-prandial tincture in the hut.

Simon and I were trying our summer sleep system again, or the 'put-everything-on-instead-of-using-a-big-heavy-sleeping-bag' technique. After our first freezing attempt, on the Bishorn, I was worried I would not sleep, and the Zinalrothorn is a great deal more taxing than the Bishorn. However, I pulled Helly Hansen long-johns over my cotton climbing trousers, zipped on fleece salopettes and Gore-Tex overtrousers. I wore one pair of socks and my Koflach boot inners loosely laced. On top, I put on a fleece and a lightweight duvet and pulled up the hood. Then I slipped into my Gore-Tex bivvy bag on my bed mat. This time, I slept solidly, warm as toast.

We woke at 2 a.m., made a brew, stripped off our sleeping gear, donned plastic boots and set off into the moonlight at 2.47 a.m. To our surprise and relief, we found the snow quite firm. The Tarot experts in Geneva had predicted, 'The next sixty hours will see the zero temperature level drop from 3700 metres to 3200 metres.' This unusually detailed forecast was more or less right and gave us confidence. We made good time.

The Schneegrat is not really very narrow or difficult, as the guide book suggested, and we quickly made our way onto the South Face, crossing a series of fluted ridges on easy rocks and lovely hard snow to the narrow couloir which leads up to the Gabel Notch. We kept moving together, front-pointing up the ice, using hand holds on the rocks on the left of the couloir and looping our rope over spikes for protection. The Gabel Notch is a prominent cut in the South-West Ridge and the wind whistled through from the west. We removed our crampons and pushed on just as the light brightened in the eastern sky. I took over the lead from Simon up the easy and pleasant rocks to the Biner slab which has a bad name for being difficult and which, as these things often do, proved quite simple. There was plenty of snow on it, but the rock was not particularly icy, when I guess it would be hard. We found a couple of pitons on the downhill side and I was able to place a chockstone to protect Simon across.

From here, we had to put on our crampons again for the steepish névé slope which leads back to the rock ridge. The exposure on this last part is not as bad as the guide book suggests. There are plenty of great deep handholds so I didn't mind hanging out for a photo.

We reached the Zinalrothorn summit (4221m) at dawn. There is plenty of room and we stayed to enjoy the superb views at all points of the compass, from the majestic Weisshorn in the north, the Mischabel chain curving from one big peak to another in the east, the massive Monte Rosa group in the south-west, the Breithorn group, the Matterhorn due south and the Dent Blanche to our west.

With the growing light, a slight wind picked up, cold enough to drive us off the top. On the way down, we unroped and I went ahead to stand on a gendarme on the ridge below so Simon could take a picture of me with the Matterhorn in the background. I felt tremendously exhilarated by our swift progress up, my confidence boosted in our climbing and fitness, by being first on the summit, alone, and the sensation of being remote from the pettiness of the world, feelings perfectly familiar to all mountaineers. I have taken drugs but for sheer excitement, this beats it all. Arms outstretched, I wanted to fly.

More prosaically, Simon wanted to do a handstand on the rock pinnacle in front of me, for another photo, till I pointed out there was a bit of a drop and we were still not roped up.

We only met three other pairs on our way down. The last two were well below the Schneegrat and, I think, extremely stupid for setting off so late in the morning, after nine o'clock, when the snow was turning soft. We got back to our tents about half past nine, making the whole trip in 6 hrs 49 min. The first two pairs we passed did not come down the glacier behind us till after 2 p.m. and we never saw the last two return at all.

This climb restored my confidence after our long sagas on the Dent d'Hérens and the Täschhorn–Dom traverse. Simon and I were up and down in better than even par time and enjoyed the varied climbing. The difficulties were not as tiresome as advertised in the guide book and the exposure not as fearsome. After forty-two mountains and 44,000 metres of up, we needed this outing, especially after the fruitless waste of energy on the Aiguille Blanche. We needed a reminder that sometimes the climbing can be fun and satisfying, and I consider it quite understandable that the first ascensionist, Leslie Stephen, the father of Virginia Woolf, who reached the summit on 20 August 1864, was the man to coin the phrase, 'The Playground of Europe' for the title of his classic book. I can recommend the Zinalrothorn.

Simon and I went down to the hut for hot chocolate and arrived just as the delightful lady warden and her two pretty daughters pulled her daily bake out of the oven, a delicious sweet and sour apricot and apple tart. Later that afternoon the weather thickened and clouds surged over the mountain behind us. George was outraged, sitting outside his tent, when the sky darkened suddenly and hailstones pulverised his fruitless efforts to turn mutton granules into a half-way decent supper.

'Don't these bloody dried peas ever soften up?' he asked plaintively an hour later.

Next morning, Simon and I were away from our tent at the same time as the day before and making for the Obergabelhorn. Clouds drifted over the moon and the temperature was not so low as the morning before. Our boots occasionally burst through the crisp surface snow, making progress slow and tiresome. Long gone were the days in May when we set out on skis with extra warm clothing on for the icy morning starts. We soon stripped off to vest and windproof jacket for the long drag over the Trift Glacier up to the East Ridge of the Wellenkuppe.

We reached the top of the snow shoulder under the Wellenkuppe Ridge in an hour, which is good going, though I did not feel on top form at all, and started on the rock ridge above. I led up broken loose rock towards the big rock step barring the way to the snow ridge.

It was hard to see the way as the moon chose this moment to hide behind dark clouds and my head-torch battery gave out. We groped our way up to the ridge and were confronted with the steep exposed slabs of the step. After some hopeful peering through the darkness round to the left (south) side we decided we must go straight up. A British climber from Nottingham in the hut the day before had mentioned the climb was exposed, rearing vertically over the big drop to the Trift Glacier below, and this step certainly seemed so, especially in the dark.

Actually, the climbing was rather good, with lovely big handholds and we came up the two-pitch face quickly. On the top is a convenient flat snowy area before the final seventy-metre push to the snow cap of the Wellenkuppe (3903m).

We walked straight over the Wellenkuppe, down the broad snow ridge the other side, and stopped. The view of the big Swiss mountains all round was impressive but an angry pink tinge was just showing on the horizon in the east, lighting layers of dark purple clouds right across the sky. Clouds pulled at the higher peaks, like the Matterhorn closest to us and even the Zinalrothorn. Far away over the Monte Rosa group flashes of lightning suggested the Italians were getting a soaking. Of more concern was a dramatic electric storm to our north-west, where the weather was coming from. We put on more clothing and our waterproof overtrousers.

We breezed along the snow ridge to the Obergabelhorn until the Grand Gendarme. There are fixed ropes up this sharp obstacle and a narrow rock ridge to negotiate before rejoining the snow arête on the other side. We noticed someone had avoided the difficulties by traversing beneath the Gendarme, leaving a track across the steep, flanking slope.

'Why don't we go that way?' said Simon blithely. 'Save fiddling about on the rocks.'

Like an idiot, I agreed. I hated it. First, the angle of the slope looked all right at the start but then became steeper and steeper as we traversed under the gendarme, most of it easily fifty-five degrees. Then, the steps were solid enough, I suppose, but they were only a couple of inches wide and I like lots more. Worse, I like to think I have a chance of stopping myself if I stumble, but the slope was either rotten snow or solid ice and I did not feel at all comfortable. For over an hour Simon, with his irritatingly good sense of balance, casually sauntered along behind me as if he was walking down 'leafy lane' in Brig to the pub, while I made a real hash of it, mincing along step by step, my attention fatally gripped by the vast open slope beneath me and cursing my imagination.

Later Simon had the grace to admit that he knew perfectly well he would not have been able to stop us had I slipped, or had the iced footsteps given way. I would not have registered quick enough if he had fallen behind me. Danger is a question of perception, each of us seeing more or less of it according to our attitudes. The crucial elements of danger on mountains are pretty obvious – steepness, snow conditions and of course the potential results of a mistake, whether injury or death – but the vital factor which creates a lasting impression is time. Not the superficiality of time or the convention of hours in a day, but duration.

Most of us have been in danger for short periods, typically on the road when we have an accident or a near-miss. We can always stop afterwards and have a cigarette or a drink to help us relax. You cannot do that on a mountain. The danger, perceived or not, may last for an hour or more, as I found on that traverse, or longer, as I was to find later. And there is no stopping for time out. You have to carry on, you have to complete the task in hand, to survive. I was discovering the essence of my journey. Time was the key to the grail of my search.

We regained the ridge and continued up snow-encrusted rocks onto the summit just after seven o'clock. The climbing was not hard but I was glad to reach the top. The morning seemed brighter, but clouds still scudded across the sky, keeping the air cool and sharp. No incentive to hang about, and we were conscious the steep snow shoulder back round the Wellenkuppe shoulder would catch every bit of sun and soften all morning.

We abseiled down the summit rocks on tapes we found sticking out of the snow, passed several other groups on their way up, and made good time till the Grand Gendarme. I flatly refused to go back across the snow traverse and followed Simon up the rock instead. This is not hard from that direction. We clambered along the narrow ridge and sidled along a narrow ledge under the topmost needle of the gendarme to the top end of the fixed ropes where we found three German lads coming up the rope. They were all absurdly safe, prusiked tight to the fixed rope, and took ages to come up, swinging about on the slack ropes and laboriously moving their prusiks round the iron pitons. This impressive safety-consciousness revealed itself as lunatic ignorance the moment they reached us perched on the ledge traverse. Here, in spite of my suggestive talk about roping up, they simply undid their prusiks and each one just walked along the ledge completely unprotected. Had they been scampering up the fixed rope hand over hand, like monkeys, this casual attitude to the traverse might have seemed normal, if foolhardy, for the penalty of a slip was a fatal slide into crevasses far below. I am not sure they even had a rope, and the last one appeared not to have an ice axe either.

After this hold-up Simon and I made good progress back to the hut, over the Wellenkuppe, abseiling down the slabby step below the Wellenkuppe and down the steep, very loose rocks to the snow shoulder which was already soft. That slope would not be any fun later in the day. We reached the hut at 11.30 after nine hours, still too early for the daily oven bake. However, we relaxed for a couple of hours in the sunshine and waited for another slice of apricot and apple tart (well worth it), which we washed down with a litre of cold lemonade. Even when we started out for the long walk down to Zermatt, we had still not seen any of the other groups descending that soft snow shoulder.

We took our time walking down, warmed by the satisfaction of two good climbs, and Bryan Adams niggled softly in my ear, 'I did it all for you.' The snowy peaks circled our horizons all the way to the Trift Hotel and I relished the splendour of isolation in the mountains, untouched by humanity. Temporary withdrawal from civilisation, not to be confused with retreat, is one good reason why we come into the hills. Would we appreciate the same exhilarations if we had been born in the mountains and knew nothing else? The taste of wine is nothing without the contrast of water.

After a deliciously cold but expensive beer (at 6 SFrs, fifty per cent more than in Brig in the valley) at the Edelweiss Café at the top of the Trift Gorge overlooking Zermatt, we walked down to our rendezvous at the station bar in Zermatt. Mike and George, who had come down earlier with the tents, were waiting with Dave and Gonzo. They had hidden the VW behind a house on the outskirts.

I could tell at once we needed to get everyone on Mont Blanc at the earliest opportunity.

'I got bored watching videos at the weekend,' said Gonzo off-handedly. 'So I went down to the kitchen to watch the washing machine going round. You get a much better picture.' He paused and added, 'Nigel had put his jeans in with a red T-shirt and I watched them gradually turn from blue to a bright pink colour. It was quite exciting really.'

Back to reality, of a sort.

And the press. In Brig, Simon's girlfriend rang up to say there was a rumour in a South Wales newspaper that two SAS soldiers had been killed climbing in the Swiss Valais. He reassured her we were still alive and kicking (and planning a night out at the Pirate to prove it).

The following morning I rang the SAS camp in Hereford.

'It's nonsense,' I was told, which was a relief, but I was unimpressed when the officer on duty added, 'Anyway, climbing isn't as dangerous as free-falling which some of the guys are doing just now.'

I thanked him and put the phone down thinking how wrong he was. There is no denying the buzz when you jump, no matter how experienced you are, but with modern gear the statistical chance of total malfunction of both main and reserve 'chutes is virtually nil. True, that faint chance concentrates the mind, but free-fall requires no real thought provided you obey the rules: scrupulously follow the parachute packing sequence and choose a safe opening height! As for static-line parachuting? Well, it is not called 'dope roping' for nothing.

In climbing, the penalty of making a mistake is the same. Yet decisions affecting your safety and survival are complex, made up of a multitude of varying elements which change all the time, and the risks may be continuous for hours. As an ex-free-fall Troop Commander, I can categorically state that the physical and mental demands on climbers at risk are much greater than those required by any parachutist. There is no comparison.

On the Obergabelhorn, I had learned that Time, or the duration of the perceived danger, is the most telling element of all.

16

THE FOUR TRUTHS

All men come to the hills,
Finally . . . .
Men come with dusty broken feet;
Proud men, lone men like me,
Seeking again the soul's deeps –
Or a shallow grave.

Roger Mais (1905–1955)

'I've not led a sheltered life,' said Mike Nutter in awe as we emerged onto the narrow snow arête from the Aiguille du Midi lift station in brilliant sunshine. 'But I've never seen anything like this!'

Chamonix regulars will be blasé, but walking down the Midi arête for the first time is like flying. On one side of the arête, the steep slope drops away to the dark green emptiness of Chamonix far below, while on the other is a steep drop over the bergschrund to the Plan du Midi and a grandstand view of the Mont Blanc Massif. It is not surprising so many tourists take the lift and stand about in the way as you emerge onto that arête, just for the experience. This time, we were lucky with the weather. The snow glittered on the jagged crevasses and tumbling icefalls of the Géant and Tacul Glaciers below. On the far side, the great Alpine North Walls of the Grandes Jorasses and the Rochefort Ridge dominated the horizon, with the sheer pillar of the Dent du Géant like a huge sentinel statue on the end. On our right, across the flat snowfield of the Midi, the North Face of the Tacul seemed impossibly steep until we noticed the tracks torn through the soft afternoon snow. Even though it was past five o'clock, people were still coming down, some of them moving terribly slowly, tired out, having walked from the summit of Mont Blanc eight kilometres away. Up there on the horizon, we could see very late parties, just tiny black figures in the distance, still high up on the Bosses Ridge.

We set up three tents on the Plan du Midi under the natty, new and extremely expensive Cosmiques Hut (tel: Chamonix 50–544016), which is perched on a rock by the Cosmiques Ridge. Simon, Peter and I planned to traverse Mont Blanc the following morning, leaving Mike and George to take the tents down and drive round to meet us in Les Houches some time later in the day. We dug out rectangles of snow and stamped about to harden them off. Mike, with short ginger hair, fit and enthusiastic, and George, powerfully built and always cheerful, were sharing next to me, beginning to learn the routine on mountains, while Peter and Simon put their tent deliberately further away, muttering something about people snoring. I was alone, and spread out inside mine.

Another ten tents dotted the snowfield and over supper (transformed with the aid of the Chamonix deli: for me, thin slices of Bressaola with black olives followed by a fish and granules bouillabaisse, goût du Curry, à la façon du chef, washed down with a pleasing half-bottle of Gamay), we discussed the problem of human waste. In scientific detail. Considering the amount of pee and shit per person per night and the (increasing) popularity of the Plan du Midi, we felt the French should grip the problem, make the Midi snowfield a designated campsite and provide proper toilets with a warden to collect fees for the pleasure of using them. Garbage and soil disposal is a serious problem on the mountains, even in the huts. The new Cosmiques Hut sleeps 200+ people, it is open several months a year, it sports real flush lavatories (NB: the seats are a bit small for those with capacious bottoms and there is a real danger of leaving your change on the counter), but the soil just slides down pipes onto steep rocks on the Chamonix side. A most atrocious smell wafts across the balcony outside the dining room and the damage to the environment can be imagined.

It is time the Alpine countries took responsibility for their mountains, as well as taking our money. The Cosmiques Hut is equipped with lovely modern view windows, so why was it not also fitted with a solar-driven unit to break down the soil? Such disposal units are common, they are fitted in New Zealand mountain huts, says Russell Brice, and should be mandatory in the Alps.

We all dug our snow pits after supper and added to the layers of poo on the Plan du Midi. The best I can say is that there was plenty of snow this year.

The sunset over the white landscape was superb, the air temperature fell encouragingly and we turned in early. We wanted to be up and away before those 200 people disgorged from the Cosmiques Hut and blocked the trail up the Tacul.

I woke in darkness. George and Mike were whispering in loud voices in their tent next to mine.

'What's the time?' George said. Half-asleep, I checked my watch. The luminous hands on the Promaster are excellent. It was midnight.

I heard some more muttering, their tent unzipped and someone clambered out onto the snow. I assumed one of them was going for a pee. Footsteps crunched over the hard snow and stopped unnecessarily close to my tent. Then a voice said, 'Time to get up!'

'It's midnight,' I stated flatly.

'Oh!' said Mike. 'Sorry.'

I grunted and rolled over in my sleeping bag. He crunched back to his tent, wriggled inside again, and I heard them arguing.

'You bloody said it was one o'clock!' whispered Mike hoarsely. 'They don't have to get up for another hour!'

'It looks like one o'clock on my watch,' said George plaintively.

Peter and Simon slept badly but there was no lying in. We were up at one o'clock for a hot brew ('this is one I prepared earlier') which we had ready in a Thermos from the night before, to save time, and we started at half past one. Even so, there were two groups ahead of us. We could see their head-torches bobbing about on the slope above us.

The snow was hard and squeaked satisfactorily under our crampons. The sky was black but starry, which augured well for a fine day. We made good progress up the Tacul by the light of our head-torches. There was so much snow we hardly noticed the big crevasses. After an hour and a half when we were near the top of the Tacul Glacier, we saw the Cosmiques crowd had set out too. A stream of tiny lights snaked back and forth up the slope far below us, like glow-worms.

We had timed our start nicely. The Cosmiques warden was a fierce lady who provides breakfast at 1.30 a.m. for the Mont Blanc route (no variation of timing allowed!), after which there is a lot of milling about as parties fit gear, crampons and rope up behind their guides.

On our right, we could see more lines of head-torches winding up the Grand Mulets route and faint lights of parties on the Dôme du Goûter. Including climbers from the Tête Rousse Hut, the Gonella Hut and other groups on the harder southern ridges, there must have been hundreds of people converging on the summit of the mountain that morning.

We climbed Mont Blanc du Tacul (4248m) in the pitch dark. After a quick photo-call by the cross (modern art, minimalist movement), we front-pointed down the icy top section and dropped off the ridge to the Col Maudit. I realised I had stupidly left my telescopic ski stick on the summit. As I stood there swearing and weighing up the pros and cons of going back, because I felt fit and had used that stick on all our climbs, Simon wandered up.

'I left my bloody ski stick on the Tacul,' I grumbled.

'I know.'

In the darkness, I could see his brown face split by a wide grin. I focused on him.

'This it?' he asked, lifting my ski stick in his hand. Leading in the dark, I had not seen him with my stick, but I was delighted. You get attached to things which go everywhere with you.

The slope up to the Col du Mont Maudit is steep but the snow was frozen and easy. We caught up with the groups ahead of us who were having difficulty finding the route to the col in the dark. We moved left and higher and found a narrow ledge which routed us under the rocks below the final sharp icy climb over the bergschrund to the ridge.

We took the rocky North-West Ridge from the col to the summit of Mont Maudit (4465), which was fun, the rock easy and the views truly impressive. Dawn was just lighting the sky when we reached the top. We perched on this narrow spire of rock and snow under a cathedral dome of dark blue sky where the stars were still just visible. Away to the east, the peaks of the Alps were racked into the distance in a magical mist of orange light spreading out from the horizon.

There is also a fine view of the Brenva Face of Mont Blanc from the top, overhung by huge gleaming white cornices. We traversed round to the Col de la Brenva and pushed on up the Mur de la Côte going like trains. The last slope past the Petits Rochers Rouges is a drag as the summit is always just out of sight. In the last hundred metres, we spotted other climbers approaching on the final section of the Bosses Ridge on our right and we caught up with the first group again just as we topped the summit. The whole walk including detours to the Tacul and Mont Maudit had taken just six hours. This is given as eleven hours in the guide book, excluding detours, so we felt pretty pleased with ourselves.

I counted over sixty people on the long, broad summit ridge, milling about in a balmy wind in a wild confusion of coloured clothing, jangling carabiners and ice axes. Everyone was chattering away, like in a bar, taking photographs of the views all round and trampling on the coils of multi-coloured ropes on the snow. I have never seen so much expensive climbing gear at one time, but at least it was being put to good use, on a fine day on the highest mountain in western Europe.

Too many people whinge about the fashion-conscious hordes 'desecrating' the purity of the mountains. What nonsense! What hypocrisy! There are precious few humans who can add much purity to anything, no matter where they are, what they do, or wear. Taken to logical conclusions, we have no business in the high mountains at all. Historically, the people of the Alpine countries never dreamed of climbing their mountains until the mid-nineteenth century when it was largely the British who started the desecration ball rolling.

We should be proud of those early British first ascensionists who climbed so bravely with such extraordinarily crude and dangerous gear, though they were quite as bigoted as any buff nowadays. When crampons came in, wearers of leather boots with tricouni nails said it was the beginning of the end. However, we should encourage people to follow their example, to take advantage of the improvements in safety in modern equipment and to explore the hills. Mountains are not just for experts and elitists – whether they wear skins, tweed or Gore-Tex – any more than the rivers, valleys or forests. Mountains are for everyone.

We loitered on the top nearly an hour and a half taking photos and enjoying the views. The whole of Europe stretched out before us in all directions. Then we set off at speed down the Bosses Ridge, passing dozens coming up, men and women of all ages, shapes and sizes, wheezing with the altitude and most plainly unfit but all determined to reach the top.

We virtually ran down to the Vallot Hut, marched over the wide snowy Col du Dôme and sat down on the broad 'summit' of the Dôme du Goûter (4304m) for breakfast. Between mouthfuls of garlic sausage, Peter peered at me darkly through his contact lenses and demanded to know, 'What shall we do now?' It was only 8.30 a.m. and the snow conditions were still good.

Simon, elegant as usual in black Ron Hills and black jacket, was fiddling about with his camera for a 'run-round' shot. He agreed. 'Mike and George won't be at Les Houches till this afternoon,' he said. 'If we go down now we'll have to hang about for hours.'

We studied our maps, ate more sausage, felt good and decided we should climb the Aiguille de Bionnassay as well, via the delicate snow arête of the East Ridge.

This thin arête from the Goûter is very impressive. It seemed to me that if the ridge were any narrower, the mountain would fall apart. The exposure is acute. Looking down on the right, there was just ten metres of brilliant white snow curving out of sight to a sharp line and then blackness hundreds of metres below on the Glacier de Bionnassay. On the south side, the drop falls into Italy hardly any less dramatically to the Glacier de Bionnassay which looks flat from above. It was gripping stuff but the snow was hard and we moved swiftly on a rope together. We reached the summit in an hour, at which point Peter announced he had not been so terrified, so many times, in so short a time in all his life. Sounded like Flying Officer Perkins again, with, 'Sir, I want to join the Few.'

'I'm sorry, Perkins, there are already too many.'

In truth, there had been too many that year. 137 people had died in the Alps during the year and we were keen not to add to these grim statistics. There is no room for pointless gestures on the summit knife-edge of the Bionnassay, so after trying to look as casual as possible for a couple of photographs, we went back the way we came. Covering ground you know requires the same degree of concentration in the climbing but always seems more relaxing. In complete contrast, the 300 metre climb from the Col du Bionnassay onto the east flank of the Goûter was a tiring, slow plod. I suppose we were running out of energy. Fortunately, the snow was not too soft so we took a short-cut traverse round the Dôme over the top of the steep Glacier du Bionnassay and rejoined the normal route to the Goûter Hut.

There are newish fixed plastic-coated wires on the rocks beneath the hut and we ran head first down the ridge hanging onto these ropes, bouncing and leaping from rock to rock. Pity they do not go all the way down. We crossed the remaining bank of snow at the bottom of the Grand Couloir, glissaded across the Glacier de Tête Rousse and carried on down on our feet and bottoms on the rough old snow in the gulley which runs steeply into the rocky valley below. The snow ran out at the Désert de Pierre Ronde, a spine of slabs overlooking the Nid d'Aigle, but saved us more than half the walk on the path and we reached the Nid d'Aigle at half past two.

The Nid d'Aigle is a bit too organised now. The rack and pinion train brings so many people that they issue coloured cards to control the numbers in the old-fashioned wood carriages. The place was seething with day-trippers burned red in the sun, picnicking, gazing at the fine view of the Aiguille de Bionnassay, drinking at the buvette or stuffing themselves in the rather good restaurant. At that time of day they were thinking of going down and the return train was full. However, the ticket controller seemed well-disposed towards climbers and we wangled ourselves on the next train. At Bellevue, we left the train, crossed the grass to the Bellevue lift which took us down to Les Houches by four o'clock, in time for our rendezvous with Mike and George who were waiting for us in the bar opposite the lift station.

We had romped round four summits (excluding the Goûter), ascended 2200 metres, descended 5500 metres, covered twenty kilometres in thirteen hours and we felt pretty chuffed. Our next outing to the Mont Blanc Massif was a complete contrast.

On Sunday, 15 August, we drove back to Chamonix and bought a picnic lunch at the delicatessen.

'You realise that it's not macho to drink strong beer,' George declared piously as Mike Nutter happily pulled several bottles of five proof off the shelves.

Armed with fresh French loaves, Mediterranean black olives, Pont l'Evêque cheese, huge tomatoes, honey cured ham and yet another bottle of Gamay, we went through the tunnel to Italy. This time we turned left at Entrèves, along the Val Ferret to Planpincieux. The two valleys which run under the mountains either side of the main road are holiday areas and car access is controlled at the weekends by the Italian police. When they saw our old blue Land-Rover they merely shrugged and waved us past. We left the road and bounced over coarse grass towards the torrent of the Doire de Ferret where we ate our picnic sitting on rocks in hot sunshine looking up at our objectives. We wanted to climb the Rochefort Ridge and the Grandes Jorasses, starting at the Pointe Helbronner and descending eventually via the Refuge Boccalatte to Planpincieux. From the bottom of the valley, this long ridge rises very abruptly to over 4000 metres for much of its length, the mass of fluted rock ridges broken only by the steep, chaotic icefalls of the Glacier de Planpincieux.

We milled round the Land-Rover changing from tourist to climber. T-shirts, shorts and flip-flops were flung in bags and we donned thin Polartec shirts, climbing slacks and plastic boots, and made final adjustments to our rucksacks. I was rather slow, which Simon said was on account of my age, but Peter seemed to think it was the Gamay. Mike and George thought this was all very funny for some reason.

I admit I was last across the snowfield at the top of the Glacier du Géant. There did not seem to be any rush. Annie Lennox crooned 'Primitive' in my ear, 'Take our fears and make us strong' and I just let it all go by. The weather was deteriorating, as the wizards had predicted. Clouds blotted out the sun and tucked around the summit of the Dent du Géant. In a haze of goodwill, I plodded round the steep bulk of the Aiguilles Marbrées onto the flat open Col de Rochefort where the others were already setting up their tents.

The jokes subsided with the weather. By the time we were huddled in our tents cooking our supper, visibility had closed to nothing, wet sleet was beating on the flysheet and thunder rattled around above us. In theory, it was supposed to clear later in the night, then freeze and provide us with good climbing weather tomorrow. On my own in my tent, I ate chocolate and typed up notes on my little Sharp PC3000 which lived in my rucksack and survived every trip.

Next morning, Mike and George kept quiet and we overslept till we heard other groups passing our tents. We clambered out to find a crisp clear morning. A few head-torches were glowing in the dark by the bergschrund and even bobbing about high in the first snow couloir which leads left-handed onto the rock spur under the Dent. Late, at half past five, we hurried after them. There had been a few centimetres of snow the night before, which had frozen; this was fine for walking on but not such good news for the rock climb itself.

The mixed rock and snow climb to the Salle à Manger (3830m) was much easier than it looks and an enjoyable way to warm up for the main effort. This was just as well. At seven o'clock, we turned the last gendarme before the snowy Salle à Manger, and saw the 200-metre rock pillar of the Dent du Géant towering over us, overhanging the ridge. It was hard to see how on earth there was a way up.

The guide book says go left, round and above a large flake, so we did and Simon found the route up at the back, confirmed by pitons which we happily used to belay ourselves. Being three on a rope, we were slow, and the steep, narrow couloir which rises on the north-west side towards the (very) flat place under the Burgener slabs was badly snowed up after the previous night's storm. We made steady progress but the rock was cold and unappealing.

The fixed ropes up the Burgener slabs are not attractive but they do speed things up. That morning, they were very iced up and slippery but the route up the series of cracks in the near-vertical rock is narrow and fiddly and would be hard without them. God knows how the first climbers managed this. Dressed doubtless in plus-fours and stout leather cleated walking boots, Fred Mummery, an Englishman from Dover, attempted the peak with Alexander Burgener in 1880, and wrote, 'Absolutely inaccessible by fair means!' Two years later, a clutch of climbers led by J.-J. Maquignaz and Alessandro Sella took four days to force a way up the rock by fixing the huge iron pitons which still carry the ropes today.

On the plus side, the view was at all times incredible. The climbing is exposed but not hard, so everyone should go on the Dent, just for the view. You cling to this narrow pillar of rock with a grandstand view of the most splendid mountains in the Alps. Dawn lit the Tacul, Maudit and Mont Blanc, the Aiguille du Midi was busy with people, little black dots on the white snowfield, the Mer de Glace far below us flowed filthy grey in a great curve to Chamonix out of sight over twenty kilometres away, the sun lit the summit snow dome of the Aiguille Verte and, when we finally reached the summit of the Dent, we could see the famous view of the great swirling cornices on the Rochefort Ridge below us and the Grandes Jorasses rising high beyond.

There is no way the guide time is right for ordinary mortals. The

Alpine Club book gives one hour for the 200-metre rock climb. I am not sure I could do that in just skiddies and sticky rock shoes if the climbing were in the comfort of the Chepstow valley. In the cold winds, wearing plenty of layers, colourful Gore-Tex jackets, nice safe modern ropes to abseil on, alloy karabiners and plastic shell mountain boots with thermal inners to keep our tootsies warm, (and crampons in the snow couloir), we took four hours up and three to come down. Three of us on our rope made us slow but we were still the fastest of the half-dozen or more groups on the rock that day. The person who wrote the guide book was either a rock star, or he had never been there at all. Actually, once we realised how long it would take, nothing mattered, for the views and experience on such a marvellous sunny day were unforgettable.

However, planning a trip with a vastly optimistic time from the guide book can land you in terrible trouble, as we were to find out.

We were back on the snow arête at the Salle à Manger at two o'clock, far too late to continue along the Rochefort Ridge. The snow was too soft in the hot sun. After some discussion over a chunk of bread and Emmental cheese, we decided to bivvy out on the Salle à Manger.

To keep boredom at bay for the remainder of the day, we dug a snowhole. We chose a site in the sun with a view of Italy, under the ridge below the rock tower of the Dent. The snow was easy on the outside but compact and ice-hard only a few feet into the bank. We gave up digging in, cut sideways instead and put up a splendid igloo palace over the entrance. Peter and I lay inside the snow bank, head to toe, and Simon lay under the igloo by the door. The weather was balmy and we ate al fresco, enjoying the views of Italy spread out to our south before the cold evening air drove us back into our snowhole for the night. We put on every bit of clothing in our lightweight sleep system and slept well.

At 4.40 a.m. next morning, we woke to the sound of crampons squeaking past our igloo on the hard snow. A French couple, who had taken hours on the Dent, had bivvied in the open and been driven to action by the cold dawn. We took our time getting up, confident we were already on top of the mountain, lying warm in our bivvy bags inside the snowhole as we brewed up our water for hot tea (and two scoops of Maxim for an old'un like me!).

We left just before six o'clock and made good time along the

Rochefort Ridge. I do not think we showed 'the perfect mastery of cramponing techniques' which a recent and very beautifully illus-trated guide book describes as necessary for this climb, but the corniced snow arête is not so exposed as the Aiguille de Bionnassay or Liskamm and we soon reached the summit of the Aiguille de Rochefort, after an icy climb up the rocks from the arête which looked harder than it was.

On the other side, we passed the French couple on the flattish snowfield by Mont Mallet and, three hours after leaving the Dent, we reached the Dôme de Rochefort. The climbing was not hard, though quite snowy after the storm, and we found lots of agreeable spikes and holds. The sun shone, though the wind continued cold, and the views of Mont Blanc, the Midi and the Aiguille Verte were stunning.

Most people turn back after the Dôme, it seems, and there was very little sign in the snow of anyone carrying on. However, the route is obvious. The ridge becomes much narrower and we carried on to the Canzio Bivouac Hut, which was our objective for the day, on the Col des Grandes Jorasses.

I can see why few people complete the Rochefort Ridge. It is not just that the ridge becomes more exposed, knife-edge at times, but there is more fiddling about to do. There are sudden drops where it is best to abseil, which means unroping, fitting up the abseil, on a worrying variety of old tape slings we found, abseiling one after the other, then roping up again, all of which uses up a lot of time with three on the rope. Some of the stances were rather short on space, notably the sharp little snow arête between the Calotte de Rochefort and the last high point above the Col des Grandes Jorasses and the Canzio Hut. In addition to roping up again after the abseil, perched on this thin curve, we had to put on crampons for the snowy climb the other side, which meant juggling rucksacks about too. My advice is take a good look at the climb out first, to assess whether crampons will be necessary, and put them on before the abseil.

From the last high point above the Col, our Alpine guide book said quite simply, 'Continue along the ridge, very easy, to the top of the step above the Col des Grandes Jorasses. Descend this in three abseils.' Sounded a piece of cake. We took seven abseils and three hours! The slope is steep, mixed and was covered with gungy weak snow. Once we were level with the col about 3850 metres but still far above the crevasses of the Glacier du Mont Mallet, we had to traverse right to gain the col. I led the first pitch to a sound-looking rock island on the open snow slope and belayed Peter over, but when Simon stepped off his rock the snow gave way and he fell in a big swooping circle beneath our rock where I had him belayed.

'I'd have done that again,' he said smiling cheerfully after climbing back up. 'Rather enjoyed it.' I grunted and Peter peered at him in amazement, totally unconvinced. Trouble is, I think he meant it.

Once again, we were not the only ones to take time. A French guide with an English client took nearly as long, and they were using a double-length rope. This lightweight 100-metre long 6 mm abseil rope gave them 50-metre abseils. Though not elastic enough for lead falls, it was ideal on this ridge. The French couple who had followed us all day took longer still. In the Canzio Hut guest book, I found comments by other people to the same effect, one from two English climbers, dated 1986, which said, 'The guide book is wrong isn't it? The abseil down took yonks!'

Maybe we should have taken the hint there, but the options at this col are all serious. The climb back up to the Rochefort Ridge is graded D and involves vertical rock pitches of V (they looked harder when we had abseiled down them). The descent into Italy, onto the Glacier de Planpincieux, is also D with lots of abseiling. The descent on the French side is steep over the heavily crevassed Glacier du Mont Mallet and the continuation along the Grandes Jorasses Ridge, which was our intended route, is D with pitches of IV.

We settled into the hut to relax and think about the next day. The Canzio Hut is another round-topped metal box, with two wide shelves making bunk-beds, one over the other, with pillows and blankets for about ten and a small living space. We were first inside, installed ourselves on the top bunk and searched about the mess on the shelves for grub. We had no food left as we had not planned to be out for three days, but we found some very ancient spaghetti in a dusty cardboard box. Even after extensive boiling, this pasta tasted like wood glue but it filled a hole while we talked over our plans.

The Alpine Club guide book casually described the eight-hour D-graded route from Canzio to the summit of the Grandes Jorasses in just ten lines. During our long abseil down to the hut I had looked across at the first daunting mountainside which lifts in a long rising traverse from the col to Pointe Young and the route was obviously more complex than these ten lines suggested. We chatted up the French guide. He was taking his client up the same route which he had done before.

'Where do you have a pee round here?' interrupted the young Englishman suddenly. We all gaped and his French guide looked at him in astonishment. *'Au dehors!'* he said waving vaguely at the world outside.

When he was outside, we burst out laughing. The relationship between guide and client is truly bizarre. The Frenchman was a full-time nanny, as well as mountain guide, and we wondered what pleasure there was for a client in being led about the mountains like a child? Roger Mathieu had always been most helpful with advice but he never came out with us, which was how we wanted it. The pleasure of climbing a mountain is not 'because it's there', as immortalised by George Mallory, but in making decisions all the way up and down: assessing, for example, the snow, the rock, the ice, the aspect, the temperature, the cloud cover, the sun's warmth, the passage of time, your own state and of course the condition of your friends with you. These factors vary continuously, sometimes by the minute, and the challenge is timeless.

A client does not have to think at all. All the decisions are taken by the guide. The client only has to follow the umbilical rope attached to his harness and do what the person on the other end tells him to. We were certainly jealous of the guide's knowledge of the next day's route, but happy to be on our own. Just before I went to bed, I stood outside and looked out over the vertical cliffs onto the tiny lights of Planpincieux far below, where Mike and George were waiting for us, and then up at the dark rock of our route the next day. A thrill of uncertainty twisted in my stomach, the fuel of fear and excitement and the essence of being in the high mountains – or maybe it was indigestion from the spaghetti. I shrugged and turned in.

For lack of knowledge or a useful explanation in the guide book, we resorted to prayer and a good night's sleep.

Next morning, there was a good deal of milling. The guide, who seemed quite an ordered person otherwise, started muddling about at 4.30 a.m., though everything must have been utterly routine for him: get up, make a brew and go. You don't even have to get dressed, or shave! Instead, we all lost valuable sleep as we did not leave till nearly six o'clock when there was enough light. None of us wanted to start climbing Grade IV in the dark.

We followed the guide and English climber with interest. I observed the guide struggling up the rocks to the left of the obvious snow couloir which starts the route and wondered how I was going to tackle the same piece. To my relief, he belayed and called down for the English guy to follow but traverse left lower down. He was also decent enough to shout down the same advice to us.

When it came to our turn, I found the route rather a blunt start to the day. After a great deal of strenuous puffing, and thoroughly off-balance with my heavy pack hanging off my back, I eased round a rock bulge that did not seem to have much in the way of holds and found a piton to belay the others. Peter followed with Simon close behind suffering from frozen fingers as his gloves were still iced solid from the wet snow the day before.

This set the pattern for the next hours. Simon and I took it in turns to lead, passing Peter at each belay, and we made our way terribly slowly up the side of Pointe Young. The climbing was at times difficult, because there was snow and ice in the crevices where we wanted to put our hands, the grade was as hard as I would like to do on big mountains with an awkward pack hanging off my back and the hardest Peter had ever done.

'You all right?' I kept asking him as he grappled with the rock.

'Fine, fine,' he always replied, lying through his teeth.

Simon always looked balanced and moved easily, talking about 'adventures'.

The main reason we took so long was simply that we were never quite sure which way to go till we got there. The route on this side of Pointe Young rises in a series of slanting shallow couloirs or cracks from low right at the col to high left and while it may be easy to see the line from a distance, the immediate next moves on the route are not so obvious.

At the end of the slanting ledges just under the ridge is a vertical chimney. It did not look inviting so Simon led on the right, climbing up some unpleasantly loose boulders to a stance out of sight above us. I could hear a lot of uncharacteristic muttering and 'for Christ's sake, hurry up!'

Peter followed and when I came up I found them sitting painfully astride a very sharp, thin rock.

'Hurry, please!' they begged. 'This is agony!'

I clambered over them and led the last pitch across some slabs to the ridge. We had taken six long hours to reach Pointe Young (3996m). We stopped for a bite of chocolate and tried to see where to go next. The guide book was quite inadequate. Two lines describe the route from Pointe Young to Pointe Marguerite. On the ground, the view is bleak. The mountain dropped away very steeply beneath us and a confusing mess of rock gulleys, ridges and couloirs curved round to the buttress of Pointe Marguerite. There was no snow where we might have seen the footprints of the guide and the Englishman and no other clue as to how to reach the narrow couloir running up behind the buttress to the summit of Pointe Marguerite.

We could see a few tattered and sun-faded coloured slings where people had abseiled in the past, though it was hard to see how they connected to make the route. Following guide-book instructions, we abseiled thirty metres down from the ridge onto a steep slope covered in loose rock. Soft snow filled a couloir below but there was no obvious route carrying on up to Pointe Marguerite. We felt cheated.

'We need to take a view,' I said, depressed.

Simon agreed. Peter waited patiently, rubbing his eyes. I guess he was prepared to follow us anywhere, but he kept his true feelings to himself.

We were standing on ledges above a rock face so steep we could only see fifty metres below us. Rockfall periodically exploded down the gulleys around us. It was already 2 p.m. The way down was serious, if there was a way at all, involving lots of abseiling, and the Planpincieux Glacier seemed miles away below us. However, the route up to Pointe Marguerite, even if we could find it, would take hours too and leave us higher still on the sharp ridge, in darkness at night with a long way still to go to the easier sections nearer the Grandes Jorasses summit. The sun was shining but our experience of the meteorological oracle in Geneva gave us no confidence that the following day would stay fine. We did not fancy being caught out moving slowly on the Grandes Jorasses Ridge in bad weather.

'We better bin this one,' I said. 'Try to find a route down.'

Simon agreed. He could see one old abseil point below and suggested we abseil one pitch further down. Any abseil point below that would be well off the route up to Pointe Marguerite and would indicate a route down. In theory.

This was easier said than done. There was no banter. There was very little talk. There were certainly no Walkmans. Just a stunned silence as we began to abseil down, gingerly finding our way from point to point, never able to see much further than the abseil we were on. Simon and I took it in turns to go first, with Peter in the middle. At the bottom of each abseil, we peered down the cliff for signs of another old abseil point below. Most times we found something. We must have been on a route of sorts, but the condition of the abseil points left much to be desired. We had to use the existing slings we found which were always faded by the sun, often torn and a few broken. We had no option. We had some slings ourselves but if we had run out we should have had to cut our forty-five-metres rope which was short enough to start with.

I lost count of the number of abseils. At each stance, we each belayed with a long sling onto the protection, Simon or I tied a figure-of-eight in one end of the rope, clipped it into a karabiner on our harness for safety (dropping and losing the rope did not bear thinking about), we pulled the rope through the top abseil point, which got harder and harder to do as the rope gunged up with grit and water, we found the middle point, threaded the free end through the sling for the next abseil, flung the coils out over the rocks below, then I stuffed the double rope into an Italian hitch on a large karabiner and swung into space.

We carried on down the face for six hours, abseil after abseil, and the glacier below seemed to get no nearer. When the existing slings looked really bad, we used one of our own precious slings. When we could find no abseil point, we set up our own with a bit of protection. As we moved out of the big gulley beneath Pointe Marguerite onto the nose of a steep ridge, the stone fall worsened.

'This must be the way down,' I said optimistically as we jostled about at one stance. 'There are lots of crampon scratches on the rock.'

'Those are scratches all right,' said Simon, matter-of-fact. 'But from rockfall not crampons.'

Later, I fitted a large hex through a thin crack between two satisfyingly solid-looking blocks and said, 'That's what I call a good placement.'

Simon nodded, 'The whole mountain will have to fall apart before that moves.' At which, a huge chunk of rock the size of a London bus fell off the face above us and burst with a roar of noise into thousands of pieces as it bounced down the face onto the glacier far below. We took cover as fragments whirred past like bullets. All of us were hit at different times during the descent, mainly on the helmet and the top of our rucksacks which provided excellent protection as we huddled down.

Living on the edge hour after hour, tempers did not so much fray as become acute. When I was leading, I hardly communicated at all to the two above me, but of course when Simon was leading I wanted to know everything.

'He's taking bloody ages!' I shouted down at Peter's purple helmet. He was stuck in the middle. 'What the hell is he doing?'

Fairly sure I could not hear, Peter called down to Simon more diplomatically, 'Mark wants to know how you're getting on.'

'Tell him to sod off!' Simon shouted up from far down the rock face. 'I'm fed up with his bloody backseat driving!'

I could see Peter's purple helmet nodding and then he looked up at me, filtered this information like the good Communications Officer he was, and called out politely, 'He says he's busy fixing a belay.'

Late that afternoon, Peter and I heard a sudden shout. Simon was out of sight over a cliff fixing another belay. The shouting was distant and frantic, 'A rock has fallen on my leg. I can't move!'

Our position was serious enough without Simon breaking a leg. I tied off my end of the rope, made sure Peter was secure and down-climbed to see what had happened. The further we dropped down the face, the looser the rocks became, often breaking away when we put our weight on them. Simon had moved down a steep gulley where big boulders hung precariously stacked on both sides, one had shifted abruptly under his foot, tumbling him on his side and two big rocks had fallen and wedged his leg below the knee.

'Are you hurt?' I asked, carefully testing each rock I stepped on.

He shook his head, but he did not look at all happy. The stone trapping him was too big for him to shift on his own. Worse, moving it risked setting off the whole lot, like pulling the wrong spillikin from the pile.

'For Christ's sake hurry up!' Simon gasped. The whole weight of the heavy rock was lying relentlessly on his leg.

He braced himself, hanging on to the rope, I stood on the safest-looking boulders and together we heaved at the rock on his leg, thankful it was small enough to move at all. As it rolled away Simon pulled his leg out and we nipped smartly out of the way as several others broke away.

Fortunately, Simon's leg was only bruised. He rubbed the circulation back as we watched the boulders bouncing down the face and smashing into tiny fragments far below.

'We're getting on,' I said further down, trying to be cheerful as we fixed up another abseil. Simon and Peter just looked at me.

At dusk, we had to traverse right across a wide snow couloir raked by stone fall. Hunched on the snow in the bottom of the gulley in the firing line, Simon took a hard blow on the arm. In darkness, we stopped on the other side by a large whale's back of snow in which we dug out flat ledges to sleep on. When Simon unpacked his rucksack he discovered his plastic mug was shattered and a close inspection of our rope, which was looking very furry indeed by this time, showed the mantle had been cut by stone fall and worn through to the core. Worse, we were only half-way down the face. The idea of more abseiling with that rope was not appealing but there was nothing we could do about it and we were tired.

We pulled on all our clothes, sleep-system style, clambered onto our ledges, slid inside our bivvy bags wearing our harnesses and safely belayed to our ice axes which were stamped in to the hilt in the snow. I passed out to the sound of Annie Lennox singing, 'Legend in my Living Room', which seemed appropriate, 'Have mercy, have mercy on me!' I had cold feet and stone fall rattled down the gulleys either side of us all night, but I slept really well.

We were up and away by six the next morning, which dawned clear. We thought we would be down on the glacier in no time, but distances and slopes are deceptively foreshortened looking down a mountain. The bergschrund appeared much closer than it was and ledges below looked flat till we reached them and found they were steep slopes.

We abseiled another six hours that morning. Every time I slid past the tear in the rope, I examined it with scientific detachment, knowing at the same time that we had little option. The logic of desperation was that as long as it seemed all right we would continue to use it. If it had not held, it would have broken and one of us would have died. This was living on the edge.

Danger is a matter of individual perception, to a degree, but there are few mountaineers who would disagree that abseiling is dangerous. That morning, not only did we continue to use other people's old abseil points, slings and pitons, but a rope which was not so much past its sell-by date as just plain knackered. The implications of a disaster were obvious, but there was no panic. Quite the opposite. We moved slowly but efficiently and our rope-work was neat, but the mental grip required to launch off at each abseil persisted between abseils and with the hours came a change.

The continual pressure, the unselfishness of thinking about each other's safety all the time, of thinking about people at home, of thinking what we would do if one of us fell or was injured by stone fall, the impact of living on the edge of life suspended on a rotten, worn rope, swinging off old abseil points on dodgy pitons, when nothing worse could happen except that something might give and we fall and die, produced great detachment. The studied repetition of our actions and the duration of that detachment produced enormous peace of mind.

Calmly, I began to understand the value of my journey. There is no pretension in this, just the quite simple statement that I recognised the elements sought by people everywhere, in the reiteration of the Name of Divinity in Sufism, distantly in 'ataraxia' in Greek philosophy, in the Hindu 'Bhagavad-Gita' of Arjuna and Krishna, and the Four Truths of Gautama Siddhartha, and I wondered if my father ever reached the same plane of detachment on his much-loved solo walks in the Alps or his yearly retreats to his old theological college near Oxford. I suspect he did, for he was an exceptional priest, but no amount of reading, academic study or listening to others can replace the actual personal experience of undergoing pressure and the effect of living on the edge. The soul cannot be tempered by talk, books or films, only by the fire of real experience. None of us choose the moment this happens, but when it does none of us would give up the understanding it produces.

Near the bottom of the face, Peter abseiled down to me as I stood on a narrow ledge belayed to a flake. He belayed himself and shouted up, 'Safe!' After a moment Simon swung into sight above us. As he joined us, he said to Peter, 'One of those pitons fell out when you were coming down.'

'Really?' said Peter conversationally. 'Yes, I did feel a slight jolt.' What it is to be British and a Guards Officer! I wondered how Simon felt following him on the single remaining piton.

With four abseils to go (as it transpired), we dropped down a deep gulley in the vertical cliff above the glacier and ran out of rope. It was Simon's turn to go first and he ended up belayed to a spike standing on his own on a thin flake, off the rope, because the next abseil point was six metres too far down. Next, Peter had to take himself off the rope too as there was absolutely no room by Simon, and I had to abseil to a place below him. He balanced precariously on the tips of his boots in the V of the gulley and nearly fell off when I passed him.

'You okay?' I asked.

'Fine,' he said darkly.

I gardened out crushed stones from a crevice, fixed a sling for my own belay and then found there was too much friction to pull the rope down. The rope was filthy with grit, twisted on itself out of sight above us (my Italian hitch twisted it every time), and it ran obstinately over rocks in at least two places. I had to jump off my stance and swing with my full weight on the end to get it to move at all. Peter helped. Between us, we dragged it down an inch at a time till the end flicked through. We took forty minutes moving to that next abseil point.

Fortune was on our side. When we finally reached the bottom of the rock face, we jumped the bergschrund and moved two hundred metres down the glacier beyond the area peppered and blackened with stones. No sooner had we thankfully dumped our rucksacks on the soft snow, when the whole mountain seemed to explode. High up right across the face, chunks of rock the size of cars fell off, bouncing and bursting like artillery shells on rocks further down and cascading a lethal shower of smaller pieces all over the area we had just crossed to reach the glacier.

On the way down the Glacier de Planpincieux, we crossed the rubble of the big avalanche which had swept eight climbers to their death the time Simon and I had been in the Eccles Hut on the Aiguille Blanche. The delight of mountains may depend on decisions, but the inherent dangers cannot be ruled out, as if by vote of committee, and sometimes all that is left is luck. Theirs ran out. Ours lasted.

We were tired out when we reached the Boccalatte Hut (2804m), a pleasant wood hut with a verandah which hides on a cliff above an impressive icefall in the glacier (I would not like to try and find this hut in bad weather). The warden, a young guide, gave us an excellent minestrone soup and beer which we wolfed down but we immediately felt full, having eaten nothing for thirty-six hours. He was intrigued with our tale, having been told by the French guide that we were on the mountain. He told us we were not the only ones to have difficulty on the Grandes Jorasses. We said nothing, but, if we had not appeared for soup and beer, we wondered how long he would have waited before doing something about finding us.

The path to Planpincieux below the hut runs over hills of strange black moraine, like coal, then turns right through a narrow gorge where you must cross a wide, wild stream. Simon and I stepped over like the Young Man of Coblenz (the length of whose legs was immense) from stone to stone, moving fast to avoid getting water in our Koflachs. I stopped on the other side to wait for Peter. He came up to the bank and peered at the water. I realised he simply could not see the stones to step on. He had lost one of his contact lenses during the abseiling. All he could see was a blur of moving water. I could almost hear him say, 'Sod it!' (though he is far too polite) and he plunged through the icy torrent up to his waist. What it must have been like with such eyesight during the previous two days hardly bore thinking about. I decided he was either extremely brave or mad as a hatter.

By the time we reached the tree-line on our way down to the rendezvous at a café in Planpincieux on the valley floor, I was nearly asleep on my feet. We reached the café at half past four and collapsed at a table where I had one of the most refreshing beers of my life. It was still too soon to talk about the previous two days, but we stripped off our sweaty and filthy gear and relaxed. All round us, refreshingly normal families sat about picnicking and we particularly enjoyed watching several very lithe young Italian girls playing volley ball with their friends.

In retrospect, I was annoyed. If the warden was right that others have similar route-finding difficulties on the Grandes Jorasses Ridge, why does the Alpine guide book not give a better idea of the problems? Ten lines for an eight-hour route suggests it is no great problem, yet if we had had any idea, we would not have gone to the Canzio Hut at all. We would have walked to the top of the

Grandes Jorasses by the normal route, come back along the ridge to the various 'tops' and descended via the Rocher du Reposoir. This would have left us in good shape to do some more climbing in the continued good weather. As it was, we had used up all but three of our slings on the endless abseils down, our rope was finished, and we needed a rest. Douglas, who had driven over to join us on his Honda CBR1000, was disappointed but there was no option.

After several very good beers, sausages and french fries in Planpincieux, Mike Nutter drove us home to Brig. Slumped against the door of the old blue Land-Rover, I listened wryly to Annie Lennox on my Walkman, 'Dying is easy, it's living that scares me to death.' The words and the title, 'Cold', seemed fitting, on a mountain.

As we climbed through the Col de la Forclaz back into Switzerland, Mike jiving on the steering wheel to the sound of his own boogie pack, I began to feel a most delicious satisfaction, savouring the value of what all three of us (when we talked about it later) had learned on the mountain.

In all the varied experiences of my life, including my time in the SAS, in firefights or free-fall, I had done nothing which had had remotely the same impact. All my experiences in the past had been too brief. Time, as I had begun to suspect on the Obergabelhorn, was of the essence. Just giving yourself a quick fright, in a car or solo climbing, is not enough.

I realised too, the commitment must be total and inescapable. I thought of parallels, all people I had written about and knew well, like the combat experience of a friend, Peter MacAleese, who has taken part in more fighting in different war zones over the years than anyone else I know, or like Hortense Daman who suffered terribly for nine months as a prisoner in Ravensbrück Concentration Camp (where she was injected with gangrene and sterilised) or like Carlo, a kidnap victim whose freedom I negotiated in Rome. He was chained, blindfolded with masking tape and beaten daily for sixty-seven days till his release.

When I finally met Carlo and we talked about his kidnapping, something made me ask him how important his experiences had been to him. He gave a little smile and replied, 'There is no doubt that this was the worst thing that has happened to me, but it was also the most rewarding. I came to terms with my life and its limitations.

I thought not just about myself but about other people and life itself. I learned that understanding is arrived at through pressure, but that this is not the important factor; it is just the vehicle that brings the human condition around us all the more sharply into focus. I consider this understanding invaluable.'*

Now I knew why. Our experiences were a tiny fraction of these three, but quite as important to us. We had learned a cheap lesson on the Grandes Jorasses. I just wish I had not had to put my new understanding to the test quite so soon.

* *The Kidnap Business*, by Mark Bles and Robert Low, published by Pelham Books, London 1987, page 65.

17

ALPINISTS

I love not Man the less, but Nature more,
From these our interviews, in which I steal
From all I may be, or have been before,
To mingle with the Universe, and feel
What I can ne'er express, yet cannot all conceal.
     Lord Byron, from *Childe Harold's Pilgrimage*

Back in Brig, Simon was sick in bed with gastric flu for three days over the weekend. George the medic took his temperature, we all blamed Dave's cooking, then left him weak and groaning in his bunk and went to town for a few beers.

We sat at a table outside the Britannia in the sun under the pale green leaves of the plane trees, drinking Pschorr and I succumbed to another Coupe Danemark which melted in the warmth. We watched a cavalcade of superbikes roar down the main street escorting two newly-weds, the girl in a billowing white wedding dress, on an enormous Honda Gold Wing. Bikers were a common sight in Brig where they stopped en route over the Simplon Pass.

Peter turned up and handed me a scrap of paper. 'I rang Geneva for the weather report,' he said, looking glum.

I read, 'Very bad weather all week. Temperature zero degrees at 2800 metres. Very high winds from the west. Snow down to 2500 metres. Do not go on the mountains.'

'You can't say plainer than that,' I said morosely.

'Chamonix says the same thing,' he added. We always rang the

French weather centre in Chamonix because they were more detailed about conditions climbers need to know about on the mountains.

This period of adverse weather came from Spain, where there had been appalling floods in Catalina, but the whole summer had been blighted. Of course Murphy's Law dictated that there would inevitably be unusually bad Alpine weather during the one year we wanted to climb all the four-thousanders, but we wondered how much the exceptional weather patterns elsewhere on the globe had affected Europe. In July, when Alpine weather was awful, there had been torrential rain in the United States which caused the worst flooding of the Mississippi and Missouri rivers this century, and on the other side of the world monsoon rains had reduced eight Indian provinces to chaos and killed nearly 500 people.

The soothsayers were right. I cannot remember when the clouds were down so low over Brig and the rain so miserably damp and cold. As the days ticked past, I grew ratty and argumentative. I found the inactivity intensely frustrating. Simon and I had climbed forty-eight mountains. We were close enough to finish them all, if only the weather held off and gave us a chance, but as the days passed with no let-up of dirty weather on the big mountains, I could feel the end of the season closing in on us.

When Simon recovered, I wanted to discuss which mountain we should do next, how we might do it, whether there was too much snow on it, what the weather might do next and a host of other imponderables. Simon merely replied to all these hectic speculations with a casual shrug and, 'How do I know?'

He was infuriating but right. With clear logic, he pointed out that there was no point wasting a lot of energy walking into any of the mountains we still needed to climb until the weather cleared. We did not want to spend days waiting out bad weather in a hut (he reminded me of our four days caught out by a storm in the Margherita Hut), we certainly did not need the exercise (having by then ascended 50,000 metres), we did not need to acclimatise, we could not afford to fritter cash paying for wasted days of food and accommodation and nor was there any point in camping out. Being stuck in a tent in bad weather is difficult enough at the best of times, but with the frustration we now felt, we would have been at each others' throats in no time.

We did some rock climbing, on the friction walls at Gamsen near Brig and again at St Niklaus, while the Base Camp party terrified themselves white-water rafting in the Lutschine river near Interlaken and canyoning in the Fuchslochschlucht river, a sport for lunatics. Dressed in a wet-suit and life vest, they were washed downriver like corks. Mindful that more SAS soldiers have died from drowning than from other causes and that a group of Germans had been drowned rafting a few weeks before, I thought I would be tempting fate to join them. Besides, I was single-minded about climbing the rest of the mountains. I did not want to injure myself like Douglas.

Bored, I followed up the publication progress of two of my manuscripts, *No Mean Soldier* at Orion and my second novel, *Hearts and Minds*, at Hodder Headline. Both editors had proofs ready for final editing and of course they 'sweetly' asked me to do the work, 'as soon as possible!'

'Send them out,' I said. 'The weather's appalling. I'd like something constructive to do.'

They arrived at the end of the week, a great pile of proofs totalling 300,000 words, whereupon the weather improved at once.

To cap it all, just before we left to try our luck on the Dent Blanche, Brigadier Mudry rang up. We spoke French as usual and after a nice chat he said, 'I have to run a course for fifty officers in your building in Brig, starting on 6 September, and I need your accommodation. You'll have to move.'

This was a serious blow. Employing a dollop of my new-found detachment, I delegated Charlie and Dave to see the new base we had been allocated in Reckingen, a small village thirty kilometres from Brig up the valley to Andermatt, and told them to plan our move. I simply did not want to think about it. Brig had been ideal. Our rooms were Spartan but comfortable and we were only a short walk along the river, up 'leafy lane', to the shops, the bars and all those Danes. Most important, Brig was closer to the mountains we still needed to climb.

I phoned the lady warden of the Dent Blanche Hut, who said that in spite of snowfall everywhere else, there had been no snow on the mountain. The walk up to the hut is long (six hours in the guide book), but the normal route to the summit is up the South Ridge which reputedly clears quicker than most after bad weather. So, spurred on by the merest suggestion of good weather at the weekend, I persuaded Simon we should try our luck.

We found a good gear shop in Sion on the way, where we replaced slings we had left on the Grandes Jorasses, and we bought an excellent new lead rope: a 55 metre long 8.2 mm rope weighing only 44g/m which was an impressive ten metres longer and thirty-three per cent lighter than our old 45-metre-long 9 mm ropes at 68g/m. Sadly, the shop only had one and we promised ourselves a second, for abseiling, when we were next in Chamonix. Meantime, I carried another 9 mm rope. We did not expect problems on the Dent Blanche, but we now had a somewhat jaundiced view of guide books and had learned our lesson.

'Why don't we ride the mountain bikes up to the hut?' Simon said just before we left. 'So we can zoom down again.' He smiled winningly, brown eyes sparkling, plainly mad, and I agreed, just to humour him. However, when we reached Ferpècle (1880m) in the Val d'Hérens where the tarmac road runs out above Les Haudères village, we encountered some difficulties with this plan. The path disappeared vertically into larch and birch trees, twisting through thick rhododendrons, blue campanula and coarse grass. Beyond we could see a steep boulder-strewn hillside above the little reservoir. Nothing daunted, Simon and I donned our Koflachs, humped our rucksacks and tried pedalling up the first slope. Dragged back by my rucksack, I fell off. Simon found it no easier, so George, in between laughing and taking photographs, helped us hide the bikes in the rhododendrons so we could cycle downhill on our return.

Mark Cowell, or Death as we called him because of his dark and lugubrious expression, merely observed, 'Good job I know where to come and find you if there's a disaster.'

In fact, after Bricola, which is a collection of derelict old farm buildings at 2415 metres, the path widens to an easily cyclable track, rising gently across the Ruisseaux de Bricola until it reaches a sharp spine of moraine at 2640 metres. It is best to follow the path around the end of this spine, rather than climb steeply over it (as we did) which gains unnecessary height before crossing the river running out of the bottom of the Glacier des Manzettes on the other side. The clouds came and went as we walked, keeping us cool, but cleared as we crossed the glacier and gave us a grand view of the Dent Blanche high above us on our left. The mountain is a massive tetrahedron tilted slightly northwards but we were encouraged to see the rocks black and free of snow.

The glacier was dry up to about 3200 metres but we climbed on the right over a series of slabs smoothed by earlier centuries of ice. We followed clear marker posts onto the Roc Noir. This ridge is sharp (ish) but easy and leads onto the last snowy shoulder below the Dent Blanche Hut.

Twenty minutes from the hut, we were hit by a snow storm. The clouds came down very suddenly, the landscape vanished, the temperature dropped and wet hail blasted at us horizontally. Frozen in our T-shirts, we stopped to pull on extra clothes, amazed how quickly our fingers numbed in the cold wind. To our dismay the hail turned to snow and settled fast, clinging to us too, and we arrived at the hut looking like something from a *Scott of the Antarctic* movie.

This small stone-built hut stands on the nose of the final rock step under the snow shoulder which rises to the Wandflülücke and it sleeps forty. Martine, blonde, helpful and straightforward, was the warden, and Monique, slight, dark-haired, and very chatty with lovely brown eyes, was her assistant. Together they ran the place properly, and provided excellent cooked food and good company. They were very pleased to see us. Their numbers were badly down owing to the weather and Martine was despondent about others who had booked places that night. Monique brewed us hot soup and asked us about our walk up.

She broke off to answer the radio telephone. Four others who had been behind us at Ferpècle called in to say they had turned back in the snow storm. Monique quite frankly told them the snow was settling and added, 'We've just had an update from two British alpinists.'

Maybe she was impressed that we only took three and a half hours to walk up but we liked that, to be called an alpinist by a real member of the 'mountain community'. I suppose by this time we had done a lot of mountaineering. We had certainly learned an immense amount, isolated from the debilitating effects of bureaucracy and the world on our quest on the four-thousanders. Our problem now (and the ultimate reason for this book) was how to bring something of what we had experienced back to sea level.

Monique and Martine told us about two Germans who were on the South Ridge. If the snow storm did not let up they might be in serious difficulties. In the event, luck was with them. In nil visibility, they holed up at the bottom of the rock ridge on the Wandflülücke till a brief break in the clouds gave them a chance to nip down the snow shoulder to the hut as it got dark.

The storm whipped up again as they stripped off their soaking clothes, and rattled the eaves all night. Rime ice built up on the flag-pole, the wind flapped and snapped at the ropes, and the snow drifted, quickly covering my footprints to the outside khazi while I was inside sitting on the hole.

I passed the time translating a splendid notice (my version is at the end of this chapter).

Avis Important

Il a été remarqué récemment une tendance de certains à uriner à côté de la cuvette.

Par soucis d'hygiène et par respect pour tous, nous vous demanderons, à l'avenir, de respecter ces conseils.

1. *Si vous pissez à côté de la cuvette, mettez-vous donc de travers.*
2. *Si vous êtes distrait, déboutonnez votre braguette, ça vous évitera de pisser dans votre pantalon.*
3. *Si vous êtes prétentieux, avancez donc d'un pas – elle est plus courte que vous ne pensez!*
4. *Si vous êtes trop petit, montez donc sur un tabouret, au lieu de pisser partout en sautant.*
   D'avance merci.

This struck me as sound advice. Long-drop shithouses are notoriously unsavoury at mountain huts, in particular at the Goûter Hut in France.

The snow fell without let-up all Saturday and time passed very slowly. We sat on benches at tables. Simon read a Gerald Seymour (he had long ago given up with *Mein Kampf*), I typed notes into my PC3000, Monique knitted, Martine played cards and we all listened to Mozart on a battery-run CD player (charged by solar panels on a good day). I was fed up not being able to make a plan because of the weather. Everyone likes throwing their watch in a drawer when they go on holiday, to forget routine and the diary for two or three weeks. But we had been wholly dependent on the vagaries of the weather for months, unable to make a plan sometimes even a day ahead. Maybe planlessness is irrelevant on a desert island where eternity stretches out for ever like grains of sand on the beach, but we were now faced with an inescapable problem. We had to climb the remaining mountains before the deadline of the end of the season, itself dependent on the weather and impossible to date.

Fourteen people turned up during the day, covered in snow, their clothes soaking, and stamped about leaving pools of melted snow on the floorboards. One group amazed us. They took off their wet jerseys and fleeces and then solemnly put on waterproofs which they had had all along in their packs. They were members of a Swiss Mountaineerng club who came out at weekends and they planned to walk round to the Tête Blanche. Watching other people in huts is fascinating but the highlight of the day was undoubtedly Monique's fruit tart, hot from the oven at teatime, with hot chocolate.

The bunk room upstairs bustled noisily as everyone settled in for the night. Simon and I lay quietly in our corner in the dark on the top bunk (always better in our view) and wished for peace. I plugged in my Walkman and dozed off to that gentle ballad 'Promises'. Eric Clapton has a knack of getting it right.

The storm blew over in the middle of our second night and we woke to a perfectly clear sky filled with stars. I looked out of the little window onto a seascape of snowy peaks sparkling in the moon and standing out like islands from a sea of clouds at 3000 metres. This is what we had waited for, a sight to excite the most jaded cynic.

As usual, all the others started bumbling about in the darkness hours early. It was impossible to sleep but Simon and I let them all go downstairs before we moved from our warm blankets. Martine gave us hot water for our coffee and we watched them strap on their gear and leave the hut. They were still fiddling about with 'rope work' outside on the terrace when we came out and set off up the ridge behind the hut.

There had been more than thirty centimetres of snow, in places on the top of the Wandflülücke as much as fifty centimetres, and it was loose, dry, unconsolidated powder which filled the crevices where we wanted to put our hands and boots. However, we made good time to the col, following a French pair ahead.

Dawn spread from the eastern sky as we started on the South Ridge and I will never forget the scenery. The Dent Blanche is in the centre of the Pennine Alps with fantastic grandstand views of the Matterhorn, the Dent d'Hérens, the Monte Rosa group, the end of the Mischabel chain, the Obergabelhorn, the Zinalrothorn and the Grand Combin, which rises massively in the west. Every one of these magnificent mountains glistened with new snow in the perfect clarity of the bright morning light, like winter. Just walk up to the Wandflülücke and see.

The first half of the South Ridge is easy, even in the soft powder. We moved fast roped together and reached the Grand Gendarme in two hours from the hut. There we sat down on the last pinnacle under the gendarme, pulled out some sausage and bread and watched the French pair trying the gendarme direct, which Monique had advised us to do. It was obvious at once that they were in difficulty. The rocks are nearly vertical, all the cracks were filled with snow and the slabs were pasted with ice. The leader seemed brash, he used no protection and, munching our sausage like old hands, we expected him to come off any moment.

I swallowed a mouthful and observed, 'Let's be realistic, Simon, I'm not going up that!' Or that was the gist of what I said.

For some reason, Simon thought this enormously funny.

The other group behind us came past and we watched them too. They wanted to try their luck at the two-pitch traverse across the bottom of the gendarme to reach the couloir which turns the gendarme on the left at the back. The wretched guide stepped out, belayed by another in the party, but he must have realised the stupidity of it. The slope is steep and was thick with unconsolidated, fluffy snow. After only ten metres of very dodgy progress, he was obviously immensely relieved when one of his clients shouted at him to come back. At least, he had made the effort, to justify his fees.

'Excellent powder for skiing,' I remarked to the world at large. 'But useless for climbing.'

'Perfect for avalanches too,' said Simon with impeccable accuracy. While we sat eating our sausage and bread watching the others slip and slide on the Grand Gendarme, thirty climbers were avalanched off Pollux not far away, three died and six were seriously injured.

Above us, the two Frenchmen had wisely clipped into a fixed bolt and were preparing to abseil down. Simon and I turned round and set off back down the ridge to the hut. Monique fed us another slice of tart and sympathised with us, but oddly, even knowing we should have to return for the summit, we were not disappointed. Long gone were the days when we were obsessed with the 4000 metre contour line, the precise height of each mountain and ticking off our list of successes. We were climbing for the sake of it, for the pleasure of place and opportunity, for the challenge of all those decisions on the way, for the experience of the moment. On the Dent Blanche, we had had the privilege of wonderful climbing in a beautiful place and I felt on top of the world. We wanted to finish the job, but suddenly the target list of 4000ers no longer mattered.

We flew all the way down. The sun was brilliant, the mountains sparkled and we mucked about like idiots on the Glacier des Manzettes glissading on the new snow right down to 2700 metres. After a quick stop to strip off, we ran on, bouncing down the path in rhythm with our Walkmans. With an almost religious delight in the repetition, I listened over and over to Elton John: 'You can shoot down the moon', tirelessly intrigued by the lyric which sings of building bridges while 'The empty space remains'.

We reached Ferpècle in two hours, pulled our bikes out of the rhododendrons and cycled at huge speed down the road to Les Haudères. This was our concession to doing the mountains 'without mechanical assistance' but, like certain other parties who brandish this fashionable deception, we slyly handed our rucksacks and Koflachs to Death whom we met coming up the road in one of our VWs. Unencumbered, we overtook everything on the road and nearly killed ourselves through the hairpins, racing down to Les Haudères.

We relaxed over a couple of frothies in the sunshine in a café and I smelled the air. All the way down the mountain we had noticed a definite tang of autumn, like the smoky cold as you cross an icy mountain stream. New snow carpeted the mountains down to 2500 metres. The pines were still green, but seemed distant now and sharply in focus in the clear air, not hot and close as in summer heat. The temperature was cooler, a few brown leaves were lying at the side of the road and the days were shorter.

Summer was over.

Visitors, like envoys of the real world beyond the mountains, were waiting for us. Nikki Hatrick was back to see us. So was Tim Spicer with his stepson Benjamin, aged 14. They arrived on the same flight as Charlie's father, Brigadier Graham Messervy-Whiting, who had just finished a hectic nine months as Lord Owen's military advisor in Bosnia and the 'former Yugoslavia'. He wanted a rest and innocently thought that climbing Mont Blanc would be the answer.

Charlie had told him I wanted to take everyone to the summit. I told the Base party that if bus-loads of Japanese tourists could step straight off a coach and climb (or be dragged by French guides) to the summit, then so could anyone. Judging by the deep silence after this remark, not everyone was convinced, but at least they were ready to try.

Amazingly, the weather favoured us. Both the Swiss and French meteoromancers foretold sun and clear skies, then spoiled the spell with a curse of high winds, but we left for Chamonix next morning anyway.

After an agreeable lunch in the Bar Nash in the main square, we changed into plastic boots in the car park and took the lift to the Aiguille du Midi. As always here, the newcomers were amazed by the views and the exposure on the arête. There were unnerving floundering tracks of someone who had fallen off the sharp ridge, and footprints climbing back on, so we moved steadily, descending onto the Plan du Midi and stopped on a snow bank curving down from the cliff beneath the Cosmiques Hut. This was home, or soon would be. We stripped off and started digging snow holes.

There is plenty of room here for snowholes and the snow was ideal: cheesy, neither too hard nor too soft. Tim and I took it in turns with ours as Benjie found that the exercise gave him a headache. Typical Etonian, I muttered, but he was suffering from his first time at altitude. We installed him as soon as we had a useful cavern because he froze standing about outside and I wanted him in the best possible shape for the next day. None of the newcomers had had a chance to acclimatise properly and I resolved to keep a careful eye on Benjie in particular. Altitude affects the young more acutely than the old.

'I can't go back to Caroline and say we've lost him,' said Tim, meaning it.

'No problem,' I said. Neither of them realised how much they would have to push themselves next day.

Everyone disappeared into a variety of snowholes by sunset as the glorious translucence of the day faded behind the towering bulk of the Tacul. As the sky darkened, the moon rose enormous above the Dent du Géant and froze the winter landscape with silver light. Until a great flash of yellow light blazed inside the snowbank as Simon nearly incinerated Brigadier Messervy-Whiting and his son trying to light a new Epigas cylinder.

Inside our ice cave, Benjie, Tim and I made ourselves real cosy on our neoprene mats with room enough to sit up, and I prepared another chef's delight of fish bouillabaisse, washed down of course with more Gamay. After a brew of hot chocolate, we settled down to sleep for an hour or two before we had to move in the morning. Fortunately, Benjie slept well but Tim did not. Maybe it was my cooking or the altitude but a blazing headache kept him awake, and he sleeplessly watched the hands of his watch tick round till he could wake us on the strike of one o'clock as planned.

We were fourteen in four groups and after some milling about roping up, we turned towards the bulk of the Tacul Glacier in the silver light of the moon which had moved round over the first ridge. The light was so bright we hardly needed head-torches and our crampons made a very satisfying scrunching noise on the crisp hard snow.

Half-way up the glacier, Tim had to stop our rope for an urgent call of nature. My bouillabaisse, the Gamay and the altitude were wreaking merry havoc on his digestive system. I apologise for this detail as there is nothing worse than coming across someone else's excrement in the snow, but when a man has to go, he has to go, and on the steep slope of the Tacul there is not much option as to where he goes. I only wish I had taken a photograph. It is not every day you find a Lieutenant Colonel and Commanding Officer of Her Majesty's Foot Guards dropping his trousers and squatting in public while numerous people to whom he has not been introduced climb past him.

Soon after this edifying sight, Tim Boyle's knee gave up on him and Simon took him back to the snowholes. At the same place, the climbers ahead stopped and a queue formed. I scrambled up a bank and saw the reason. An impressively large and bottomless crevasse three metres wide split the slope from side to side. We had seen no sign of this hole when we were last there, but now the only way over was a narrow plank. No one minds walking along a couple of floorboards at home, but confidence evaporates high over a dark blue crevasse. There was a lot of arm-waving and wobbling in the moonlight and Nigel our second chef nearly fell in.

After the crevasse we made better progress, but I had to remind myself that the three behind me, Benjie, the youngest in the party, Graham, the eldest and Tim were neither acclimatised nor mountain fit. They were soon convinced that I was forcing them uphill at a breathless pace. I tried to recall the awful feeling the first time I climbed Mont Blanc some years before. We plodded on, at 'guide pace', which derives from a balance of time against a measure of the total energy of the weakest member of the party for the day's activity. I constantly turned to check how they were coping. Benjie was not weak, but he was the youngest and I was particularly aware that there was a point on Mont Maudit which would be the last time to make a decision on whether to go on right up to the summit, and commit them all the way down via the Goûter, or turn back.

The effort was all theirs. All we could do was watch and encourage (quite fiercely near the top!). Their headaches worsened, their muscles drained of strength and they felt increasingly tired and sick with the altitude. We crossed the Tacul Ridge, dropped into the Col Maudit (4035m) and started up the steep slope of the North Face of Mont Maudit at dawn. To offset the shock of being able to see the drop below them, I expected the sun to improve morale. Not that morning. The winds picked up unpleasantly and never abated, battering us continuously, exactly as forecast.

The route from the Midi over the Tacul and Mont Maudit is about the same distance as the Goûter route but more interesting. The Goûter route is relentlessly boring all the way up until the last excitement of the Bosses Ridge. Even so, Benjie periodically threw himself down on the snow declaring, 'This is ghastly! I'm not going another step. In any direction!'

Graham and Tim thankfully slumped to the snow too. They were stoically British and never complained but they were more than happy to use Benjie's honest reaction to the altitude for a good rest themselves. Benjie was strong for his age and his youth enabled him to recover much more quickly than the others at each rest stop.

After traversing the sides of Mont Maudit, they all found the sudden steepness of the Mur de la Côte back-breaking. The wind was viciously cold and whipped surface snow against our faces. We were terribly slow, zigzagging up the last long slope to the summit. We found some shelter in the lee on the Italian side. Benjie and Graham sat down like puppets with their strings cut and went straight to sleep. I very much doubt they have any recollection of the magnificent clear views in every direction but Graham and Charlie, father and son, have a photograph to remind them they once stood together on the highest point in western Europe.

They had done well, completing the route in something over eight hours, but the trick on mountains is coming down again safely. Douglas went on ahead with Charlie and Gonzo Martin, who was showing remarkable form for a serious smoker with an intimate knowledge of Brig's park-benches and bushes where he frequently finished up after a good night out. Tim led my group but Graham was so tired on the way down the Bosses Ridge that several times he simply went to sleep. His legs buckled, he fell flat on his face and slid off down the slope. I walked at the back, ice axe ready for this, but Benjie normally beat me to it. He looked and was tired out, but he was still aware.

We stopped in the Vallot Hut (4362m) for a respite after ten hours in the wind. This aluminium box hut is indescribably mucky, for which the French have really no excuse. Graham and Benjie went to sleep again on a pile of filthy mattresses and Tim was forced to brave the unspeakable conditions of the khazi. The hut may be a life-saver, but I suspect everyone is relieved to quit the Vallot.

At three o'clock, we stopped at the Goûter for a late lunch. After hours in the debilitatingly cold wind, the warmth had a dramatic effect and various people nodded off over their soup until Peter turned up unexpectedly with Dave Moore and George Roper. We had been looking for their rope behind us on the way but seen nothing and assumed they had turned back. Indeed, the Swiss liaison officer in Brig had said to Dave, 'You're just a cook! You'll never get to the top of Mont Blanc!' Furious, Dave was utterly determined 'to prove the bastard wrong!' They had been slow but they made it.

Beers were ordered, glasses clinked together and toasts made. A definite feeling of triumph took over and everyone started telling their stories. True, thousands reach the summit of Mont Blanc every year, but millions more never try, and no matter how many succeed, the effort is entirely individual. This route may not be technical, but it is long, arduous and high, with inherent risks. It was a delight to see how everyone began to appreciate their personal achievement, and to think how we had been able to help make it possible.

We stayed the night at the Tête Rousse Hut and woke early to a perfect dawn next morning, bright but very cold. I could smell the woodsmoke of autumn again. On the walk down the rocky path to the Nid d'Aigle, Tim asked if we had seen much wildlife.

I told him about the ibex on the Gornergrat and the chamois on the Weingarten Glacier but said, 'The animals seem very chary of humans in Switzerland.'

'I'm not surprised,' Tim laughed. 'The Swiss like shooting them.'

As we spoke we turned a corner and saw several chamois on the path. They glanced up disdainfully and carried on grazing, quite unconcerned. We approached to within ten metres while they nibbled sparse tufts of grass between the rocks or snuffled at the sandy track for salt. Plainly, these very wise French chamois had read the National Park regulations: no shooting. Pity the Swiss do not follow this example too.

We drove back to Brig to find the Swiss liaison officer wanted us to move out of our building at once, that night. The telephone had been cut off and Simon had already begun to supervise the move. Everything broke up. Charlie drove his father Graham, Tim and Benjie to Geneva airport and by the time he returned, our accommodation was cleared, our boxes of equipment were on the road in the eight-tonner and Mike Nutter had called out for the last time to the girl who passed our window every evening at supper. It was September, the end of the season, and Coupe Danemark was no longer being served at the tables under the plane trees outside the Britannia.

Douglas took me on the back of his Honda CBR1000 up the valley, fast, through tight bends past Mörel and Fiesch to Reckingen where next day snow dusted the low hills and the weather closed in for ever.

Translation of lavatorial advice:

Important Notice

It has been noticed recently there is a tendency for certain people to miss the hole while pissing.

For reasons of hygiene and out of respect for others, we ask you in future to take heed of the following advice.

1. *If you are missing the hole, move over.*
2. *If you are absent-minded, unbutton your flies first to avoid pissing in your trousers.*

3. *If you are pretentious, come a pace forward – it isn't as long as you think it is.*
4. *If you are short, stand on a step instead of jumping up and down and pissing all over the place as you try to piss in the hole.*

EPILOGUE

The sense of danger must not disappear:
The way is certainly both short and steep,
However gradual it looks from here;
Look if you like, but you will have to leap.
                                                    W.H. Auden

Reckingen was monkish. No flowers grew now in the grass meadows of the broad Goms valley. At 1325 metres the ground was cold, 640 metres higher than Brig. Snow whitened the dark pine slopes on the hillsides and the ridges above were in cloud. Black wood chalets with bright red geraniums at their windows straddled the railway and the river. Traffic on the main road from the Furka and Grimsel Passes went through the village on higher ground flanked by modern concrete buildings, a store, two chalet hotel-restaurants and a white Palladian Gothic church topped by a slate-grey onion dome: complete with a fine clock which chimed every quarter, and a full set of bells.

We lived in a three-storey house under the church, with the luxury of single or double rooms and hot showers, we were fed well and drank in a bar on the other side of the road, but we were woken by the bells regularly on the hour, every hour, all through the night. I decided they tolled for bad weather. Autumn was in the air, and snow on the hills. Lots of it.

The days without climbing were intensely frustrating. Our gear lay unused on spare beds in our rooms, a catalogue of economy born of experience, but storms continued to thrash the high mountains and the weak autumn sun was not strong enough to consolidate the new snow. Roger flew across the Monte Rosa in a Swiss Army helicopter and reported huts at only 3000 metres almost covered with snow, like one expects to see in mid-winter.

I decided we would wait another week, to see if the weather pattern changed. Keyed up, extremely fit and ready to climb, the waiting produced a sense of unreality. We went to a chamber concert in the church, of Vivaldi, Telemann and Albinoni, we ate superbly in the Hôtel Croix d'Or in Münster (where the crêpes Suzette 'Schmeckts were outstandingly good) and we drove down the valley to see the Danes in Brig.

After one long night celebrating Charlie's twenty-first birthday, we assembled in uniform feeling less than robust for a press call at the behest of Brigadier Mudry. He was pleased with our achievement and so was I. We had climbed forty-eight summits, we had done it on our own without guides, starting with virtual beginners who had learned fast, and we had often been three on a rope. We had not been supported by an experienced Base Camp team who could supply us in the mountains. Our base team had supported us in Brig. We had climbed just as anyone else would do on holiday in the Alps. Sometimes we had camped, sometimes we had stayed in huts.

'And you've avoided injury,' said Jean-Daniel Mudry smiling genially for his photographer who was busy snapping away. Dressed as a Scots Guards Major, I tried desperately to look crisp. Douglas ignored me.

'You realise 52 climbers have died this season in Switzerland while you've been here?' Brigadier Mudry went on.

I wondered at the number in France and Italy.

In the next days, the temperature dropped a few more degrees and we woke one morning to see the Furka Pass white with fresh snow down to 2000 metres. The wardens in the Hörnli Hut, the Schreckhorn Hut and Monique in the Dent Blanche Hut all gloomily reported so much new snow on the hills they expected no more climbing. The high priests of meteorological clairvoyance in Geneva and Chamonix gave us no hope. Even the Glishorn above Brig was dusted white as it had been when we had arrived in April. The climbing season was over.

At dawn on 20 September, after several hectic farewell parties, Peter took the convoy of our gentian-blue trucks up the valley to Andermatt, over the Furka Pass in fresh snow on their way north to Germany and England.

I went in the other direction on the Furka-Oberalp train to Brig where I changed for Geneva and a flight back to Heathrow. I was leaving after five months in the Alps. The little red train rattled down the valley, on time at each stop as usual. The air was wonderfully clear, for the first time in weeks of foul weather. The ridges above the valley were sharp dark lines against the pale blue sky. Wet autumn mist hung over the fields and ice-cold spray rose like steam from the rivers tumbling down from the mountains on either side.

The leaves were turning, lying damply on the roads. We had arrived in winter when the trees were bare and seen them through to fall, yellowing birch, cherry and apples and bright red splashes of maple among the dark green pines.

There is something reflective about autumn. I thought about all the mountains we had climbed. On the horizon in the distance, far above the surrounding mountains, the Weisshorn and Bishorn were shrouded in white, my last glimpse of the four-thousanders. Even though we had been unable to reach all the summits we had so bureaucratically listed at the start, I was now certain that all the Alpine four-thousanders can be climbed by ordinary climbers in one year. Only the weather, the one factor quite outside our control, had spoiled our chances.

I had no regrets. We had made lasting friendships. Each of us had discovered something of ourselves. Yet the journey was not over. On some climbs we had lived on the leading edge of experience for a short while and we had learned that sometimes in life our dreams of safety have to disappear. We have to commit ourselves, and sometimes, whatever or wherever the circumstances, we must leap before we look.

On the mountains, beyond the reach of bureaucracy, we were privileged to experience exceptional freedoms and challenges, and memories which leave us with an enormous sense of achievement at having climbed so much, in such varied conditions, on some of the finest mountains in the world.

APPENDICES

Appendix 1 A Summary of the Climbs

MOUNTAIN	ALTITUDE		GRADE max. diff for route	DATE CLIMBED
	metres	feet		
Allalinhorn	4027	13,217	F	3 May
Breithorn	4164	13,666	PD–	4 May
Pollux	4092	13,430	PD/II	5 May
Mönch	4099	13,453	PD/II	8 May
Jungfrau	4158	13,647	PD+/II	9 May
Gross-Fiescherhorn	4049	13,289	PD+/II	10 May
Hinter-Fiescherhorn	4025	13,210	PD/II	10 May
Castor	4228	13,876	AD	17 May
Signalkuppe	4556	14,953	PD	18 May
Zumsteinspitze	4563	14,976	PD	21 May
"				22 May
Jungfrau	4158	13,647	PD+/II	24 May
Gross-Grünhorn	4044	13,272	PD+/III–	25 May
Finsteraarhorn	4273	14,024	PD/II	26 May
"				27 May
Bishorn	4153	13,630	F/I	29 May
"				30 May
Alphubel	4206	13,804	PD/II	1 Jun
Strahlhorn	4190	13,752	PD	3 Jun
"				4 Jun
Rimpfischhorn	4199	13,781	PD+/II+	5 Jun
Grand Combin	4314	14,159	AD+	8 Jun
"				9 Jun
Nordend	4609	15,127	PD/II	15 Jun
"				16 Jun
Dufourspitze	4634	15,209	PD/II+	16 Jun
"				17 Jun
Liskamm	4527	14,858	AD	18 Jun
"				19 Jun
Parrotspitze	4436	14,559	PD	19 Jun
Ludwigshöhe	4341	14,247	F	19 Jun
Schwarzhorn	4322	14,185	PD	19 Jun

NOTES ON THE APPROACH	THE CLIMBING				
	ASCENT		DESCENT		
	Start	Finish	Start	Finish	Kms
Skied fm Felskinn. Metro closed!	09:05	12.10	12:30	13.53	13.5
Skied fm Klein Matterhorn lift.	11:00	12:30	12:55	14:00	12.2
Skied fm Klein Matterhorn lift.	09:08	12:04	12:35	15:30	17.4
Skied fm Jungfraujoch station.	10:56	13:29	13:45	15:06	4.0
Fm Mönch Hut. First attempt.	07:00	08:30	08:30	13:40	8.5
Out & back fm Mönch Hut, both	06:54	10:17	10:30	11:01	
on same excellent day.	11:01	12:40	12:50	16:16	14.9
Lift to Klein Matterhorn.	09:05	13:25	13:35	18:13	16.4
Fm Monte Rosa Hut after Castor	05:57	11:46	Stayed on summ		10.0
In Margherita Hut all week.	09:03	10:30	10:30	12:55	1.4
Fm Margherita Hut on Sig'kuppe.	06:30	07:40	07:55	11:22	16.7
Started fm Jungfraujoch rlwy.	10:20	13:15	13:25	16:25	15.5
Fm Konkordia Hut.	06:04	10:25	10:40	15:40	16.5
Fm Finsteraarhorn Hut	05:57	10:45	10:55	12:10	6.0
Descent over Fiesch Glacier.			08:13	15:44	18.5
Walk up to Tracuit Hut.	08:57	14:13			8.5
Summit day descent to valley.	06:13	08:58	09:20	12:29	16.5
Fm Langflüh lift station.	08:50	12:10	12:45	13:11	7.5
To Britannia Hut fm Langflüh.	15:20	17:05			5.5
Fm hut to summit, then to tents	06:16	10:08	11:15	11:55	11.5
Straight fm tents on glacier.	04:17	07:33	07:55	11:35	18.0
Long ski approach fm Pindin.	09:28	15:25			8.8
Summit climb & ski out.	04:15	07:31	07:50	12:14	14.6
Ski via Gornergrat to 3670m	08:46	15:33			10.0
Summit ski, then st to Dufour.	04:55	08:50	09:05	10:09	
Long ridge climb, then to tents	10:09	14:13	14:30	17:10	10.0
Nil vis at Lisjoch, so exfil.	05:00	08:30	08:30	14:00	18.6
Drive to Italy, to Gnifetti Hut.	15:15	16:30			2.0
Summit ski, then st to Dufour.	04:00	07:55	08:15	09:25	
We did all these one morning	09:25	11:00	11:10	11:45	
after Liskamm (excellent snow	11:45	12:00	12:05	12:15	
ridge), then skied and walked	12:15	12:42	12:46	12:55	

MOUNTAIN	ALTITUDE		GRADE max. diff for route	DATE CLIMBED
	metres	feet		
Balmenhorn	4167	13,676	PD	19 Jun
Vincent Piramide	4215	13,834	PD	19 Jun
				24 Jun
Piz Bernina	4049	13,289	AD/I	25 Jun
Gran Paradiso	4061	13,328	PD–/exp II	27 Jun
"				28 Jun
Madonna Summit	4058	13,318	PD–/II	28 Jun
Lagginhorn	4010	13,161	PD/II	30 Jun
Weissmies	4023	13,203	PD	1 Jul
Aletschhorn	4195	13,768	PD	3 Jul
"				4 Jul
Dent d'Hérens	4171	13,689	AD/III	15 Jul
"				16 Jul
Dürrenhorn	4035	13,243	AD/II +	26 Jul
"				27 Jul
Hohberghorn	4219	13,847	PD/II	27 Jul
Stecknadelhorn	4241	13,919	PD/II–	28 Jul
Nadelhorn	4327	14,201	PD/II +	28 Jul
Aig. du Midi camp.	3532	11,592		29 Jul
Mont Blanc du Tacul	4248	13,942	PD	30 Jul
Mont Maudit	4465	14,654	PD	30 Jul
Mont Blanc	4807	15,777	PD	30 Jul
Dome du Goûter	4304	14,126	PD	30 Jul
Aig. de Bionnassay	4052	13,299	AD/II	30 Jul
Aiguille Blanche	4112	13,496	D + /IV	1 Aug
"				2 Aug
"				3 Aug
Zinalrothorn	4221	13,853	AD–/III–	6 Aug
"				7 Aug
Obergabelhorn	4063	13,335	AD/III	8 Aug
Täschhorn	4490	14,736	AD/III	10 Aug
"				12 Aug
Dom	4545	14,917	AD/III	12 Aug
"				13 Aug
Dent du Géant	4013	13,171	AD/III	15 Aug
"				16 Aug
Aig. de Rochefort	4001	13,131	AD/II	17 Aug
Dôme de Rochefort	4015	13,177	AD/II	17 Aug
(Descent fm Dôme, via Pte Young)			D/IV	18 Aug
				19 Aug
Dent Blanche	4356	14,296	AD/III	27 Aug
"				29 Aug
Aig du Midi camp.	3532	11,592		31 Aug
Mont Blanc	4807	15,777	PD	1 Sep
"				

| NOTES ON THE APPROACH | THE CLIMBING | | | | |
| | ASCENT | | DESCENT | | |
	Start	Finish	Start	Finish	Kms
all way to down to Alagna	12:55	13:08	13:12	13:20	
village.	13:20	13:44	13:54	19:20	30.2
Walk down fm lift station.	16:30	17:30			0.5
Summit day. Back to station.	03:50	11:00	11:15	17:20	20.5
Walk up thru woods to hut.	15:15	17:15			5.3
Summit day, on skis, superb.	04:31	07:55	08:06	08:11	
Same day as Gran Paradiso	08:11	08:19	08:45	11:45	16.1
Lift to Hoh Saas Restaurant.	07:15	11:51	12:15	14:56	7.6
Fm tents at Hoh Saas.	03:53	07:15	07:40	08:35	7.8
Approach march to biv hut.	13:20	18:45			12.0
Summit day and walk out again.	03:56	07:13	07:35	13:14	21.0
Walk up to Aosta biv hut.	14:15	16:43			7.8
Summit and v long walk out.	04:06	12:11	12:20	23:27	15.0
Walk up past Dom hut to biv.	10:06	15:48			6.0
Summit via Festi & Hoberg gls.	05:01	10:58	11:05	11:30	
Traverse fm Dürrenhorn.	11:30	13:21	13:25	13:45	
Traverse fm Hohberghorn.	13:50	14:43	14:50	15:24	6.6
Fm bivvy on ridge at 4190m	08:14	10:15	10:30	15:20	9.6
Lift to Midi, tents on Plan	16:45	17:15			1.5
Summit. Early start, no moon.	01:31	03:23	03:35	03:55	
Romped full traverse Mt Blanc	03:55	05:49	06:00	06:10	
fm Col du Midi via Gouter and	06:10	07:31	07:55	08:20	
Bionnassay down to Les Houches	08:20	08:38	08:55	09:08	
Tiring but superb day.	00:08	10:16	10:25	14:35	19.8
Walk to Monzino hut fm Freiney	16:30	17:58			3.8
Hut to Eccles bivouac.	02:21	07:44			2.6
Eccles down; v soft warm Foehn			08:15	10:55	6.4
Walk up: Zermatt to Rothorn hut	11:00	15:30			7.4
Summit. Up & back to tents	02:47	6:41	07:00	09:36	6.0
Fm Rothorn hut too, next day	02:38	07:12	07:30	14:51	16.0
Walk up to Mischabel biv hut	11:08	16:39			4.5
Full Täschhorn–Dom traverse	04:55	09:12	09:20	14:59	
Fm summit of Dom to Dom Hut	14:59	19:33	19:45	22:47	6.9
Dom Hut down to Randa			08:20	11.00	4.3
Lift to Torino, walk to camp	16:00	16:30			1.6
Tents to summit, then ridge	05:34	11:09	11:30	14:12	3.0
Fm snow-hole bivvy under Dent	05:55	07:30	07:45	08:00	0.7
Along Rochefort Ridge fm Aig	08:00	09:02	09:20	14:50	0.4
Took 2 days; 6 hrs abseiling	06:00	13:30	14:00	21:30	2.1
each day. Down to Planpincieux			05:45	16:50	4.8
Walk up to hut. Snowstorm start	12:35	16:44			8.0
Attempt after two days. Powder	05:27	08:10	08:10	13:10	11.6
Lift to Midi, all in snowholes	15:40	16:10			1.5
Early but brilliant full moon	01:50	10:40	11:05	19:45	16.5
Took all base camp party onto			06:30	08:30	3.2
Mont Blanc including the chef					

Appendix 2

Map Reference

Rather than give a large scale map of the general area of the entire Alps, the following shopping list of maps for each mountain will be more useful, giving codes of each map for ordering.

SCALES: unless otherwise given, scales are as follows:
1 All Swiss LKS maps numbered 1200–1300+ are 1:25,000
2 All Swiss LKS maps numbered 5000+ are 1:50,000 combination maps
3 All Swiss LKS maps numbered 200+ are 1:50,000
4 Most French IGN maps are 1:25,000

A. GENERAL AREA MAPS

Peak	Map	Scale
Piz Bernina	LKS 44 Maloja	1:100,000
Gran Paradiso	Kompasskarte No 86 Gran Paradiso	
Barre des Ecrins	IGN foot and ski no. 6, Ecrins et Haut Dauphine	1:50,000
Bernese Oberland	LKS 5004	
Matterhorn-Mischabel	LKS 5006	
Mischabel	LKS 248	
Gressoney	LKS 294	

B. DETAILED MAPS OF INDIVIDUAL PEAKS

Peak	Map	Scale
	OUTLIERS	
Piz Bernina	LKS 1277 Piz Bernina	
	LKS 44 Maloja	1:100,000

Gran Paradiso	IGC 62003 Gran Paradiso	1:50,000
	Kompasskarte No. 86 Gran Paradiso	
Barre des Ecrins	IGN 241 Massif des Ecrins	1:25,000
	IGN foot & Ski 6,	1:50,000

CENTRAL BERNESE OBERLAND

Aletschhorn	LKS 1269 Aletsch Glacier	
	LKS 5004 Berner Oberland	cf Jungfrau
Jungfrau	LKS 264 Jungfrau	
Mönch	LKS 264 Jungfrau	
	LKS 1249 Finsteraarhorn	
Gross-Fiescherhorn	LKS 1249 Finsteraarhorn	
	LKS 264 Jungfrau	
Hinter-Fiescherhorn	LKS 1249 Finsteraarhorn	
Gross-Grünhorn	LKS 1249 Finsteraarhorn	
	LKS 1269 Gr Aletsch Gletscher	

EAST BERNESE OBERLAND

Schreckhorn	LKS 1299 Grindelwald	
Lauteraarhorn	LKS 1250 Ulrichen	
	LKS 1229 Grindelwald	
	LKS 1249 Finsteraarhorn	
Finsteraarhorn	LKS 1249 Finsteraarhorn	cf Aletschhorn

EASTERN PENNINE ALPS

Lagginhorn	LKS 1309 Simplon	
	LKS 5006 Matterhorn-Mischabel	
Weissmies	LKS 1329 Saas	

NORTHERN PENNINE ALPS – MISCHABEL GROUP

Nadelhorn	LKS 1328 Randa	also
		LKS 5006
Duerrenhorn	LKS 1328 Randa	
Hohberghorn	LKS 1328 Randa	
Stecknadelhorn	LKS 1328 Randa	
Lenzspitze	LKS 1328 Randa	
Dom	LKS 1328 Randa	
Täschhorn	LKS 1328 Randa	

NORTHERN PENNINE ALPS – ALLALIN GROUP

Alphubel	LKS 1328 Randa	
Allalinhorn	LKS 1328 Randa	
	LKS 1329 Saas	
Rimpfischhorn	LKS 1348 Zermatt	
Strahlhorn	LKS 1348 Zermatt	

LKS 1328 Randa

NORTH-WEST PENNINE ALPS

Bishorn	LKS 1327 Evolene
	LKS 1328 Randa
Weisshorn	LKS 1328 Randa
Zinalrothorn	LKS 1328 Randa
	LKS 1348 Zermatt
	LKS 1327 Evolene
Obergabelhorn	LKS 1328 Randa
	LKS 1348 Zermatt
	LKS 1327 Evolene
Dent Blanche	LKS 1347 Matterhorn
	LKS 1327 Evolene

EASTERN PENNINE FRONTIER CREST – MONTE ROSA GROUP

Nordend	LKS 1348 Zermatt
Dufourspitze	LKS 1348 Zermatt
Zumsteinspitze	see Signalkuppe (next)
Signalkuppe	LKS 1348 Zermatt
	LKS 248 Mischabel
	LKS 294 Gressoney
Parrotspitze	see Signalkuppe
Ludwigshoehe	see Signalkuppe
Schwarzhorn	see Signalkuppe
Balmenhorn	see Signalkuppe
Vincent Piramide	see Signalkuppe

CENTRAL PENNINE FRONTIER CREST

Liskamm	see Signalkuppe
Castor	LKS 1348 Zermatt
	LKS 294 Gressoney
Pollux	LKS 1348 Zermatt
Breithorn	LKS 1348 Zermatt
Matterhorn	LKS 1348 Zermatt
	LKS 1347 Matterhorn
Dent d'Hérens	LKS 1347 Matterhorn

WESTERN PENNINE FRONTIER CREST

Grand Combin	LKS 5003 Mont Blanc-Grand Combin

EASTERN MONT BLANC RANGE

Aig. Verte	IGN 1 Massif du Mont Blanc 1:25,000 number 3630 ouest
Grande Rocheuse	see Aig. Verte

Aig. du Jardin	see Aig. Verte
Les Droites	see Aig. Verte
Grandes Jorasses	IGN 1 Massif du Mont Blanc 1:25,000
Dôme de Rochefort	see Grandes Jorasses
Aig. de Rochefort	see Grandes Jorasses
Dent du Géant	see Grandes Jorasses

MONT BLANC MASSIF

Mont Blanc du Tacul	IGN 1 Massif du Mont Blanc 1:25,000 number 3630 ouest
Mont Maudit	see Mont Blanc du Tacul
Mont Blanc	IGN 1 Chamonix-Mont Blanc 1:25,000
	IGN 2 St Gervais les Bains
Aig. de Bionnassay	IGN 2 Mont Blanc-Trélatête 1:25,000
Mont Brouillard	see Grandes Jorasses and Mont Blanc
Punta Baretti	see Grandes Jorasses and Mont Blanc
Aig. Blanche	IGN 2 Mont Blanc-Trélatête 1:25,000

Appendix 3

Climbing Grades

Rock Climbing Grades

Britain		France	Germany	USA	UIAA
Moderate		1	I	5.2	I
Difficult		2	II	5.3	II+
Hard Difficult		2	II	5.3	II+
Very Difficult		3	III	5.4	III
Hard Very Difficult		3	III	5.4	III+
Mild Severe		4	IV	5.5	IV−
Severe	4a, 4b	4	IV	5.5	IV
Hard Severe	4a, 4b, 4c	5	V	5.6	V−
Very Severe	4b, 4c, 5a	5	VI	5.7	V
Hard Very Severe	4c, 5a, 5b	5+	VIIa	5.8	VI−
	5a, 5b	6a	VIIb	5.9	VI

The Alpine Grades

Routes are given an overall grade, with rock pitches graded on the UIAA scale (see above). Grades given for a particular route are a guide only. The actual difficulties encountered on the mountains vary with conditions.

F– facile, or easy.
PD– peu difficile, or moderately difficult.
AD– assez difficile, or fairly difficult.
D– difficile, or difficult.
TD– très difficile, or very difficult.
ED– extrêmement difficile, or extremely difficult.
ABO– abominable, which needs no translating.

Appendix 4

Equipment

This annex, for the use of future expeditions, details the equipment used during the winter, ski mountaineering, and during the summer, when the weather was, in theory, warmer.

A. Ski Mountaineering

1 Skis, Swiss Army touring. These weighed 6.825 kg, twice as much as civilian skis.
2 Ski touring safety bindings, Swiss Army.
3 Ski poles, Swiss Army. Also heavier than civ ski sticks.
4 Touring ski boots, Dynafit 'Tourlites' (excellent).
5 Skins, Swiss Army.
6 Flat ski ice blades, Swiss Army harscheisen.
7 Rucksack, 50–55 litres. Needs side straps for skis.
8 Rucksack liner (poly bag).
9 Sleeping bag, 4 season.
10 Compression sack for bag.
11 Neoprene roll mat.
12 Tent, lightweight 2-man. (Vaude 'Hogan', 2.2 kg)
13 Aluminium cook pot, 2 litres plus lid (vol for melting snow).
14 Mug, plastic and large.
15 EPI-gas high altitude mix, appliance (140g) and cylinders.
16 Lighter and spare matches.
17 Wind shield, aluminium lightweight.
18 Wood spoon.
19 Rations. A selection fm 24hr Arctic (plus civ packet sauces, curry powder to make the bloody granules taste of something).
20 Bread/chocolate/salami for snacks en route.
21 Water flask, 1 litre, plus neoprene insulated jacket.

22 Rope, 8.2mm, 55 metres, one per pair (or three).
23 Sit, or Alpine, harness.
24 Crampons, plus crampon bag.
25 Ice axe (flat adze). 2 ice tools as nec.
26 Snow shovel. For snowholes, or avalanche emergencies.
27 6ft slings, 3 or more as req.
28 Karabiners, 2 or 3 snap, 1 screwgate.
29 Altimeter; Thommen Classic, or Citizen 'Promaster' watch-cum-altimeter (both excellent).
30 Outer shell jacket, Gore-Tex.
31 Inner jacket, fleece.
32 Outer gloves, mitts, Gore-Tex.
33 Inner gloves, mitts, Dachsteins (excellent combination).
34 Outer shell trousers, Gore-Tex, zip all way up side.
35 Inner trousers, fleece, or tracksuit bottoms.
36 Emergency Helly Hansen long-sleeved vest and long-johns.
37 Emergency Duvet jacket.
38 Hat, woolly or fleece balaclava.
39 Lightweight baseball cap (for sun-protection).
40 Sunglasses, plus spare pair in group.
41 Sun block cream and lip cream.
42 Scarf.
43 Socks, 2 pairs, Fox River (excellent)
44 First aid kit; shell dressing, 'Spenco' blister kit and paracetamol.
45 'Pieps' avalanche transceiver.
46 Camera and film. 28mm lens ideal.
47 Note book and pencil, or light computer e.g. Sharp PC3000.
48 Radio transceiver, light, for heli rescue.
49 Loadstraps, eg for crampons on top of rucksack.
50 Penknife.
51 Head-torch (Petzl good), spare battery and bulb.
52 Maps, 'fabloned'.
53 Lightweight thermal survival sheet.
54 Photostats from guide book and topo.
55 Snow gaiters, a matter of personal choice.

B Summer Climbing

The equipment here reflects the increased climbing on rock routes, when more protection is required and abseiling expected. Plus, with the 'sleep system' we used, hoped-for increased temperatures.

1 Helmet, Petzl, with elastics for head-torch. Stone fall a real problem.
2 Thin balaclava.

3 Rucksack, 50–55 litres. Needs side straps for skis.

4 Rucksack liner (poly bag).

5 Sleep system.
   Instead of carrying a heavy tent and 4 season sleeping bag, we chose to carry a bivvy bag, no sleeping bag, and wore every bit of clothing we had, much of which we carried anyway in case of emergencies, sleeping of course on a neoprene mat. This worked in the summer weeks, even on snow.

6 Sleeping bag, 1 season lightweight, depending on temperatures (see sleep system para 5).

7 Compression sack for bivvy bag (not really nec).

8 Neoprene roll mat.

9 Gore-Tex bivvy bag.

10 Aluminium cook pot, 2 litres plus lid (vol for melting snow).

11 Mug, plastic and large.

12 EPI-gas high altitude mix, appliance (140gms) and cylinders.

13 Lighter and spare matches.

14 Wind shield, aluminium lightweight.

15 Wood spoon.

16 Rations. A selection fm 24hr Arctic (plus civ packet sauces, curry powder etc to make the bloody granules taste of something).

17 Bread/chocolate/salami for snacks en route.

18 Water flask, 1 litre, plus neoprene insulated jacket.

19 Rope, two × 8.2mm, 55 metres per pair. Makes good long abseil.

20 Sit, or Alpine, harness.

21 Fig 8 descender. An Italian hitch twists the rope.

22 Telescopic ski stick, as walking stick. Useful and light.

23 Crampons (with metal toe bar is best, as toe straps get worn easily on rocks) plus crampon bag.

24 Ice axe (flat adze). 2 ice tools as nec.

25 Snow shovel. For snowholes, or avalanche emergencies.

26 Slings. 6ft slings, 3+ as req. per person on 2-man rope.

27 Spare tape, for making abseil points.

28 Protection: 6 to 10 items – a mix of different sized 'Friends', chocks, hex's or nuts, and 1 or 2 lightweight titanium ice screws.

29 Karabiners, 1 snap per item of protection.
   plus 3 spare.
   plus 3 screwgate, two for harness tie in and abseil, both large offset 'D'.

30 Altimeter; Thommen Classic, or Citizen 'Promaster' watch-cum-altimeter (both excellent).

31 Outer shell jacket, Gore-Tex.

32 Inner jacket, fleece.

33 Gloves, leather, Gore-Tex. Good for climbing on icy rocks.
34 Spare outer shell gloves, mitts, Gore-Tex, plus light wool inners.
34 Outer shell trousers, Gore-Tex, zip all way up side.
35 Inner trousers, fleece, or tracksuit bottoms.
36 Emergency Helly Hansen long-sleeved vest and long-johns.
37 Emergency Duvet jacket.
38 Hat, woolly or fleece balaclava.
39 Lightweight baseball cap (for sun-protection).
40 Sunglasses, plus spare pair in climbing group.
41 Sun block cream and lip cream.
42 Scarf.
43 Socks, 2 pairs, Fox River (excellent)
44 First aid kit; shell dressing, 'Spenco' blister kit and paracetamol.
45 'Pieps' avalanche transceiver.
46 Camera and film. 28mm lens ideal.
47 Note book and pencil, or light computer e.g. Sharp PC3000.
48 Radio transceiver, light, for heli rescue.
49 Loadstraps, e.g. for crampons on top of rucksack.
50 Penknife.
51 Head torch (Petzl good), spare battery and bulb.
52 Maps, 'fabloned'.
53 Lightweight thermal survival sheet.
54 Photostats from guide book and topo.
55 Plastic shell mountain boots, Koflachs (excellent).
56 Snow gaiters. These need to be the toughest avail.
57 Duvet socks, as part of 'sleep system'. Light and warm.

Appendix 5

Sponsors

The following sponsored the expedition with equipment and funds.

1 Britannia Sports Ltd (47 Poulters Lane, Worthing, Sussex, BN14 7ST). Gloria Vanderper Cloren very generously supplied fleece and Gore-tex shell garments to the climbers, and sportswear to the base support team. This clothing was invaluable as some of us had nothing to start with.

2 Citizen Watch UK Ltd (Quoin House, Fishponds Road, Wokingham, Berkshire, RG11 2QJ). The Marketing Director, Mr Andrew Martland, kindly gave us four *Citizen Promaster Watches*.

These watches combine full altimeter functions and memory capacity for seven time and altitude points en route with normal watch functions. This watch is expensive, more than a Thommen Classic say, but over five months I found mine more accurate (3m out between the Midi and the summit of Mt Blanc), more convenient because it is on the wrist, you can tell the time with it, the night luminosity is excellent, and it looks good. The best altimeter you can have on the hills.

3 Revue-Thommen (CH-4437 Waldenburg, Basle, Switzerland). Mr Ph. Schaer gave us 6 Thommen Classics (to 6000m) and 6 electronic Altitronic Traveller altimeters, to compare them, and another computerised altimeter which Douglas used for a while but we sent it back as it was really designed for engineering uses, too complex and not 'soldier-proof' on the mountains.

The Thommen Classic is well known. Our small crib was that the string is the wrong side, so when it's hanging round your neck you can't just lift it up to see the dial; you have to twist it round. It is also bigger than a watch altimeter and means carrying another bit of gear. Plus, you can't tell the time with it. But it rightly remains an attractive item: it is very good.

The Altitronic Traveller did not measure up to the rigours of mountaineering. The buttons kept switching on or off or changing functions, the info window had a habit of misting up, and if the battery konks out, as happens in the cold, you lose all its memory.

4 Fox River Socks (Moonraker Marketing, The Old Warehouse, Finnimore Industrial Estate, Alansway, Ottery St Mary, Devon EX11 1AH). Mr and Mrs Michael Moore supported us with more than 60 pairs of socks and we all agreed that these were the finest socks we had ever worn, without exception.

I have a pair which did 600kms and nearly 60,000m of up and by all the rules should be crushed, worn and extremely smelly. In fact, you would be pressed to tell this pair from a new pair (and it smells sweetly).

The wicking properties are excellent. I thoroughly recommend these jobs.

5 Calange Outdoor Clothing Ltd (PO Box 61, Stockport, Cheshire, SK3 0AP). Caroline Croft and Charles Moss gave us a Calange *balaclava* which was a good design, colourful, comfortable to wear for long periods and bloody warm.

Their Peruvian-style pixie hats were not very popular. They may be made of jolly warm stuff, but they look silly.

6 DIP Systems Ltd (2 Frederick Sanger Road, Surrey Research Park, Guildford, GU2 5XN). Oliver Tucker gave me a *PC3000 pocket sized IBM compatible computer*. All the innards are designed by DIP Systems and this 480gms gadget is stuffed with first class, leading-edge, British, solid-state technology. There are no wobbly working parts. Only the batteries and the keys rattle around slightly when you give it a good shake. It was quite excellent. It was just big enough for me to touch-type its keyboard. It lived in my rucksack. It suffered every fall, being flung about, dragged up mountains, dropped down them, abrupt falls skiing, extremes of temperature, freezing at night (and day), and warmth in the sun. It always worked. (I got some weird looks using it in the huts).

When I got back to the office, I merely Lap-linked my notes onto my IBM desktop. I could not have written this book without it. A real boon.

7 Relum Tents Ltd (Carlton Park Industrial Estate, Kelsale, Saxmundham, Suffolk IP17 2NL). Peter Stockdale kindly loaned us two 14' × 14' frame tents which were most useful extra accommodation. I can't say they were 'by appointment' but they were vital during the visit of HRH the Duke of Kent when it poured with rain.

8 AMS Ltd (South Lea, Balkholme, Howden, North Humberside, DN14 7XH). Steven Jennings gave us 50kgs of *Maxim [TM]* fuel energy powder.

This is an 'altodexin made from a special blend of short, medium and long chain glucose polymers'. Whatever that means, it is (virtually) tasteless, dissolves easily in warm drinks, and supplies energy you would otherwise get from carbohydrate food.

4 scoops (about equal to two heaped tablespoonfuls) is the equivalent of 6 slices of wholemeal bread, 1 large plate of cooked pasta and 1.5 large baked potatoes. Not a menu you could easily face without gagging at 3 a m in a cold alpine bivvy, but I regularly dissolved 2 or 3 scoops in my early morning hot chocolate which gave me a good breakfast and set me up for the day.

I reckon it worked. I carried Maxim [TM] on most trips and I have never been as fit in my life, even passing SAS selection years ago when I was a lot younger.

One problem on mountains is that you cannot eat Maxim [TM] on the recommended little-and-often principle as you normally only have a litre of drink in a flask for the whole day.

At the end of a day, you are recommended to slug down some Maxim [TM] within half an hour of finishing exercise or the day's climb, to enable the body to recover for the next day. I did this and I guess that worked too as I never had any problems bump-starting myself the next day, but I can tell you that Maxim [TM] does not dissolve at all well in cold beer.

9 VauDe Tents UK Ltd. John Anderson kindly arranged a healthy discount for us to buy 3 VauDe *'Hogan' tents*.

These tents are lightweight (2.2kgs), easy to put up in all winds, and take down, neat for two people, and good value. They served us well. Good alpine tents.

10 British Army Cash Sponsors A number of funds generously gave us varying amounts of money without which we would not have been able to afford to climb more than a fraction of what we did. They may have some odd-sounding names to the civilian ear, but all deserve our gratitude.

(a) Scots Guards
(b) The Commander's Fund
(c) Adventure Training Grant
(d) GOC's Grant
(e) 7 Armoured Brigade
(f) C in C BAOR Fund
(g) Brigadier of Infantry
(h) The Ulysses Trust

11 British Industry and Commerce I know recession-awareness peaked in 1993, but only one company gave us any money, and that was not for want of trying to persuade a host of others: Mercury donated a sizeable sum to the Foundation for cot death research.

12 Private Donations This list of sponsors would not be complete without thanking all the individuals who gave money to the Foundation for cot death research. Some of them took great trouble 'rattling the box' or gave considerable sums and we are most grateful to them all.

14 Swiss Army The sponsorship of the Swiss Army has been mentioned in various ways in the text. All I can say is that the expedition, as mounted, could not have taken place without the exceptional generosity of the Swiss Army.